The Lives of the
KINGS & QUEENS OF FRANCE

The Lives of the
KINGS & QUEENS
OF FRANCE

DUC DE CASTRIES
of the Académie Française

Translated from the French
by Anne Dobell

Alfred A. Knopf
New York 1979

THIS IS A BORZOI BOOK
PUBLISHED BY ALFRED A. KNOPF, INC.

Copyright © 1979 by
George Weidenfeld and Nicolson Limited

All rights reserved under International and
Pan-American Copyright Conventions.
Published in the United States by Alfred A. Knopf,
Inc., New York, and simultaneously in Canada by
Random House of Canada Limited, Toronto.
Distributed by Random House, Inc., New York.
Originally published in Great Britain as *The lives of
the Kings and Queens of France* by Weidenfeld &
Nicolson Ltd, London.

Library of Congress Cataloging in Publication Data
Castries, René de La Croix, duc de, [date]
 The lives of the kings and queens of France.
 Translation of *Rois et Reines de France*.
 1. France—Kings and rulers—Biography.
2. France—Queens—Biography.   I. Title.
DC36.6.C38513 1979   944'.00992 [B] 79-2205
ISBN 0-394-50734-7

First American Edition

❧ CONTENTS ❧

CONTENTS

✁ CONTENTS ✁

℘ PREFACE ℘

THIS BOOK IS BROADLY MODELLED on the parallel work, *Kings and Queens of England,* by Antonia Fraser. As in the English book, a concise biography of each king is given and through this the general history of the period is traced.

But the history of royalty in France began earlier and also came to an end sooner than in England. In France it began in the fifth century with the Merovingian dynasty; this disappeared in 754, to be replaced by a second dynasty, the Carolingians, which was in turn eliminated in 987 by a third dynasty, the Capetians. This third dynasty reigned for more than 800 years through four branches: the direct Capetians, the Valois, the Bourbons, and the Orléans.

As in England, revolutions caused interregnums and also brought about the rise of a fourth dynasty, the Bonapartes, who reigned sporadically for two periods in the nineteenth century. But this book concentrates on the true kings of France and ends in 1848, with the abdication of Louis-Philippe.

Clovis is baptized by archbishop Remi.
(*Grandes Chroniques de France*)

Part One

THE MEROVINGIANS

450?~768

From tribal myth
to Christian kings

THE MEROVINGIANS

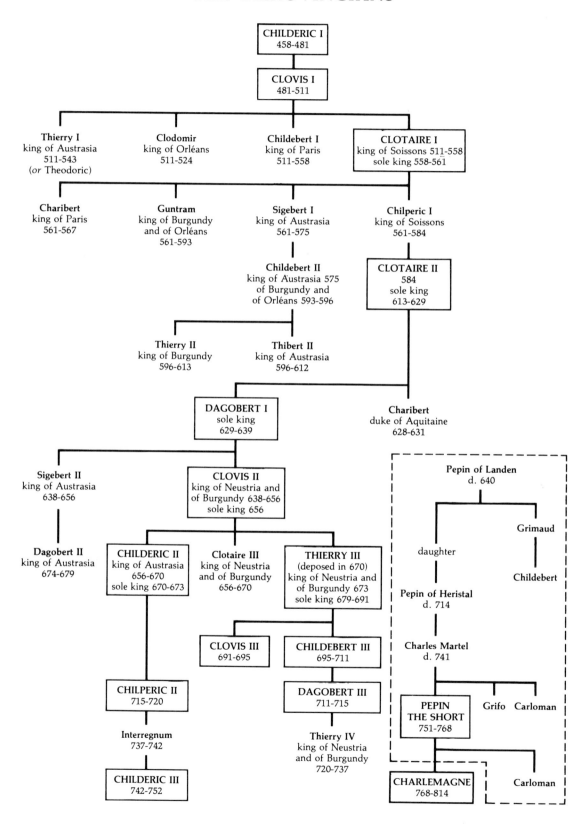

❦ MEROVIUS, CLODION ❦ AND CHILDERIC
(450–481)

ROYALTY IN FRANCE was not a spontaneous phenomenon: in fact it took root at a fairly late date. In Gaul the tribal system prevailed, and little is known of the names of the tribal chiefs. From a period covering thousands of years, history has recorded only one name, that of Vercingetorix, the son of a man called Celtilles, who was killed by his compatriots for having tried to become king of the Arverni.

After defending his country heroically, Vercingetorix was defeated by Julius Caesar. Gaul became a Roman colony, a situation from which it profited greatly, and it was run for four centuries by able administrators. These men brought with them the benefits of a well established civilization and, more importantly, a long period of peace, during which the fate of Gaul reflected that of the Roman Empire.

Under the pressure of invasions during the fourth century the empire began to crumble and Gaul saw the establishment in part of its territory of a people from the lower Rhine whose arrival was to alter its whole destiny: the Franks.

It was at the beginning of the fifth century that Gaul suffered most from invasions: the Visigoths occupied the south of the country, and then in about 450 a more fearsome threat appeared in the east: the invasion of the Huns. They were repelled by the Roman general Aetius, who defeated them soundly at the battle of Châlons in 451.

One of Aetius's general officers, Merovius, is considered to have played an equally important part in that day's victory. Merovius is a semi-legendary figure. He was the son of a certain Clodion the Hairy, of whom practically nothing is known; he may have been descended from one Pharamond, reputed to have been the ancestor of the kings of France.

Although little is known of Merovius, other than the fact that he was to bequeath his name to the dynasty he founded, several facts are known about his son Childeric, whose existence is evidenced by the grave found in 1653 at Tournai: he was buried in full regalia, together with his arms, his jewels and his royal signet bearing the inscription *Childerici regis*. But this factual proof casts little light on his life.

Childeric had been in the service of the Roman empire, as had Merovius, and helped Count Paul to recapture Angers from the Saxons in 468. He has had attributed to him, without proof, the siege of Paris during which St Genevieve saved the city from starvation. We also know for certain that Childeric ruled over Tournai, and that he died in about 481, leaving his inheritance to his son Clodovic, whose name has been corrupted by modern historians into Clovis.

❦ CLOVIS ❦ AND ST CLOTILDA
(481–511)

LITTLE IS KNOWN of Clovis, as he left no records. His reign can be reconstructed, but only in part, from the almost hagiographic writings of the historian Gregory of Tours, recorded towards the middle of the sixth century. Allowing for the author's obvious bias in favour of Clovis, certain aspects of his character, epitomized by the famous episode of the Vase of Soissons (see p. 29), remain disturbing.

Clovis succeeded his father without difficulty

Clovis and *right* Saint Clotilda. (From the church of Notre-Dame de Corbeil)

but he was not the only king of the Salian Franks. At least two of his relatives ruled at the same time: Ragnachair at Cambrai, and Chararic, apparently at Saint-Quentin.

Clovis, whose territory consisted only of Tournaisis, attacked Syagrius, the son of the Roman general Aegidius, king of Soissons. As Clovis was not powerful enough to lead the attack, he contracted an alliance with Ragnachair and Chararic. Syagrius fled the onslaught and escaped to Toulouse, where he was given shelter by Alaric II. Clovis insisted that the fugitive be handed over to him and then had him secretly put to death. He was now master of the Soissons area, which he pillaged thoroughly. Then, when he felt powerful enough, he had his two allies Ragnachair and Chararic put to death, and annexed their territories. The two victims had a brother, Rigomer, who ruled in the region of Le Mans; he too was sacrificed.

Despite his partiality for Clovis, even Gregory of Tours is obliged to admit that Clovis had several more of his royal relatives put to death, enabling him to extend his authority over most of Gaul, but the number of these murders gives us no information on the precise importance of the conquered territories. However it would appear that towards 486 Clovis ruled all the land north of the Loire, and those territories to the south were paying him tribute.

A few details are known about the siege of Verdun, a few more about the siege of Paris, which must have lasted ten years. According to Gregory of Tours, Clovis waged war on the Thuringians and brought them under his authority, which seems doubtful to say the least; the area in question was most probably Tangres in Belgium.

In 491 Clovis, now twenty-five years old, fathered a bastard child, Theodoric (or Thierry), by an unknown woman who was not of royal blood. He began to consider a political marriage, and his eyes lighted on the daughter of Gondebaud, king of the Burgundii. The girl's name was Clotilda; she was Arian by religion, but with strong Roman Catholic tendencies. This marriage was of primary importance, as the real shape of France dated from it. Clotilda, who was later canonized, converted her husband to Catholicism and henceforth the Church played a decisive role in the history of the kings of France.

According to tradition, Clovis's conversion was the result of his victory over the Alemanni, a fearsome people whose capital was Cologne. They first attacked the Ripuary Franks in the region of Trèves, and then in 496 they attacked the Salian Franks, which posed a direct threat to Clovis. The decisive battle took place at a place known as Tolbiac, which would appear to have been situated at the borders of Alsace and Lorraine. The fighting was fierce and Clovis despaired of winning. Then, reports Gregory of Tours, he wept, lifted his eyes to heaven and uttered the following prayer: 'Jesus Christ, who Clotilda says is the son of the God of life, you who deign to help those who submit to you and grant them victory if they put their hope in you, I devoutly call for your assistance. If you deign to grant me victory over my enemies, and if I find that power of which your believers say you give such plentiful evidence, I will believe in you and will be baptized in your name.'

No sooner was this prayer uttered than the Alemanni yielded; their king was killed, and the routed army submitted to Clovis. On his return he told Queen Clotilda that he had won the victory by invoking the name of Christ. The queen called Saint Remi, bishop of the town of Rheims, and asked him to instruct her husband in the Christian religion. The priest taught him the rudiments of the faith, and called upon him to repent of his past sins. Clovis made an act of contrition, but warned the bishop that his people would not be willing to give up their gods. However, on the insistence of Saint Remi, he assembled his troops, and miraculously his soldiers announced: 'We reject our mortal gods, pious king, and are ready to follow the immortal god preached by Remi.'

So the bishop of Rheims had the baptismal fonts prepared and the king asked to be baptized first. Saint Remi's words have gone down in history: 'Bow your head gently, adore that which you have burned and burn that which you have adored.' After the holy water had touched Clovis's brow, three thousand of his soldiers were also baptized.

In baptizing Clovis, Saint Remi created a precedent which was to become a feature of the history of the kings of France, namely canonical investiture: in France henceforth the king would be not only a military but also a religious leader, *dux et sacerdos.* This is the generally accepted version of the circumstances of Clovis's baptism; others exist which seem at least equally dubious.

Despite having become a Christian, Clovis remained a tireless warrior and soon went to attack the country of the Burgundii, his wife's homeland. This intervention was the result of sinister plots within the royal family, due to the rivalry between Godegisèle and his brother Gondebaud. Godegisèle betrayed Gondebaud to Clovis, and in a battle near Dijon, Gondebaud's troops were defeated. Gondebaud took his revenge by having Godegisèle assassinated, and was reconciled with Clovis. A military alliance was sealed and Clovis, with the aid of Gondebaud, set off to conquer Aquitaine, which was then Visigoth territory. Their king, Alaric II, gathered his troops together and marched out to face the invaders. They met near Poitiers in 507, on the vast plain of Vouillé. No details of this battle are known, although Gregory of Tours reports that Clovis won a total victory 'with God's help'.

Franks and Burgundii met at Toulouse; Clovis's son Thierry occupied Auvergne and Gondebaud occupied Septimania. Clovis, established in Bordeaux, undertook to subdue everything south of the Garonne. On his way back north Clovis stopped at St Martin's basilica at Tours, where the emperor of Byzantium, Anastasius, granted him not, as was wrongly recorded, the *imperium*, but the insignia of the consulate. Clovis then left Tours and established himself in Paris, which he made his capital. There he formulated a code which became known as the 'Salic Law'.

He then consolidated his eastern frontiers and attacked his blood brothers, the Ripuary Franks. Faithful to his old habits, he cleft the head of their chief Chloderic in two at the very moment when the latter was displaying his treasures to him. After this final conquest, he was master of a territory roughly corresponding to that of France today. Clovis spent the last years of his life in Paris supervising the completion of his code.

In 511, the year of his death, he gathered his bishops in council at Orléans. Thirty-two prelates attended, and a serious analysis was made of problems arising from the right of asylum and the recruitment of the clergy. Freemen were authorized to belong to the clergy with the king's consent, whereas serfs were declared unsuitable to be priests.

The Council of Orléans was Clovis's last political act: he died shortly afterwards in Paris and was buried in the basilica of the Holy Apostles which he had had built on the mountain of St-Geneviève, and where Queen Clotilda was laid to rest beside him.

Clovis's achievement was a tremendous one: he had created France. Unfortunately he did not realize this, and the problems of the succession once again threatened the unity which he had brought about.

❦ THE HEIRS OF CLOVIS ❦
(511–629)

IN ADDITION TO THEODORIC, Clovis left three sons by Clotilda. Theodoric, the eldest son, brought about the partition of the *regnum francorum*. The eldest of Clotilda's sons, Clodomir, got the Loire from Orléans to Tours, plus the cities of Chartres, Sens and Auxerre; Childebert got Paris, the valleys of the Seine and the Somme, and the Channel coast as far as Brittany; Clotaire received Soissons, Laon, Noyon and the old Frankish country: Cambrai, Tournai and the lower side of the Meuse. Theodoric kept for himself the most exposed portion, that of the Ripuary country, the Moselle valley with Metz and Trier, French Hesse, Champagne and the Alemanni protectorate. When the Goth territory was divided Theodoric took the lion's share: Quercy, Albigeois and Auvergne. Clodomir received Poitiers, and Childebert Bourges.

This system of sharing out territory, which took no account of ethnic and political factors, was absurd, and an agreement was necessary to maintain some kind of unity by mutual support.

l bône rome
croasde demo
roit a donc
a paris la
nouvrissoit

il luy sembloit que ilz les
amoient et quilz auoiēt
son conseil seuers eulx
furent liurez aux messag
qui de par les roys estoiēt

'How king Clotaire and king Childebert killed their nephews in front of queen Clotilda.' (*Grandes Chroniques de France*)

This indeed was the first thought of Clovis's sons, but it was short-lived, and they began to practise the methods with which their father had succeeded so well. Political assassination became the rule of the day. When Clodomir died he left three young sons; Childebert and Clotaire had them killed or, to be precise, Clotaire took charge of the operation when Childebert hesitated. Having murdered the children, they also killed their servants and tutors. Clodomir's third son, Clodoald, managed to escape the massacre; he is said to have founded a monastery and was canonized as Saint Cloud.

Theodoric, interested by these methods, tried to have his brothers assassinated but failed. He died shortly afterwards, leaving a son, Thibert, who defended himself and allied himself to Childebert against Clotaire, who escaped only after a tragic flight in the forest of Bretonne. Queen Clotilda was still alive, and is said to have spent her life praying to God not to allow a war between her sons.

Thibert died in about 548, leaving a degenerate son who was incapable of reigning for long and died in 555. Clotaire succeeded his great-nephew. Childebert was jealous, and favoured a revolt against Clotaire, but he died childless in 558. Clotaire seized his territories and the unity of the kingdom was re-established by the sum of these crimes. But this reunification did not last for long, as Clotaire died in 561.

These criminal kings were nevertheless great

warriors, and during their reigns France acquired Burgundy through a new series of political crimes. Theodoric seized Provence and Childebert routed the Visigoths. Thibert occupied Bavaria and advanced as far as Pannonia. However, Clotaire was unable to defeat the Saxons. Expeditions into Italy penetrated quite far but were stopped by the Alemanni.

It is difficult to give a coherent account of all these events because of a complete absence of documentation. In contrast the period from 561 to 591, covering the grandsons of Clovis, is the best known in Merovingian history because Gregory of Tours documented it with precision.

As Clotaire I left four sons, the dividing of the *regnum* began again after only three years of unity. The succession was to prove difficult, as differences of opinion between the successors immediately revealed themselves.

Chilperic was the son of Clotaire's incestuous relationship with Queen Ingund's sister. Fearing to be outdone, he moved first, seized his father's treasure and established himself in Paris. Ingund's legitimate sons rose against him and Chilperic had to be content with the smaller share, Soissons and the region around it. Charibert received his uncle Childebert's kingdom together with Paris; Guntram received Clodomir's kingdom, with Orléans as its capital, and including Burgundy; his seat was usually therefore at Chalon-sur-Sâone. The last son, Sigebert, received Theodoric's old estate, i.e. the dangerous eastern marches.

Charibert died young, in 567, and his share was divided. Sigebert, as king of Austrasia, took Vendômois, Tours, Poitou and part of Aquitaine. Guntram took Saintonge, Angoumois, Périgord, Agenais and Nantais. Chilperic received territory from all sides: the lower course of the Seine, Normandy, Maine and Anjou, Limousin, Toulouse and Bordeaux, Dax, Bigorre, Comminges and Béarn. By common consent, Paris and its territory were declared neutral. This chaotic division was clear proof of the Merovingians' political ineffectiveness.

Sigebert, the only brother with decent morals, made a fine match in Brunhilda, the king of the Visigoths' daughter. Not to be outdone, Chilperic married Brunhilda's sister, Galswintha. The marriage was not a success: Galswintha was found strangled in her bed, probably by Fredegund, Chilperic's mistress, whom he subsequently married. The rivalry between Brunhilda and Fredegund has gone down in history.

For all his domestic virtues, Sigebert was unscrupulous in politics and tried to grab Arles from his brother Guntram, but failed pitifully. Even less scrupulous than he, Chilperic refused to return Galswintha's dowry and demanded compensation should he have to give it up. His sons by Queen Audovère, Clovis and Thibert, declared war on Sigebert, who called on the Rhine nations for help.

In 574 Chilperic refused to fight at Havelu and restored the territories conquered by his sons. But the Rhine forces unwisely summoned by Sigebert plundered the Ile de France. Chilperic had second thoughts and Sigebert called back the Rhine nations. After marching on Rheims, Chilperic took refuge in Tournai. His son Thibert had been killed in battle. Sigebert seemed certain of victory when he was assassinated in 575 by two fanatical supporters of Fredegund.

Chilperic planned to seize Childebert's kingdom but Childebert's son Heudebert had been miraculously saved and, although only five years old, he was proclaimed king.

In another *coup de théâtre*, Merovius, youngest son of Chilperic and Audovere, married Brunhilda. Sigebert's widow was young and attractive, and this accounted in part for the union, which was considered incestuous. Chilperic dissolved the marriage, imprisoned his son and pardoned Brunhilda.

Merovius' brother Clovis incurred Fredegund's hatred and she had him killed. The excesses of this wild queen were about to become more serious and make her name notorious.

Having lost his children, Chilperic adopted his nephew Childebert II. He soon regretted this, as another son was born to him who was to become Clotaire II. Shortly afterwards, in 584, Chilperic was assassinated.

As Gregory of Tours' chronicle ends in 591, subsequent events are less well documented. We do know, however, that Fredegund tried to have Childebert II and Guntram assassinated, and that Brunhilda eliminated everyone who got in her way at Childebert's court. This was a horrific period, during which, according to the saying, 'absolute power was moderated by assassination'.

faisant ce qui appartenoit a tel office · ɔ
ffine le second liure des cironiques de france des
faiz z histoires aux iiij · filz le fort Roy clouis ·

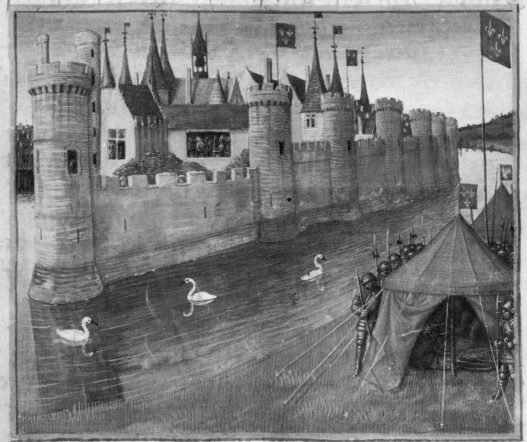

Cy commence le iij· liure coment les quatre
filz au Roy clotaire partirent le Royaume en iiij·
parties sique chun ỽnt au sien Royaume ;

                    prez la mort au Roy clotaire
                    fu le Royaume departi aux
                    quatre freres / mais chilperich
                    qui le plus fause z le plus ma
                    licieux estoit que nul des au
                    tres a qui il ne souffist mie tele partie comme
                    il deuoit auoir par droit sort / ala ala nuit au
                    plustost quil pot z saisy les tresozs de son pere

ABOVE Near Orléans, Guntram transfers his kingdom to his nephew Childebert.
(*Grandes Chroniques de France*)

Childebert II and Guntram, having joined together in the face of Fredegund's ferocity, contracted an alliance at Andelot, and Charibert's succession was once again shared out. This new division was possibly more chaotic than all the others, as Paris was split into three. However, for the first time ever, the exact frontiers of the different kingdoms were established, and the delicate problem of transit rights was settled.

Relations between Guntram and Childebert II became stormy again, but Guntram died on 28 March 592. Childebert II succeeded him but followed him to the grave shortly afterwards, aged only twenty-five, in 595.

Subsequent events are not clearly reported. Childebert II left two sons, of whom the elder, Thibert, received Austrasia with Metz as its capital, and the younger son, Thierry, received Burgundy, with Orléans as capital. Their rival was Chilperic's son Clotaire II. He had lost his mother, Fredegund, which increased the influence of Brunhilda at her grandson's court.

OPPOSITE Chilperic and his three brothers divide up Clotaire's kingdom between them at his death.
(*Grandes Chroniques de France*)

21

The death of Brunhilda.
(Vincent of Beauvais' *Miroir Historial*)

Clotaire II wanted to regain Thierry's territory between the Seine and Loire, but in a battle fought in 604 near Etampes he was defeated and his son taken prisoner.

Despite their success, Childebert's sons turned on each other. In 610 Thibert invaded his brother's territory of Alsace and Thierry had to yield; but he joined forces with his cousin Clotaire II and in 612, at the battle of Toul, Thibert was defeated, taken prisoner and stripped of his royal status. Brunhilda had him tonsured and probably killed.

Clotaire II decided to demand his share of the alliance. Thierry responded by declaring war on him, but he died of dysentery at Metz. Brunhilda retained the throne of Austrasia and tried to have one of her great-grandchildren, Sigebert, recognized. She was thwarted by the bishop of Metz, Arnulf, an important person whose descendants were to be the race of the Pepinids, future Carolingians. Clotaire II, when called on for help by Arnulf's party, invaded Austrasia, seized Brunhilda and killed Thierry's sons.

Brunhilda's death has gone down in history: the wicked old queen was tortured for three days, paraded in front of the army riding a camel, then tied by one arm and one leg to the tail of a wild horse which trampled her to pieces.

Clotaire II was quite clearly an outstanding man. His brutal policies bore fruit, since by physically removing all his rivals he re-established unity and, like his grandfather and namesake, reigned over the whole kingdom of the Franks. From his reign dates the administrative division of the kingdom into Austrasia and Neustria, representing roughly east and west.

The major event in Clotaire II's reign was the council he held in Paris in October 614. Seventy-nine bishops attended and from it emerged the text of the *Constitutio Cloteriana,* which determined the main principles of government.

To secure the succession, Clotaire II had his son Dagobert crowned king of Austrasia in 622. When Dagobert came of age in 625, he married him to Gomatrude, sister of Queen Sichilda.

Two days later a violent quarrel erupted between father and son: Dagobert demanded the whole of the kingdom of Austrasia. Clotaire II had to cede Champagne, but he kept Aquitaine.

An attempted revolt by Neustria was the last event to mark the reign of Clotaire II, who died in 629, after a reign of forty-six years, and was buried in the basilica of Saint Vincent near Paris.

ᑶᔓ DAGOBERT ᑶᔓ
(629–639)

THE REIGN OF DAGOBERT, which lasted only six years, was the last flicker of the Merovingian dynasty. After his death everything declined, and the country entered into the period of the 'lazy kings', during which power passed gradually into the hands of the great civil servants, the 'mayors of the palace', who were eventually to start a new dynasty.

Dagobert was a dynamic man, well supported by his minister Saint Eloy. His private life was lively: he had several queens, including Nanthilda, Vulfégund and Berthilda, not to mention numerous concubines, all with the knowledge of the legitimate wife. Nothing is known of these queens, indeed the events of the reign itself are dubious, but enough is known to draw the conclusion that this was an important reign, which affected the whole kingdom.

Dagobert had a younger brother, Charibert, who lived in Paris and immediately hatched a plot, with the help of his uncle Brodulf, to supplant Dagobert and reign in his place. Without hesitation, Dagobert raised troops in Austrasia and ordered Burgundy and Neustria to obey. He had himself recognized sole king at Soissons by the bishops of Burgundy and Neustria.

Brodulf's plot had failed. But Dagobert, more humane than his ancestors, did not have his brother Charibert put to death, as he was considered a simpleton. Dagobert constituted, for the first time, an appanage for him: Charibert was given the task of administering Toulousain, Cahorsin, Agenais, Périgord and Saintonge with all the territory as far as the Pyrenees. It was agreed in a family pact that he would demand no part of his father's kingdom, and his residence was fixed at Toulouse. Since Charibert died in 632, it would seem that Dagobert had found the perfect solution to a difficult problem

which then disappeared, since Charibert's son, Chilperic, died young. Some chroniclers believe that Dagobert was responsible for this.

When he had dealt with his younger brother, Dagobert made a tour of Burgundy which further established his authority, particularly since he had Brodulf put to death for conspiring against him. It was also during this journey that he repudiated Queen Gomatrude, married a seamstress, Nanthilda, and made her his queen.

After Burgundy Dagobert visited Austrasia. Arnulf had become a monk and been replaced by Cunibert, bishop of Cologne, whose adviser was one of the 'mayors of the palace', Pepin of Landen, a close relation of Arnulf's and one of the earliest known Pepinids. Dagobert judged Pepin's advice to be sound and readily followed it, with important consequences.

Dagobert took up residence in Paris and the Austrasians resented this; they demanded a king and Dagobert had to comply. He placed on their throne a three-year-old boy, Sigebert, whom he had fathered on his concubine Raintrude. To prevent his illegitimate son from one day trying to seize the whole of the *regnum* he made the Austrasian magnates swear to guarantee the throne of Neustria and Burgundy for the son he had by Nanthilda, and who was to reign under the name of Clotaire III. Thus occurred the partition of Neustria and Austrasia which had been brought about on a purely administrative level by Clotaire II.

Being on the whole surer of his power than his predecessor had been, Dagobert was able to wage several successful wars both at home and abroad. In 637 the Gascons revolted and ravaged the regions under Charibert's authority. Dagobert raised a Frankish army in Burgundy, under a general named Chadoind. The Gascons refused to fight and dug in in the valleys and gorges of the Pyrenees. Dagobert's army pursued them into their lairs, killed many of them, burned their houses and took their flocks. This brutality bore fruit, and the following year (638) the leaders of Aquitaine and their duke, Aegina, came to submit to Dagobert at Clichy and, surprisingly, remained faithful to their oath.

The Bretons, whose activities were also suspect, took note of the lesson learned by the people of Aquitaine and their leader Judicael went of his own accord to make his submission at Clichy, preceded by Saint Eloy.

Dagobert's reputation at home was greatly strengthened by these acts of authority; he was looked upon as a great sovereign with whom it was unwise to trifle. He was therefore able to conclude a treaty of perpetual peace with the emperor of Byzantium.

In Spain, Dagobert helped Sisenand to oust King Sointila in a military operation led by a Frankish army raised in Burgundy, mustered at Toulouse and which he led as far as Saragossa. As well as a matter of prestige this was a financial transaction, as Dagobert was anxious to obtain the golden *missoire* which had previously been offered to King Thorismond by Aetius, a piece weighing 500 pounds, which was the pride of the Visigoth kings' treasury. He was not offered it, but received in compensation 200,000 golden crowns, which today would probably represent several millions (633).

Some Frankish merchants had been robbed and murdered by the Slavs, and Dagobert demanded reparation; he raised an army both in Austrasia and from among his Alemanni subjects. This was the only unfortunate action of his reign, as his army was thoroughly defeated by the Slavs, who ravaged Thuringia and threatened Austrasia.

Dagobert's prestige can be measured by the fact that despite their military success the Slavs came the following year to submit to him, after hearing that he was mustering forces to take Thuringia. Dagobert installed there duke Radulf, who seemed at first a good choice but soon, consumed by ambition, threatened young Sigebert in Austrasia.

Though Dagobert had not completely defeated the Slavs, he had at least halted their advance, which Byzantium subsequently

King Dagobert hunting. (Extract from the *Roman de Godefroid de Bouillon*)

proved incapable of doing. In 638, the sixteenth year of his reign over Austrasia and the tenth over the *regnum,* Dagobert, in his residence of Epinay near Paris, began to suffer from dysentery. He had himself immediately taken to the basilica of St Denis. Feeling that his end was near, he gave his final words of advice to Queen Nanthilda and charged her with helping their son Clovis to ascend the throne. He was buried at Saint Denis, which he had magnificently enriched and decorated.

Thanks to the efforts of Queen Nanthilda, the child-king Clovis II was recognized by the lords of Neustria and Burgundy. The Austrasians then demanded part of Dagobert's treasure and had to be satisfied.

Nanthilda reigned as regent with the help of Aega, a man trusted by Dagobert and who in fact became a mayor of the palace; but he died in 642. After his son-in-law Ermenfred had put to death a high dignitary named Chainulf, a rising took place during which Queen Nanthilda was unable to prevent pillaging and massacres. Ermenfred fled to Austrasia and took refuge in the basilica of Saint Remi at Rheims. Through his ill-judged murder he had lost all hopes of succeeding Aega, whom Nanthilda replaced by Erchinoald, who became mayor of the palace. Two years before, Pepin of Landen had died at Metz, and Austrasia was becoming restless.

A difficult period was beginning, that of the 'lazy kings', or the mayors of the palace.

⮷ THE LAZY KINGS ⮷
(639–741)

THE CENTURY BETWEEN the death of Dagobert and the founding of a new dynasty falls readily into two sections, the first consisting of the rivalries between Austrasia and Neustria and the second showing once again a fairly well unified France, but in which power had passed from the hands of inconsistent kings into those of the increasingly powerful mayors of the palace.

When Pepin of Landen died in 640, his son Grimald had succeeded him with the approval of Queen Nanthilda, who named as Aega's successor in Burgundy the Frank Flaochat, to whom she gave her niece in marriage. When she died, Flaochat became the true ruler under the nominal king Clovis II. After a series of dramatic incidents, Flaochat died in mysterious circumstances at Saint-Jean-de-Losne in about 642. After this date, the only known documentary evidence, the *Liber Historiae Francorum*, proves very mediocre and must be used with caution.

It is fairly certain that Clovis II died in 657 virtually insane. A son of the mayor of the palace Erchinoald, successor to Flaochat, and born of an English palace servant-girl, Bathilda, reigned over Neustria and Burgundy under the name of Clotaire III.

At about the same time Sigebert III (brother of Clovis II) reigned over Austrasia, with Grimald as mayor of the palace. This reign, about which very little is known, was marked by an unfortunate war against Duke Radulf of Thuringia. The purely nominal King Sigebert III died on 1 February 656, aged twenty-seven. He left a son, Dagobert, by Queen Himnechilda; but now a surprising event took place. Grimald, Pepin of Landen's son, had planned to take over the throne, and to this end he had had his own son, Childebert, adopted by King Sigebert III, in uncertain circumstances. As he was young Dagobert's guardian, he had him tonsured and sent to a monastery in Ireland, and Grimald reigned under the name of his son Childebert 'the adopted'. This was the first sign of the Pepinids' vocation for the throne; their only mistake was in trying a century too soon. But this ploy failed. Grimald was overthrown by a group of magnates, handed over to Clotaire III and thrown into prison, where he died; his son Childebert mysteriously disappeared (662).

Dagobert II was (wrongly) thought to be dead, and the kingdom should have been handed back to Clotaire III, but Queen Bathilda, his guardian, decided to propose her second son, Childeric II, to the Austrasians as king. Then in about 665 Bathilda was removed by Neustrian magnates and sent to the monastery of Chelles. She died there in 680 and was later canonized.

A sinister character, Ebroin, had succeeded Erchinoald as head of Neustria. At the death of Clotaire III, Ebroin placed the brother of the dead King Thierry III on the throne of Neustria. He was mentally retarded, and the Neustrian magnates realized that Ebroin was after the crown for himself. With the help of the Austrasian King Childeric II, Ebroin was removed, tonsured and sent to the monastery of Luxeuil. He was replaced by Bishop Leger of Autun, who soon fell from favour and was sent to join Ebroin at Luxeuil.

An anti-Austrasian party was formed in

The battle between Charles Martel, newly escaped from the prison in which he had been placed by his stepmother Plectrude, and Chilperic, at Vinci, near Cambrai. (*Grandes Chroniques de France*) 27

Neustria. Thierry III was replaced on the throne and Erchinoald's son Leudesius was named mayor of the palace; but his ministry was a short one, as Ebroin escaped from Luxeuil, had Leudesius put to death and became mayor again, holding power with Thierry III as a front. Ebroin was to become a merciless tyrant; he began by torturing Bishop Leger, whose tongue and lips he had cut off, then had him indicted before a council, which ordered his execution. Ebroin then decided to subdue the Austrasians, and they brought Dagobert II out of his Irish monastery, but he was assassinated shortly after being replaced on the throne.

The vacancy on the throne of Austrasia favoured the return of the Pepinids as mayors of the palace. One of them, Pepin of Heristal, the son of Ansegisel (himself the son of Bishop Arnulf's marriage before he entered orders) and of Grimald's sister, seized power in Austrasia, and governed under Thierry III.

Conflict with Neustria erupted and Austrasia took the upper hand. Shortly afterwards Ebroin, defeated, was beaten by his lieutenants.

War erupted again between Austrasia and Neustria. Pepin of Heristal won a victory at Tertry in 687 and Thierry III fled. This confirmed the ascendancy of Austrasia over Neustria, where Pepin judged it wise to maintain the royal fiction through the 'lazy kings' Clovis III, then Childebert III and finally Dagobert III, puppet kings of whom virtually nothing is known.

The country's unity, effectively re-established under the hand of Pepin of Heristal, made it possible to face new invasions, and to take in hand again the region south of the Loire, which royal insolvency had allowed to become virtually autonomous. When Pepin of Heristal died in 714, his widow Plectrude undertook to rule in the name of her grandchildren and the imprisoned Charles, a son of Pepin by his concubine Aupaïs.

Charles, who was to make his mark as Charles Martel, had an exceptional destiny before him which was to change the course of events. He escaped from the prison where he had been kept by Plectrude and began an unsuccessful war against the Frisians. The Neustrians, angered at Plectrude's usurpation, took advantage of the death of Dagobert III in 715 to bring one of

Childeric II's sons out from his monastery and proclaim him king under the name of Chilperic II. But the Neustrians ran into Charles's troops; he defeated them at Ambleve in 717, and refused to make peace. Then he obliged Plectrude to hand over the treasure of Pepin of Heristal, and to consolidate the situation he placed one of Thierry III's sons on the throne under the name of Clotaire IV (718); but he was incapable of ruling and all trace of him has disappeared. Charles then agreed to replace Chilperic II on the throne, but the king died shortly afterwards in 721.

Always cautious, for the memory of Grimald haunted him, Charles sought another Merovingian, and they brought out from the monastery of Chelles a supposed son of Thierry III, who became king Thierry IV. With this insignificant man as king, Charles Martel was mayor of the palace. He repulsed the Saxons three times but was unable to annex their territory. He also interceded in Bavaria in 725 and nominated a king there, Odilo, having Bavarian law promulgated by Thierry IV.

Charles Martel's political objective was to dominate his dangerous neighbours by converting them to Christianity; he was encouraged in this by Pope Gregory II and supported by the famous English missionary Boniface, who became archbishop and oversaw the bishoprics of Würzburg, Erfurt, Eichsstadt, Salzburg, Passau and Regensburg.

All Charles Martel's great achievements are overshadowed in history by his successful struggle against the Muslims; because of this he is considered the saviour of Christianity. Duke Eudes of Aquitaine, after fighting Charles Martel for many years, saw a new danger approaching across the Pyrenees. In 711 the Arabs had occupied Visigothic Spain; in 719 they attacked Septimania and seized Narbonne in 720. Defeated by Eudes in 721, they took the offensive again and in 725 Carcassonne fell to them; a Muslim raid penetrated as far as Autun.

In 731 the situation deteriorated. Chief Abd-el-Rahman crossed the Pyrenees and marched on Bordeaux, which he pillaged; Eudes came for help to Charles Martel, who gathered his troops and marched south. He failed to prevent the pillaging of the abbey of St Hilaire at Poitiers but he halted the Muslim force north of

Coment le fort roy dodonee
fut conzonne apres la mort
son pere et coment il rendit
lorrel a sainct Remy

The notorious episode of Clovis and the vase of Soissons: after his victory at Soissons, Clovis was requested by its bishop to return the vase which one of his soldiers had stolen from a church. The soldier refused to comply and smashed the vase. Clovis later personally split the soldier's skull in two. (*Grandes Chroniques de France*)

'How, after Clovis's death, his kingdom was shared out between the four brothers.' (*Grandes Chroniques de France*)

L · omment charlemaine fist logier :
son ost et se reposerent toute celle nuit mes
mes la ou le corps gisoit mort / Et comment

Charlemagne finds the body of Roland at Roncevaux.
(*Chroniques de Saint Denis*)

there in a bloody battle (732) in which Abd-el-Rahman was killed.

The Muslims scattered and fled back over the Pyrenees. The battle of Poitiers, a simple incident in Charles Martel's life, destined him for glory. But this indefatigable warrior also subdued Frisia in 734, tried to annex Aquitaine at Eudes' death (735), suppressed a revolt in Burgundy in 736 and occupied Marseilles. In 736 the Muslims again tried to occupy Septimania and infiltrated the valley of the Rhône; they were stopped by Charles at Leucate near Narbonne.

In 737, Thierry IV died. Charles did not replace him but neither did he seize his crown or try to impose his sons Pepin (called the Short) or Carloman.

To finance his massive military expeditions Charles Martel, a pious man, had been reduced to taxing the clergy and seizing certain church property. This spoliation revealed a streak of brutality which made the ecclesiastical world rise against him. For the sake of comparison, the confiscation of church property carried out by Charles Martel was equalled again only during the Revolution.

Although he had not worn the crown, Charles disposed of the heritage of the *regnum*. To his eldest son, Carloman, he gave Austrasia, Alemannia and Thuringia; to the younger, Pepin, he gave Neustria, Burgundy and Provence. From a Bavarian concubine named Swanchilda he had a bastard son named Grifo. To him he assigned scattered territories in Neustria, Burgundy and Austrasia, but without giving him any political authority. In the testament of this true head of State, no title of king was allowed for. He died in 741, having achieved a tremendous amount, from which his descendants were rapidly to benefit; and it was to lead them finally to sovereignty.

❧ PEPIN THE SHORT ❧
AND THE PEPINIDS
(741–768)

WITH CHARLES MARTEL DEAD, it seemed that everything must begin again. The established unity was once again at risk through partition. Family difficulties complicated things even further: Hiltrude, sister of Pepin and Carloman, fled to Bavaria and, against her brothers' wishes, married Duke Odilo, whom Charles Martel had invested. On top of this, Grifo was causing problems and his half-brothers had him interned at Neufchâteau in Luxemburg.

Aquitaine rebelled, and a punitive expedition set out which ended in the sacking of Bourges; on their return from the campaign the Alemanni declared war, then submitted. The following year, the two brothers declared war on their unwished-for brother-in-law, Duke Odilo. When the Frankish army arrived on the River Inn, Odilo fled and his kingdom was taken over. Pepin and Carloman then had the sense to see that an empty throne breeds trouble. They brought the last Merovingian out from a cloister and placed him on the throne under the name of Childeric III; he proved even more powerless than his predecessors (743).

To counteract a new Alemanni rebellion, the two brothers resumed the task of Christianization, which was carried out by Archbishop Boniface with the benediction of Pope Zacharias. Having tamed the Alemanni, they had to subdue Aquitaine again. Then in 747 Carloman, weary of power and tormented by scruples of conscience, turned his back on the world and became a monk at Monte-Cassino. He placed his son Drogo in the guardianship of Pepin, who henceforth ruled alone.

Pepin the Short was a great man, but little is known of his private life. His nickname was due, presumably, to his brief stature. He is depicted as an extremely brave man, not afraid of taking on wild animals in circus games. His achievement proves that he had strong political intuition, probably the best of all his dynasty.

LEFT Pepin the Short and his brother Grifo fight in Bavaria. RIGHT Pepin is crowned by Pope Stephen at Soissons. (*Grandes Chroniques de France*)

He fully understood the power held by the Church and realized his father's mistake in alienating it. It was impossible to go back on Charles Martel's confiscations, as the nation's finances would have crumbled. A transaction was sought which had originally been instigated by Carloman. Ecclesiastical establishments which had had property confiscated were to be allowed rights of ownership. This principle granted, it was understood that the bishoprics and monasteries should concede their appropriated property to the warriors, and this under an uncertain title bringing on average an annual 'quit-rent' fixed at one golden sou per family

holding. At the death of the temporary title holder the property would revert to the Church, unless affairs of state made it necessary to renew the title for the benefit of another titulary owner. These principles, which allowed for the reconciliation of Church and State while retaining great advantages for the latter, were codified by Pepin at the Neustrian synod at Soissons (2 March 744). As the new régime gave the church a reasonable subsistence, Pepin won it to his side, an advantage from which he rapidly profited.

When his brother retired, he had judged himself strong enough to give Grifo his freedom. But he miscalculated: Grifo first of all incited the

Saxons to revolt, then tried, at the death of Odilo, to take over Bavaria. The Bavarians rejected him, and delivered him to Pepin, who, after establishing his nephew Tassilo III in Bavaria, pardoned Grifo and granted him an endowment of twelve Neustrian counties, with Le Mans as capital. Not content with his lot, Grifo fled to Aquitaine and left Pepin sole master of the game.

In 750, weary of agitations and rebellions, Pepin felt the time was ripe to consolidate his authority. In the course of the year, he sent two trusted men to confer with Pope Zacharias, chaplain Fulrad and Burchard, bishop of Würzburg. Their orders were to discuss a matter of principle: 'In France, kings no longer exert their royal power – is this a good thing or a bad?'

The official chronicler adds: 'Pope Zacharias replied that it was better to give the name of king to the man who in fact held power than to the man who merely did so nominally. He recommended that Pepin be made king to keep order.' This is the official version. The pope did not, in fact, issue an order, but he made a wise move. He was well aware of the power of the Pepinids and was counting on their help against Lombard incursions.

Pepin was therefore elected king 'according to the tradition of the kings of France', i.e. lifted on to a shield during an assembly of magnates and bishops which was called at Soissons in November 751. For the first time in France's history and with papal consent, the new king was anointed at Soissons by Archbishop Boniface. This was an important precedent which would apply to all the kings of France up to the Revolution. Clovis had already acquired a sacred character by being baptized; but the kings only truly became religious leaders by the anointing of the coronation, which made them into the chosen of God.

Before he was crowned, Pepin, considering himself to be a true king by divine right, felt it unnecessary to encumber himself with Childeric III any longer; he had him tonsured and sent to a convent, a fate to which the Merovingians had become well accustomed. The change of dynasty therefore happened smoothly and it would seem that no serious opposition occurred.

The Papacy's agreement to this arrangement concealed deeper motives which were soon to come to light. On Christmas day 753 Pepin was informed that the pope was about to cross the Alps to visit him. Zacharias's successor, Stephen II, was a Frank by birth and was coming to ask the new king for his military support to repel the Lombards, who were occupying the north of Italy and threatening to invade Rome. Pepin sent his son Charles, the future Charlemagne, ahead to meet the pope. Charles accompanied the pontiff to Ponthion (in the Aisne), where Pepin received him on 6 January 754.

After unsuccessful negotiations with the Lombards, Pepin resigned himself to war. Before setting out, he had himself, his wife Bertha of the Big Foot, and his sons Charles and Carloman solemnly anointed again by the pope. This politically significant ceremony further consolidated his power and its sacred nature.

Pepin crossed the Alps, defeated the Lombards and presented the pope with the territories he had won from them, the duchy of Rome and the exarchate of Ravenna. Then, continuing the work of Charles Martel, he seized Gothia (Mediterranean Languedoc) and occupied Nîmes. He then undertook to subdue Aquitaine and extended his territory as far as the Pyrenees. Finally, he turned to Bavaria and defeated Duke Tassilo III, who was contesting his vassaldom.

To these military successes were added diplomatic successes, of which the most important was an agreement with the emperor of Byzantium, who could well have legitimately protested at the loss of the exarchate of Ravenna, one of Byzantium's last possessions on the Italian peninsula.

At the end of his reign, the totality of Pepin's kingdom (apart from France itself), consisted of Belgium, Holland, the Rhineland and Bavaria. But, in true Merovingian style, he meant to share this immense territory between his sons, which would have compromised the results of this tremendous achievement.

After a wonderfully eventful life, this founder of a dynasty, the mayor of the palace who had become the first real Christian king, died at Saint Denis on 24 September 768. He could well be proud of what he had achieved.

Et comence le ſecond liure des hiſtoires chu
lemaine · premierement coment il fut cou
ronne a empereur en leglise ſaint pierre
de romme · Apres coment il condampna
par cuil ceulx qui auoient laidi la apostoll
lyon · Et puis des troules des terres qui
fuent par le monde · et des meſſaiges et pꝛie
aaron le roy depeꝛſe ·
z our de la natiuite en
tra lempereur en leglise
ſaint pierr de romme
droit en ce point que on

Part Two

THE CAROLINGIANS

768~987

Empire and division

The coronation of Charlemagne by pope Leo III in
St Peter's, Rome. (*Grandes Chroniques de France*)

THE CAROLINGIANS

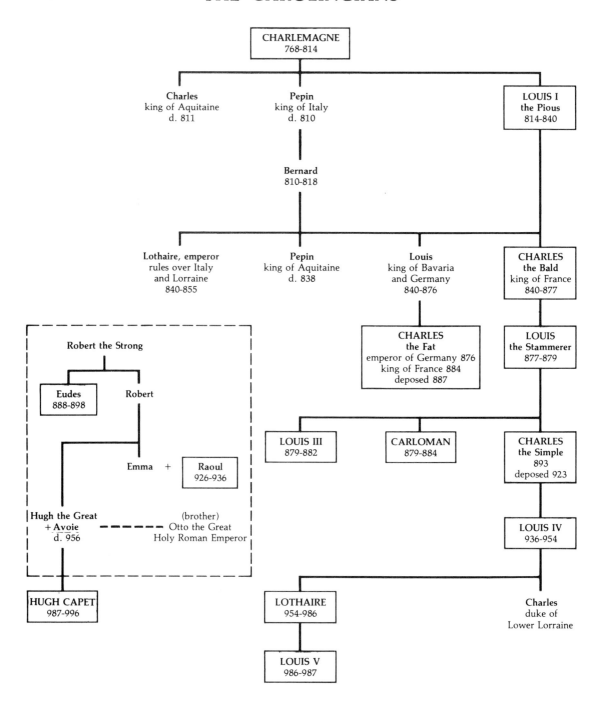

CHARLEMAGNE
768-814

Charles
king of Aquitaine
d. 811

Pepin
king of Italy
d. 810

LOUIS I
the Pious
814-840

Bernard
810-818

Lothaire, emperor
rules over Italy
and Lorraine
840-855

Pepin
king of Aquitaine
d. 838

Louis
king of Bavaria
and Germany
840-876

CHARLES
the Bald
king of France
840-877

CHARLES
the Fat
emperor of Germany 876
king of France 884
deposed 887

LOUIS
the Stammerer
877-879

Robert the Strong

Eudes
888-898

Robert

Emma + **Raoul**
926-936

LOUIS III
879-882

CARLOMAN
879-884

CHARLES
the Simple
893
deposed 923

Hugh the Great
+ **Avoie**
d. 956

(brother)
Otto the Great
Holy Roman Emperor

LOUIS IV
936-954

HUGH CAPET
987-996

LOTHAIRE
954-986

Charles
duke of
Lower Lorraine

LOUIS V
986-987

❧ CHARLEMAGNE ❧
(768–814)

WITH CHARLEMAGNE, who gave his name to the Carolingian dynasty, we come to a legendary figure belonging as much to the history of Germany as to that of France.

The illegitimate son of Pepin, born in 742, he was legitimized by a subsequent marriage. His physical appearance is quite well documented, and does not fit the picture of the huge emperor with the long white beard of the *chansons de geste*. In fact he was of medium height, with a tendency to portliness. It seems his nose was too long and he had a substantial moustache. He was descended through his mother Bertha from the Merovingians, and this established a close link between the dynasties.

Charlemagne has gone down in history as a political and military genius, which is far from being the truth. Aided by exceptional circumstances, he had a far greater destiny than his personal capacities in fact warranted. His education had been neglected to such an extent that for a long time he could not write, and all we have of his writings are a few childish scribbles. But he had an inquiring mind and was not above taking lessons in middle age.

Shortly before his death, Pepin had divided his kingdom between his two sons, Charles and Carloman. The division was a strange one from the geographic point of view: Carloman got Septimania, Toulousain, eastern Aquitaine (Auvergne, Limousin and Berry), Burgundy, Provence, Paris and Soissons, Rheims, Metz, Trier and Strasbourg; a coherent whole, and fairly safe from invasion.

Charles's kingdom was in the shape of a crescent around that of Carloman: it started at the Pyrenees, reached the Garonne at Agen, covered all of western France, Belgium and Frisia, then turned east to take in, on the right bank of the Rhine, Hesse, Bavarian Nordgau and Thuringia, in other words, as they were at the time, western Aquitaine, Neustria, Austrasia and Bavaria.

The two brothers were crowned on the same day, 9 October 768, Charles at Noyon and Carloman at Soissons. To maintain a semblance of unity an agreement was essential, but it was broken in 769 when Carloman refused to help his brother quell a rebellion in Aquitaine.

A more serious disagreement erupted the following year over the Lombards. Carloman supported their king, Desiderius, while Charles was on the side of Pope Stephen III. To reconcile the two brothers, King Desiderius offered them his daughters in marriage. Charles was married to Queen Himiltrude; he repudiated her to marry Desiderius's daughter Desideria. This was not an isolated event in his private life: he was to have many mistresses and illegitimate children. Carloman also had mistresses, but he was not yet married.

Once these marriages had been celebrated, Desiderius marched on Rome in 771, had the principal figures of the pontifical curia handed over to him, and had them tortured, then put to death. Charles, horrified at his new father-in-law's conduct, repudiated Desideria and joined forces with Carloman to punish the Lombards. During this expedition Carloman died suddenly on 4 December 771, leaving two young children from his marriage with Gerbergia, Desideria's sister.

Charles, who should have protected his nephews, adopted the line of a true politician rather than a devoted guardian: he had himself recognized by Carloman's subjects, and Gerbergia was forced to flee to Lombardy with her two young children, of whom nothing more was heard. By this debatable action, Charles re-established unity. He was to be the sole ruler of this huge kingdom for forty-three years, extending it through new conquests and shifting its centre from Paris to Aix-la-Chapelle, where he established a new capital; the Carolingian race thus acquired Germanic influences.

This long reign was marked by fifty-three military expeditions of varying success, which are not well documented. Only one has become famous, the celebrated intervention in Spain in 778, which was in fact of secondary importance. Immortalized in the *chanson de geste* which made famous the names of Roland, Ganelon and Roncevaux, it was a disaster, and had to be com-

Charlemagne's vision: Saint James orders him
to deliver Spain from the Saracens.
(*Grandes Chroniques de France*)

pleted in 793 by a further expedition to liberate
Corbières, which had been invaded by the
Moors. The credit for this expedition goes to
Guillaume au Courb-nez, the famous William of
Orange, who became a monk and retired to the
abbey of Gellone (Saint-Guilhem-le-Désert).
There are several far more important events in
Charlemagne's life, such as the war against the
states of Germany and his relations with the
Papacy.

The troubles with Germany were the result of
the war against Desiderius. Duke Tassilo of
Bavaria was his son-in-law, having married one
of his daughters, Liutbergia. He was twice called
to order to renew his oath of fealty, in 781 and
787. Having broken his promises and allied himself to the pagan Avars of Pannonia, he was
brought to trial by the assembly of Ingelheim
and sentenced to death in 788. Charlemagne
repealed his death sentence but imprisoned him
in a monastery.

This unfortunate affair fades into the background when compared with the war against the
Saxons, which lasted for thirty years, with very
differing fortunes, including one defeat reminiscent of the adventures of Varus's legions in the
Teutonburg Forest. On this occasion, Charlemagne proved himself formidable. In one
single day at Verdun 4500 Saxons were killed.
Finally, after three successful campaigns (783,
784, 785), Witiking, king of the Saxons, surrendered. He was converted to Christianity, and
Charles became his godfather. The Christianization of Saxony, which became part of the
empire, can well be considered the most important of Charlemagne's conquests.

But the most interesting aspect of his reign
was his relationship with the Papacy. Having
temporarily neutralized the Lombards,
Charlemagne went to Rome in 774. Pope
Stephen III had been a very mediocre pontiff. His
successor, Adrian I, was an able politician who
succeeded in ensnaring Charlemagne. Adrian
showed Charlemagne a text which is possibly
the most famous of all political frauds, the *Con-
stitutum Constantini*, appearing to grant the pope
tremendous rights over Italian territory. On
seeing this false piece of evidence, Charlemagne
felt obliged to comply with papal demands,
which gives one a poor opinion of his diplomatic
talents. He solemnly confirmed the illegal gifts
made by his father and added to them Tuscany,
Benevento and Pentapolis. But he was less
amenable when Adrian also demanded Corsica,
Venetia, Istria and Friuli.

Charlemagne was named Patrician of the
Romans and concluded his war against
Desiderius, whom he defeated, and who was
obliged to surrender the iron crown of the
Lombards.

Charlemagne was recalled to Italy in 780, subdued the duke of Benevento, and took Capua,
which he presented to the Papacy, together with
Grosseto, Orvieto and Viterbo.

Adrian I died in 795 and was succeeded by
Leo III, a mediocre and strongly opposed pope,
who nevertheless took an astonishing initiative
which was to affect the fate of the Western
world.

At the beginning of his pontificate a rebellion
broke out in Rome (25 April 799). The pope
managed to escape and sought refuge at

Charlemagne's court at Paderborn. Pontiff and king embraced each other in tears. Then, with an escort of Frankish soldiers, the pope returned to Rome, but another attempt was made against him, and he called for help on Charlemagne, who arrived in Rome at the end of November 800.

On 1 December he gathered at St Peter's a solemn tribunal to try the pontiff's accusers. Leo III defended himself by a purgatory oath and his accusers were handed over to the executioner. The pope asked for their sentence to be commuted, which removes any doubts as to their true guilt and makes even stranger the event which took place on 25 December 800.

It was the evening of Christmas day. Charlemagne was praying in the basilica of St Peter's when, in front of several bishops and great lords, the pope placed the imperial crown on the king's head and proclaimed him Emperor of Rome.

Even today this seems an astonishing action. The pope had no lawful right to confer a crown which belonged to the senate of Byzantium; and Leo III's bad reputation certainly did not give him the moral authority to take such a vital decision. This papal initiative was on the whole badly received. Charlemagne insisted several times that he had no inkling that he was to be crowned, but that he dared not refuse the honour, even though it might have seemed contestable.

The pope then encouraged him to ask for the appalling Irene, empress of Byzantium, in marriage, which would have made of him a sort of emperor-consort. Charlemagne, to whom one

The Carolingian cavalry. (Saint Gall Psalter)

ET SYRIAM SOBAL· ET CONVERTIT
IOAB· ET PERCUSSIT EDOM IN VAL
LE SALINARUM ·XII MILIA·

woman more or less would hardly have made much difference, accepted this in principle, but the extravagant idea was nipped in the bud in 802 when Irene was deposed. Charlemagne remained emperor, and in his later years dedicated himself to internal policies, leaving his three sons to wage the wars in his place.

These internal policies deserve a mention. Charlemagne is justly credited with building churches, founding schools and restoring monasteries – images of him which were spread by the chronicler Alcuin – but the most important point was that Charlemagne had created an empire too rapidly for it to be ruled with his limited means. His counties were overseen by special envoys, the *missi dominici*, who travelled in pairs, one layman and a clergyman, and reported their trips to him, confirming the oaths of fealty. But this oath implied that when the vassal died his fief should be returned to the crown. For lack of means to impose this, this formality was later neglected by the parties concerned, who left the fief to their heirs. It was through this abuse that, during following centuries, the division of power which is called feudalism came about.

In 806 Charlemagne took steps to arrange an eventual partition of his estates between his three sons, to be carried out in true Merovingian style. The elder, Charles, was to receive Austrasia, Neustria, northern Burgundy, northern Alemannia, Bavarian Nordgau, Frisia, Saxony and Thuringia, and the valley of Aosta in the Alps, to establish communications. The second, Pepin, was to receive Lombardy, Bavaria, southern Alemannia and Rhaetia. Finally Louis, the youngest, was to inherit Aquitaine, Septimania, the Spanish marches, southern Burgundy, Provence and the Susa valley, for passage into Italy.

This dismemberment was prevented by the deaths of Charles in 810 and Pepin in 811. Louis was now sole successor to the empire, and in 813 Charles had him crowned. The ceremony took place at Aix-la-Chapelle. The emperor placed the crown on his son's head himself, and the crowd shouted, 'Long live Emperor Louis.' Then Louis returned to his kingdom of Aquitaine until his father's death. This came about fairly quickly. After hunting in the Ardennes on 22 January 814, the emperor contracted pleurisy and died on 28 January 814, at the age of seventy-two.

His immense achievement was fragile, as was to become clear under his successor. But Charlemagne's prestige remained intact. He is buried at Aix-la-Chapelle in a circular church, and both Charles V and Bonaparte, on the eve of becoming emperors, came to kneel before this tomb.

ᗧᗧ LOUIS THE PIOUS ᗧᗧ
(814–840)
AND JUDITH

LOUIS I, called the Pious and also the Affable, was born in the year of the disaster at Roncevaux, 778. His father marked out the kingdom of Aquitaine for him when he was only three (781). While ruling effectively over his southern kingdom from his majority, Louis was also associated with his father's activities. He took part in expeditions to Saxony and Spain. This military training served him in good stead during his reign, during which the empire was not free from serious external threats.

Louis ascended the throne in 814. He was certainly emperor and sole inheritor of the crown by his father's wish. But Pepin had left a son, Bernard, who held power in Italy. Fearing that he might be supplanted, this young prince rebelled. He was arrested, taken to Aix-la-Chapelle, tried and condemned to death. Louis I granted him his life, but authorized the Byzantine punishment of blinding. Bernard died in prison as a result of having his eyes gouged out.

Charlemagne had left many bastards. Louis had them all tonsured and sent into monasteries. These tough measures heralded an authoritarian reign. Determined to put an end to the moral laxity which had prevailed at Charlemagne's court, Louis took the counsel of the reformer St Benedict of Aniane, who pushed his laudable but impolitic influence too far.

The sovereign's piety led him at first to a certain weakness with regard to the Papacy; he virtually gave up his right to intervene in papal elections, a right which he held from the title of Patrician of the Romans conferred on his father. In 816 he invited Pope Stephen v to come to Rheims to crown him, implying that his previous coronation had been insufficient, and suggesting the concept that the imperial crown depended on the pope's goodwill. In 823 he also had his eldest son Lothair crowned by the pope.

Louis' concessions gave rise to trouble among the more ambitious Lateran prelates. At the death in 824 of Pascal I, Louis' son Lothair favoured the election of Pope Eugene II but imposed the Roman constitution on him to restore imperial authority in Rome; in this he appeared to go against his father. Louis' power was initially consolidated by this move, but he was shortly to lose the benefit of this reform by his mistakes.

In 818, Louis the Pious lost his wife, Empress Irmengard, by whom he had three sons, Lothair, Pepin and Louis. In 819 he married Judith, daughter of Count Welf of Bavaria. She was the first queen of France to have influenced the course of history, but unfortunately in a scarcely favourable direction.

The new empress soon gained the upper hand over her husband. On 13 June 823 she gave birth to a son, who was to become King Charles the Bald. Judith found her way round the eldest son Lothair: he agreed to be godfather to his half-brother and undertook to provide him in time with land.

Six years later, at the assembly of Worms, Louis announced that he was presenting his third son with a territory comprising Alemannia, Alsace, Rhaetia and certain counties in Burgundy. Although this was a modest endowment and did not entail the title of king, Lothair forgot his promises and protested. Louis decided to send Lothair into exile and announced that he would give his son no role in the empire. Judith took pleasure in exacerbating the situation. On top of this she was in league with Bernard, son of William called 'of Orange'; she

obtained the post of chamberlain for him, and it was rumoured that he was her lover.

Louis was accused of weakness and blamed by the entire episcopate; his natural piety prevented him from defending himself as he should have done. He was also deeply repentant of the punishment inflicted on his nephew Bernard. Under the influence of the episcopate he agreed to do public penance at the assembly of Attigny, which undermined his power to such an extent that, at a council in 829, the episcopate proclaimed that ecclesiastical power was superior to lay power, and that the latter should submit. The consequences of this were felt immediately; a military revolt against the emperor erupted in 830 to obtain the dismissal of Bernard of Orange, who fled to Barcelona; Judith was imprisoned in the cloister of St Radegarde in Poitiers.

The emperor was nearly deposed, and his power diminished in favour of his son Lothair, who became the only effective emperor. This operation revived the rivalry between Louis' sons and he was able to resume his authority, bring his wife out from the convent and clear her of the accusations of adultery. In 832 the jurors who had condemned Judith and humbled Louis were sentenced to death. The king gave them their lives but sent them into monasteries.

Having regained her power over her husband, Judith tried to influence the sharing out of territory for the benefit of her own son. But the emperor was obliged, to appease his opponents, to make concessions to all his children. The youngest, Louis and Pepin, received the bigger shares. Pepin had Aquitaine and the region between the Loire and the Seine, while Louis earned his nickname 'the German' by getting Bavaria, Saxony, Frisia and Austrasia. In view of these concessions made to the sons of his first marriage, Louis had to make up for Charles a portion consisting of Burgundy, Provence, Septimania, Woëvre, Rheims, Laon and Trier. Lothair was sent back to Italy after making honourable amends to his father.

By making these anticipatory shares Louis committed the mistake of ruining the concept of empire. Despite the considerable advantages he had gained in the 831 partition, Pepin rebelled, his father disinherited him, and he fled to England. His brothers took his side, and war

Louis the Pious punishes his son Pepin by sending him to prison.
(*Grandes Chroniques de France*)

broke out between the emperor and his sons. They met near Colmar. Disconcerted by the presence of the pope with his sons, Louis surrendered.

An ecclesiastical assembly took place at Compiègne on 1 October 833; it accused Louis of having compromised the empire and demanded his abdication. Louis was imprisoned in the monastery of St Médard near Soissons, made honourable amends to his sons and became a monk, while Judith was kept in the monastery of Tortona and Charles in that of Prüm.

Lothair became emperor and refused the concessions which his brothers demanded. In 834

they joined together against him. In view of this disorder the clergy felt it preferable to have Louis back, so on 1 March 834, Louis the Pious became emperor again. He was reconciled with his sons and, hoping to strengthen his position, had himself crowned for the third time in the cathedral of St Stephen of Metz (28 February 835).

Once freed, Judith resumed all her former influence and succeeded in her aims by winning an advantage for her son Charles. In 837, Louis granted his younger son Frisia, the land between the Seine and the Meuse, northern Burgundy and Champagne, which bit into his brothers' shares. Later on, Louis added Neustria and Brittany to Charles's lot with the consent of Pepin who, home from exile, still hoped to become Charles's protector.

In 836, Charles attained his legal majority at the age of sixteen. At the assembly of Quierzy he was made a knight with Pepin's agreement. but when Pepin died suddenly on 13 December 837, Louis added his share to Charles's.

The intriguer Judith then dealt her masterstroke: she was reconciled with Lothair and at Worms the empire was split into two, between Lothair and Charles. This treaty could not be carried out, as Pepin had left sons. Aquitaine revolted, and Louis the German also took up arms. The unfortunate Emperor Louis, at risk from so many directions, defeated his son Louis, but on returning from this expedition he fell ill. He was put on a boat which sailed down the Main, and was carried to an island in the Rhine near Ingelheim, where he died on 20 June 840 at the age of sixty-two.

He left behind him a disintegrating empire, The rivalry between his sons was to dismember it completely.

ᢟ CHARLES THE BALD ᢟ
(840–877)

IN APPEARING TO ACCEPT the last partition by Louis the Pious in 839 Lothair had yet again proved insincere. He immediately tried to win over his brother Charles's supporters with bribes. Charles was kept in Aquitaine by a rebellion in support of Pepin's sons. A section of the population declared their support for Lothair, who prepared to attack the armies of his half-brother and godson.

However, before hostilities began, negotiations were entered upon, and a truce was agreed which saved Charles and gave him time to restore order in Aquitaine. But Charles was aware now of Lothair's falseness, and determined to ally himself to Louis the German.

The postponed battle took place at Fontenoy in southern Auxerre, and Lothair's forces were defeated (25 June 841). This battle resolved nothing, but gave a breathing space to Charles, who made for Strasbourg, where he joined up with his half-brother Louis the German; in front of their armies the two kings took an oath. Louis spoke in a Romance language, Charles in Frankish, i.e. practically German.

This Oath of Strasbourg, the oldest known Romance text, is of such importance that we quote it here:

For the love of God, for the salvation of Christendom and the common good, from this day forward, and as long as God grant me the knowledge and power to do so, I will defend my brother Charles and will help him in all circumstances, as one must in equity defend one's brother, on condition that he deal the same with me, and I will never conclude with Lothair any arrangement which, to my knowledge, would prejudice the interests of my brother Charles.

This understanding was witnessed by the two armies, who in turn took a similar oath.

From Strasbourg the two kings headed for Worms, where they awaited Lothair's reply. As he refused to receive their emissaries, they attacked him on 18 March 842 at the passage of the Moselle, and Lothair fled. Thereupon the two brothers signed a provisional treaty of partition valid until 1 October. Lothair then came to terms with them. On 15 June 842 the three brothers met on an island in the Saône and finally swore to live together in peace. They appointed a committee of 120 members to set about the partition of Louis the Pious's heritage.

Despite Lothair's ill will, the treaty of Verdun in 843 accepted this partition, the most important one in French history, as it marked the birth of the nation. Charles the Bald, despite being practically Germanic by race and language, was about to become the first real king of France.

What he was inheriting was really the whole of the western empire, that is the country between the Atlantic, the Rhône, the Saône and the Meuse, but stretching as far north as Frisia and as

Charles the Bald fights his brothers at Fontenay-en-Bourgogne. (*Grandes Chroniques de France*)

far south as Barcelona. It was in fact today's France minus Provence, Dauphiné, Franche-Comté, part of Burgundy and Alsace-Lorraine, and a sector on the right bank of the Rhône corresponding to the Ardèche.

Louis the German had the western part of the empire: starting from the right bank of the Rhine, he had Austrasia, Saxony, Bohemia, Bavaria, Styria and Carinthia.

Emperor Lothair reigned over the sector between the lands of his two brothers: a long strip of territory extending from Frisia to the Arno, and encompassing Holland, eastern Belgium, Rhineland, Franche-Comté, the valleys of the Saône and Rhône, Provence, Lombardy, Venetia and Tuscany. This unnaturally long territory received the name of Lotharingia. Although it corresponded to no ethnic or geographic logic, it was a crucial piece of land, which has affected a vast stretch of history.

Charles the Bald was to reign over France for thirty-five years, and in difficult circumstances,

as his era was marked by new invasions. The Normans pillaged Rouen, and on Easter Day 845 they took Paris. For lack of military resources, Charles was obliged to pay them a huge and humiliating ransom in silver.

In 847, at the council of Meerson, Lothair tried in vain to make vassals of his brothers in order to restore the unity of the empire. His efforts were even less successful in view of the fact that feudalism was gaining a stronger hold, and that sovereigns were beginning to have power only over vassal fiefs which by now were practically independent.

In 848 Charles the Bald subdued Aquitaine; he had the sons of his half-brother Pepin II handed over to him and sent them to a monastery.

He had other problems, as from 852 to 867 the Normans made new incursions which nearly ruined the country. It seemed that weak royal power was playing into the enemy's hands. In 853 Tours, Vannes and Orléans were pillaged by the Normans.

From this time onwards a figure appears by the side of the king whose descendants, 180 years later, were to change the course of history. His name was Robert, nicknamed the Strong. Legend has it that he began as a butcher in Paris. But there is documentary evidence that he was the lay abbot of the abbey of Marmoutier, where he succeeded Le Vivien, count of Tours. The following year (854) he was *missus dominicus* to the counties of Tours, Angers and Le Mans.

Count Robert was therefore already a considerable personality. But it was as a warrior, and not an administrator, that he was to make his mark. In 858 Louis the German violated the treaty of Verdun and invaded Lorraine, which was in Lothair's portion. Then he penetrated into France. This operation could only have been carried out with intelligence from Charles the Bald's court. Evidence points to Robert, who was no doubt pursuing some ambitious plot for his own personal benefit. It seems too that it was thanks to this semi-treachery that Robert put a halt to the invasion. In 860 the Germans retreated and a peace treaty was signed at Koblenz; this consolidated Robert's position with the king. Henceforth he acted as a mayor of the palace; he subdued the Bretons and was given the county of Autun.

In 866, during a new Norman invasion, he defended the territory and defeated the invaders at Brissarthe near Angers in a famous battle in which he was killed. But he became a national hero; having acquired new territories, including Blois, he left a considerable heritage to his sons Eudes and Robert, who were brought up by their half-brother Abbot Hugh, son of Robert's wife by a first marriage and a relative of Charles the Bald. Hugh took Robert's place at the king's side and used his power to augment the possessions of his wards, who were to become dukes of France and counts of Paris.

In 877 Charles the Bald published the Capitular of Quierzy, ratifying the status of the lords while guaranteeing their loyalty to him. His own status had grown tremendously; with his brothers dead, he reigned over their possessions and became emperor. He went to Rome to be crowned by Pope John VIII, but died on the return journey at Modano on 6 October 877.

Charles the Bald's merits have been much discussed, generally unfavourably; but he was the last Carolingian king to have truly reigned.

❦ THE DECLINE OF THE DYNASTY ❦
AND THE EMPIRE
(877–987)

CHARLES THE BALD'S SON LOUIS II the Stammerer was a mediocre sovereign known only for having received Pope John VIII in France, where he held a council at Troyes. Louis II died after a two-year reign, leaving two sons, Louis III and Carloman, from a first marriage, and from a second a posthumous son who was to become Charles III the Simple.

The great lords had the two sons crowned while they were still minors. Louis III died in 882 and Carloman in 884. The imperial crown returned to the descendants of Louis the German, whose son, Charles the Large, crowned by Pope John VIII, became the guardian of young Charles and therefore administrator of French interests. At the time these were seriously threatened by the Normans, who came up the Seine and threatened Paris.

The duke of France, Eudes, son of Robert the Strong, now came into prominence. Having inherited the possessions of Abbot Hugh, he had become a powerful feudal lord. He was moreover a man of great courage and an experienced soldier. On 24 November 885, forty thousand Normans appeared in front of Paris and laid siege to the town. Eudes kept up the Parisians' spirits and called on Charles the Large for help. When the call was ignored, Eudes crossed the enemy lines to bring Charles to his senses, then returned to the besieged city. Instead of sending reinforcements, Charles the Large offered the Normans a ransom: Burgundy. The Normans left Paris and headed for Burgundy in 887.

Eudes had won glory by his heroism, but Charles the Large's cowardliness was such that he was deposed by the magnates. He died shortly afterwards, in 888, leaving the crown of France to a minor, the posthumous son of Louis the Stammerer, Charles, whose legitimacy was contested by the feudal lords. They wanted to name one of their own people king, and the choice fell fairly naturally on Eudes, who was crowned at Compiègne.

This year, 888, brought about significant changes in France's history: although the throne had been properly inherited and the regency was working well, elective power superseded heredity and a feudal choice was preferred to a king of royal blood. It would have seemed more likely that Eudes, rather than accept a crown to which he had no right, would be named regent. If he had succeeded during his ten-year reign in getting rid of the Normans, he could probably have founded a new dynasty. But despite an important victory at Montfaucon his attempts were finally unsuccessful and the magnates, having a legitimate king to hand, had Charles III the Simple crowned at Laon on 8 July 893.

However, Eudes' personal position was so strong that he continued to rule and Charles did not assume the title of king. Aware of the delicacy of his situation, he did not attempt to perpetuate his succession, and before dying in 898 he advised his younger brother Robert to recognize the Carolingian.

The reign of Charles the Simple began with a period of military calm, and the Normans agreed to a truce. With Robert's help, Charles III ruled wisely and planned to join Lorraine to France. Then he searched for a solution to the Norman problem. It was obvious the invaders could maintain their bridgehead in France. Why not try to draw up a treaty with them during a period of peace?

This was codified in the famous treaty of St-Clair-sur-Epte in 911. Normandy was put in the charge of the Viking chieftain Rollo, who immediately became a great feudal lord, on a par with a duke of France or of Burgundy. The solution was a good one and the line descended from Rollo was to prove worthy of its founder: a century and a half later one of his descendants, William the Conqueror, was to assume the crown of England.

Charles the Simple's last years were tragic and he effectively lost his throne, as did his wife Queen Eadgifu. He died in captivity in 929, leaving a son who would later become Louis IV d'Outre-Mer.

This succession did not take place straight away. Robert, who in his turn had become a true mayor of the palace, had a son-in-law, Raoul, the son of the duke of Burgundy. He was an ambitious but muddle-headed man, who managed to persuade his father-in-law Robert and brother-in-law Hugh the Great that the time was ripe for a change of dynasty. As early as 922, while Charles was still alive, though weakened by illness, Robert had himself elected king and was crowned at St Remi of Rheims by Archbishop Gautier on 29 June 922. For a while France had two kings, both consecrated by the Church, although the situation was soon resolved with the death of Robert in combat in 923.

The family did not give up and Raoul had himself elected king in his turn on 15 July 923, in open defiance of Charles III. He was crowned at St Médard-de-Soissons by Archbishop Gautier, who had become a real king-maker.

Raoul attacked Charles the Simple, seized him and had him imprisoned in the dungeon at Péronne until his death in 929. Charles's son was naturally unable to take over the throne on his father's death, and Raoul reigned until 935, rather mediocrely, leaving no issue. His brother-in-law, Hugh the Great, did not claim the throne, feeling his position to be too weak. He sent to England for Charles the Simple's son, who had been brought up there and who ruled under the name of Louis IV d'Outre-Mer.

This king was then fifteen years old, and through his mother Eadgifu was the nephew of an English king, Athelstan. Athelstan was very reticent when a delegation came to claim his nephew; he insisted that the magnates should pay homage to him as soon as he set foot in France, and only when he obtained these guarantees did he let his nephew go. Hugh received the young king in person at Boulogne and led him to Laon, and then, on 19 June 936, had him anointed at Rheims by Archbishop Artaud.

LEFT The Normans set fire to Saint Martin de Tours. RIGHT Herbert has Charles the Simple imprisoned, and Raoul is crowned. (*Grandes Chroniques de France*)

Having thus served the cause of legitimacy, Hugh the Great found his position much strengthened, and this duke of France was considered as the king's equal. He married King Athelstan's sister Eadhild and thus became the king of France's uncle.

But Louis IV had a strong personality, and also that truly royal characteristic of ingratitude. Fully aware of all he owed to Hugh the Great, he set about trying to free himself from his influence. Hugh felt this coming and opposed it adroitly. Realizing that all royal power in France depended on the Church, he followed ecclesiastic policies strictly and won the friendship of the principal Church dignitaries. While Louis IV still felt an obligation towards him he managed to persuade him to grant him Burgundy and Aquitaine, which made him the greatest western feudal lord, and allowed him, if necessary, to dispense with the king's goodwill, as he was now in effect the more powerful of the two.

To many people Hugh seemed to be the arbiter of Europe, and therefore a candidate for emperor. But this honour was to fall to his second wife Hadwig's brother Otto. An ambitious man, he took advantage of the cool relations between Hugh and Louis IV and judged the moment right to attack France. But common interest brought Hugh and the king together, and the invasion which had reached the royal palace of Attigny in the Aisne in 940 was neutralized; a treaty was signed, based on the old treaty of Verdun.

Then feudal conflict began again. The archbishop of Rheims, Artaud, who had become Louis IV's chancellor and chief adviser, was imprisoned by Hugh the Great, the duke of Normandy, William Long-Sword, and by Herbert of Vermandois. Thanks to his good relations with the clergy, Hugh won the approbation of Pope Stephen VIII.

Having tried to subdue the duke of Normandy, Louis became his prisoner. Hugh intrigued to have him freed, but Otto intervened and obtained his release. Louis IV had been in some danger, and one would have expected Hugh to try to depose him, since the throne was so fragile, but Louis reacted quickly and had Hugh condemned by an episcopal assembly at Ingelheim on 28 November 946. The influence of the future Emperor Otto had been decisive.

The condemnation of Hugh allowed the king of France to take back Laon, which Hugh had seized. But Hugh was not a man to be left in check and on 14 April 950 he was reconciled with the king.

The king of France had shown himself superior to and more able than the duke of France, but he had no chance to profit from his success, as he was killed in a riding accident at the age of thirty-three, in 954, and was buried at St Remi of Rheims. The succession presented no problems, and although he was only thirteen the king's son Lothair was crowned on Sunday, 18 November 954 by Artaud, who had been reinstated at Rheims.

Hugh the Great thought it wise to accept this new sovereign with good grace, and was once again in full favour when he died after a short illness at Dourdan in June 956; he left a son named Hugh, and nicknamed Hugh Capet because of the abbeys whose 'cappa' (or cape) he wore. His role was to be a vital one. Hugh Capet lacked his father's stature – he was a timid and rather strange person. Yet by an extraordinary chance he was to be brought to kingship by a

The iron crown of the Lombard kings.

singular sequence of events. But two reigns were to elapse before this surprising change of fortune.

Europe at that time was in the grip of a serious crisis: the Hungarian invasion was arriving from the east. And it was Otto who was to have the glory of warding it off. On 10 August 955 he defeated the Magyars in the battle of the Lechfeld in southern Augsburg, and on 16 October 955 he repelled the Slavs in the battle of the Recknitz. This dual success brought him Swabia, Helvetia and the kingdom of Arles from the Jura to Provence.

In 951 Otto had already assumed the iron crown of the Lombard kings. Thanks to this success he was to obtain a great deal more and in 962, in Rome, Pope John XII, crowned him Germanic Roman emperor, the beginning of an empire which was to last for eight centuries.

Otto was King Lothair's guardian, but as Hugh the Great's brother-in-law he was also the guardian of his nephew Hugh Capet. The extraordinary situation arose of Europe's most powerful ruler having the dual guardianship of the Carolingian race, which was expiring, and of the Robertian one, which was approaching its zenith.

Lothair's personality was a good deal stronger than Hugh Capet's, and circumstances seemed to improve the chances of the king of France. By his marriage in 965 to Emma of Italy, daughter of Otto the Great's second wife, the links between France and Germany were tightening to the detriment of the power of the great feudal lords. But Lothair, like his ancestor Charles the Simple before him, was attracted to Lorraine, and wanted to consolidate the Rhine border. These intentions were to bring about the end of the Carolingians.

In 978 the king attempted a raid on Aix-la-Chapelle to try to imprison Emperor Otto II, son of Otto the Great. He did this against the advice of Hugh Capet, who had become his adviser. The emperor was forewarned. He marched on France, and Lothair's own brother, Charles of Lorraine, a Germanophile, handed Laon over to the invaders. The route to Paris was open and Lothair fled to Etampes.

The Germans continued their march and the emperor besieged Paris, establishing his headquarters at Montmartre. Then Hugh Capet lived up to his family's reputation: he organized a defence and saved Paris from the Germans as his ancestor Eudes had saved it from the Normans ninety-three years before. This feat subsequently acquired a symbolic significance: as long as the Capetians remained on the throne of France, the Germans never returned to the gates of Paris.

Lothair realized the danger, and to assure the continuity of the dynasty he associated his son Louis to the throne in Compiègne, in other words had him crowned as his colleague and successor. Capet approved this decision. More than ever he wished to be a lay abbot, and on 9 June 980 he had the relics of St Valéry taken to Amiens Cathedral. Legend has it that the waters of the Somme divided to allow the procession to pass, and Hugh Capet saw the saint in a dream, predicting that he would not only become king, but that his family would remain on the throne for at least seven generations. Subsequent events made these predictions disconcertingly accurate.

When Emperor Otto II died in 983, Lothair took an interest in German affairs and tried to intervene in the guardianship of his young nephew Otto III, although many people tried to dissuade him. To discourage Lothair the Germans used the influence of the archbishop of Rheims, Adalbéron, an important and devious character. With their support, Adalbéron placed his nephew on the episcopal see of Verdun without consulting Lothair. Outraged, the king of France marched on Verdun and captured Adalbéron's family. The archbishop's supporters, who were numerous, began to feel it might be worth while substituting Hugh Capet for Lothair. The king discovered this, accused Adalbéron of treason and ordered that he be put on trial.

Then occurred a turning point in history: on 2 March 985, Lothair, aged only forty-four, died suddenly from a stomach complaint which some believed was due to poisoning. However, Lothair's succession posed no problems. Louis v, already aged nineteen, was associated to the throne and effectively became king on the death of his father. He was as energetic as his father and

Hugh Capet had no wish to dethrone him.

Adalbéron's trial followed its course. Capet was called and did not dare withhold his agreement, whereas Adalbéron had been hoping for his opposition to the royal decision. This collusion made the archbishop think, and he declared himself ready for any concessions; he was obliged to accept that his trial should take place at an assembly at Compiègne.

The assembly was called and the business put in hand, when an unforeseeable event occurred: Louis v fell off his horse and was killed at the age of twenty. It was the end of the Carolingians. The assembly called to judge Adalbéron was faced with a new and far more urgent problem, to fill the vacant throne, as no one imagined that Charles of Lorraine, the pro-German traitor, could be called upon to rule France.

Hugh Capet, the most powerful lord, who had been adviser to the young king, was master of the hour. The change of dynasty was welcomed by the feudal lords, and easily prevailed. The judicial assembly became an electoral college, and Capet, presiding, had Adalbéron declared innocent – a favour which was duly returned: Adalbéron and the people of Rheims were to declare Capet king of France. The electoral principle superseded heredity, as no one wanted Charles of Lorraine, not even Emperor Otto III.

One factor in favour of Capet was his very ordinariness: it was thought that such a king would be easily swayed, and when he died, what was to prevent another election? It was not for his virtues but for his lack of qualities that Hugh Capet, far inferior to his ancestors, was to be chosen. Adalbéron conferred the regency on him at Compiègne. A few days later, at Senlis, he was elected king, and on 3 July 987 Hugh Capet, acclaimed by his peers, was crowned at Noyon and took the oath.

Those who elected him could not know that they had decided the fate of France and that nearly forty kings descended from him were to succeed each other for more than eight hundred years.

The coronation of Hugh Capet.
(*Grandes Chroniques de France*)

Part Three

THE DIRECT CAPETIANS

987~1328

Birth of the nation

THE DIRECT CAPETIANS

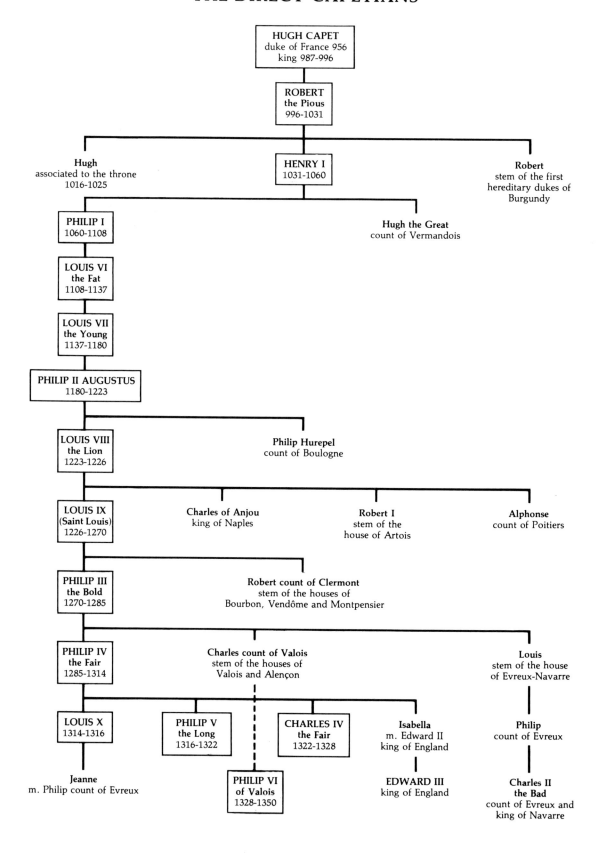

HUGH CAPET
(987–996)

VERY LITTLE IS KNOWN about Hugh Capet the man; there are no portraits of him, and no text of his exists other than the oath he took when he became king, and which was repeated by all his successors up to the Revolution:

> I, Hugh, who am about to become king of the Franks, by divine favour, on this day of my coronation, in the presence of God and the saints, promise to each one of you to preserve for you the canonical privilege, law and justice which are due to you, to defend you with all my power with God's help, as it is just for a king to behave in his kingdom towards each bishop and towards the Church which is committed to him. I promise to distribute justice to the people who are in my care, according to their rights.

This coronation oath established beyond the shadow of a doubt the supremacy of the Church in the election, and seems to offer a definite commitment to it.

The contemporary historian Richer, who recounted the discussions leading to the choice of Hugh Capet, indicates that he was singled out by opportunity and in particular as an alternative to Charles of Lorraine, of whom they wanted to be rid. But this setting aside of the legitimate Carolingians was not to everyone's liking, and Charles of Lorraine still had his partisans. The reign therefore got off to an uneasy start.

Hugh Capet, a man of experience and common sense, immediately bolstered his fragile position by associating his eldest son Robert to the throne. This system, by which Robert became *Rex designatus* (or king designate), was to facilitate the succession. To further consolidate his son's position, Hugh arranged a marriage for him which would neutralize the Flemish threat: Robert married Rozala, daughter of King Berengar of Italy and widow of the count of Flanders, Arnulf II. Robert did not get on well with this princess, who was older than himself, and this was to cause serious problems later on.

Hugh Capet was confronted with other difficulties caused by Charles of Lorraine, who

contested his defeat, and by the death of Adalbèron, the king's most loyal subject.

A famous monk, Gerbert, was seeking the archbishopric of Rheims; instead of giving it to him, Capet let himself be taken in by a rival, Arnulf, bastard of Charles of Lorraine (some writers believe he was actually the bastard of Charles of Lorraine's brother, King Lothair). Arnulf promised to deliver to him Laon, his father's capital, and he won the day. Gerbert, disgruntled, went to Rome to complain, causing a disagreement which lasted throughout the reign.

At the time it seemed more practical, before solving this problem, to defeat Charles of Lorraine, who had immured himself in Laon. Hugh and Robert began by having him excommunicated, then Laon was handed over to them by Bishop Ascelin, who was Arnulf's creature: Charles of Lorraine and all his people were taken prisoner. In 992 he died in prison, probably poisoned. The dynastic problem had been resolved, but in a scarcely honourable fashion.

On the other hand the problem of the archbishopric of Rheims remained unresolved. Despite Gerbert's advances the pope had supported Arnulf. Hugh and Robert decided to defer the case to a sort of national council held at Verzy on 17 and 18 June 991. This assembly, attended by very few bishops, gave the see of Rheims to Gerbert. The decision was a gesture of defiance both to the Papacy and to the Empire, which supported Arnulf. Pope John XV, a difficult member of the Crescenti line, opposed this decision and summoned the king of France and his son to Rome. Hugh Capet refused to attend the convocation and a second assembly held at Chelles in 993 confirmed Arnulf's eviction.

Another betrayal by the bishop of Laon, Ascelin, complicated the problem even further: he intended handing France over to Emperor Otto III in return for the archbishopric of Rheims. But the French bishops strongly supported Hugh Capet, and this display of national independence ruined Ascelin's plans. Gerbert returned to Rome and, to put an end to the problem, gave up his claim to Rheims and had himself granted the archbishopric of Ravenna, which he was soon to leave to become Pope Sylvester II.

With the conflict of Rheims finally settled, the king had to put down a rebellious vassal, Count Eudes of Blois, over whom he triumphed fairly easily. Then, stricken with smallpox, he died in August 996 and was buried in front of the altar of the Trinity in the basilica of St Denis, after nine years of an inglorious reign.

ROBERT THE PIOUS
(996–1031)

A HAGIOGRAPHY OF ROBERT, called the Pious because of his devotion, exists thanks to the monk Helgaud, of Fleury-sur-Loire. The nickname, which the king's private life seems not to have justified, stems from this work.

Crowned in his father's lifetime, Robert succeeded him without the slightest argument in 996. His first act was to repudiate his wife, whom he did not love, while keeping her dowry, the city of Montreuil-sur-Mer, which gave the king of France a gateway to the Channel. He then immediately married Bertha, widow of the count of Blois, who already had five children. Pope Gregory V intervened because quite apart from bigamy there was also a question of incest, as the newly-weds were too closely related.

To conciliate the Papacy, Robert confirmed the investiture of Arnulf after the siege of Rheims. This proved a useless gesture, and the Pope excommunicated Robert. After resisting for five years, Robert gave up and contracted a third alliance with the count of Arles's daughter, Constance of Provence; he later tried to dissolve this marriage so as to marry Bertha again.

Constance of Provence was a dreadful queen, cantankerous, miserly and jealous. Nevertheless she gave her husband four sons, Hugh, Henry, Robert and Raoul. Hugh, like Robert before him, was associated to the throne, but died before his father. Queen Constance then demanded that the crown pass to the youngest, Robert, whom she preferred to the elder, Henry.

Robert strongly opposed this wish and had Henry crowned. The youngest of all, Raoul, received the duchy of Burgundy, where he started a dynasty which lasted for more than three centuries.

These events created an important precedent: from Henry I onwards succession by primogeniture became unquestionable, and was made law.

But the queen disagreed with this and encouraged her sons to rise up against their father. These arguments cast a shadow over the end of a reign which would be considered mediocre had it not seen the union of Burgundy to the kingdom, a union which unfortunately proved ephemeral, since Robert, just like a Merovingian or a Carolingian, divided up his territories.

The reign as a whole was marked only by difficulties with vassals which, apart from the successful Burgundy affair, imposed a limit on all territorial expansion of the kingdom; it remained bordered in the south by the Loire.

Too weak to accept the crown of Italy which was once offered to him, Robert lived up to his nickname 'the Pious' through a meeting with the German Emperor Henry III the Saintly at Ivois, in 1023. They tried in vain to reach an agreement in order to put an end to the disorders which were afflicting the Papacy.

Robert the Pious died in 1031 after an unspectacular thirty-five-year reign, leaving a difficult situation brought about by Queen Constance's intriguing.

OPPOSITE Robert the Pious sings in church. (*Grandes Chroniques de France*)

Cy conmancent les chapitres du roy
robert Le pmier comt le roy huc cap
pet se fist couroner et de son trespassement

uant la generation
du grant roy char
lemaine fu faillie

⚜ HENRY I ⚜
(1031–1060)

HENRY I IS THE LEAST-KNOWN of all the Capetian kings; no one wrote about him in his lifetime, and the destruction of the archives shortly after his time has left a huge blank over this period. All that is known is that Queen Constance contested his right to the throne, which she wanted to go to Robert; this resulted in a war between the two brothers, of which little is known. Henry won it by buying the support of his vassals, which cost him French Vexin and the total renunciation of the duchy of Burgundy in favour of his brother, in 1034.

Without the benefit of the coronation it is likely that Henry, who appears to have been a mediocre man, would have been brushed aside. But the anointing brought him respect and won time for concessions. Managing to remain in power is after all a sign of stability, and despite the obscurity of his reign it saw a strengthening of the dynasty.

Like his father before him, Henry I had an interview at Ivois with the Germanic Roman emperor. The intention behind this was not to reform the Papacy, which was going through a revival (with German popes), but to study the question of Lorraine, which haunted Henry I as it had haunted Louis IV d'Outre-Mer. Henry I considered Lorraine to be strictly French territory, but seven centuries were to elapse before it was to become so.

The most interesting aspect of Henry I's life was his attempt to bring about a Franco–Russian alliance by marriage. After the death of his wife Matilda (Emperor Henry II's niece), he married, rather late in life, Anne of Kiev, daughter of the Kievan Russian head of state. This marriage produced one son who bore the name, oriental in origin, of Philip. His father had him crowned at Rheims, although he was only a child, on 23 May 1059.

When Henry I died in 1060, Philip, though already crowned, was only eight years old and too young to rule. For the first time in Capetian history, the problem arose which was unfortunately to recur only too often later on, namely that of a regency. This was assumed by one of the young king's uncles, Baldwin, count of Flanders. (Anne of Kiev refused to be regent, and the rest of her life was interesting: she was abducted by Raoul of Crépy, lived with him as his wife and married him when his wife died. Widowed a second time, she lost her title as queen and was henceforth referred to as the queen mother.)

Of Baldwin's regency little is known, although it appears to have been fairly lacking in incident; this shows that the Capetians were beginning to carry some weight. But Burgundy, over which Robert ruled, took advantage of the situation to assert its independence from the French crown; this was to recur frequently in the course of the various Burgundian dynasties.

⚜ PHILIP I ⚜
(1060–1108)
AND BERTRADE OF MONTFORT

THIS OBSCURE FORTY-EIGHT-YEAR REIGN is mostly remembered for Philip's lively private life, which resembled rather curiously that of his ancestor, Robert the Pious.

Philip first of all married Bertha of Holland, and had a son, Louis. He then fell in love with Bertrade de Montfort, wife of count Fulk of Anjou. His dramatic abduction of her happened well into the reign, in 1092. There was a tremendous scandal, but Philip was king and found

The Norman army passes Rennes. (Bayeux tapestry)

bishops in France to absolve him. In revenge the Holy See rose in protest and convoked a series of synods. Philip promised to give up Bertrade, but did no such thing.

The pope was a Frenchman, Urban ii, who had preached the Crusade. He was patient at first but finally excommunicated Philip, who resisted. An interdict was then placed on his kingdom. France was morally shattered, and contemporary chroniclers left poignant tales of the closure of churches and the prohibition of the sacraments. Philip was obliged to give in, but he did so only on the surface, and Urban's successor Pascal ii, another French pope, found himself obliged to take a hard line. It was only in 1104 that Bertrade ceased to live with the king, but she continued to be treated as queen.

These domestic upheavals are practically all that history has retained of Philip i's reign, which in fact was uneventful at home, but very eventful abroad.

In 1066, William the Bastard, duke of Normandy, crossed the Channel, defeated the English army at Hastings, and took the place of King Harold, who was killed during the battle. A danger was born which was to trouble the history of France for seven centuries. The conflict began in Philip's lifetime: the Anglo–Normans took the offensive and got as far as Nantes, which they pillaged completely. With the death of William the Conqueror in 1087 the situation eased, and Philip's relations with Robert Curthose, the new duke of Normandy, seem to have been peaceful.

A minor war had broken out before the Norman affair: it took place in Flanders in 1070–71. The Flemish had the support of the Germanic Roman emperor, and on 22 February 1071 Philip was defeated at Cassel. This was the beginning of a conflict with the Flemish which was to last to the time of the Valois.

The most important factor of Philip's reign was his refusal, in the light of his strained relations with the Papacy, to take part in the First

Crusade. This un-Christian attitude was to be of benefit to France, as many of the great crusading lords got into financial difficulties, and the crown was later to profit from this state of affairs.

Philip I associated his son Louis to the throne, then died, reconciled with the church, on 29 July 1108.

After his death the course of history was to take a drastic turn.

⧫ LOUIS VI THE FAT ⧫
(1108–1137)

LOUIS VI, AS HIS NICKNAME SUGGESTS, was a very corpulent man, an intrepid eater and great drinker. Brought up on physical exercise, he never knew tiredness; he was also a great sensualist. Beneath the rough exterior he was a sensitive man, capable of pity and of forgiving his enemies, who were numerous. He was indeed one of the first to realize the dangers and vices of the feudal system, and he tried to improve it. He did not baulk at attacking his more dangerous vassals, and some of his military operations were against domestic enemies.

Louis VI was born around 1081 and had been called Thibaud at birth. It was only at his baptism that he was given the name Louis, in accordance with Carolingian tradition. The only son of Bertha, Philip I's first wife, he was soon the object of persecution by Bertrade of Anjou (Montfort), the mistress whom the king had married while repudiating the legitimate queen. Bertrade went as far as trying to have one of her own sons substituted for Louis, the legitimate heir, and it is to Philip I's credit that he absolutely opposed this plan. But because of the family conflicts, Philip abandoned his son as early as 1098, then sent him off to the wars in the Vexin to be rid of him.

This military training was a good one and proved very useful. While Philip indulged his sensual fantasies, his son waged several successful local wars. He fought against the Norman encroachment in the Vexin, subdued a troublesome feudal lord, Bouchard of Montmorency, and resolved a quarrel between the bishop of Chartres and the countess of Chartres. At Agincourt he settled a difference between lord and burghers, an episode which confirmed his support for the notion of free towns.

All this happened in an atmosphere of some tension, as his stepmother Bertrade not only wished him ill but even tried to have him poisoned. When, therefore, he acceded to the throne in 1108, he was already a mature and hardened young man. After burying his father at the abbey of Fleury-sur-Loire, he proceeded to his own coronation, to avoid new problems with Bertrade. He was the first Capetian who, though designated, was not crowned during his father's lifetime. This shows a consolidation of the dynasty, both moral and material, for during the wars of his youth Louis had substantially increased royal territory: the original domain had been greatly augmented by the incorporation of Gâtinais and other acquisitions, despite the feudal enclaves which still dotted the land.

Louis married first Lucienne of Rochefort, then Adelaide of Savoy. He suffered the loss of his eldest son Philip, already *rex designatus*, and then associated his second son Louis, the future Louis VII, who was called the Younger precisely because he was the younger brother for such a long time.

It is impossible to divide up Louis VI's long reign into sections because the king's struggles all took place simultaneously: against the feudal lords, against England and Germany, against heresy, the emancipation of towns, let alone the squabbles of court favourites. But he was lucky enough to find an exceptional minister in the person of the monk Suger, who built the basilica of St Denis and wrote the history of the king he served. Thanks to him, we are able to date precisely the complex events of his reign.

The most important of these was the struggle against the feudal lords, which lasted throughout Louis' reign. The battles ranged from the submission of Bouchard of Montmorency in 1102 to that of the Garlande in 1135. In between these, Louis had subdued such dangerous elements as Hugh de Puiset (1111–1118), Thomas de Marle and Enguerand de Coucy, between 1103 and 1132. These internal wars not only did away with dangerous feudal lords but permitted expansion by annexation and an increase in royal power.

But Louis the Fat must be given credit for more than just these activities; his foreign policy too was remarkable. However, his intervention in Flemish politics nearly ended in disaster: he began by making the mistake of discarding Count Thierry of Flanders in favour of an Anglo–Norman, Guillaume Cliton. But when Cliton was killed during his siege of Alost, Louis changed sides and supported Thierry, of whom he made an ally.

The most important military engagement took place in 1124. Emperor Henry v allied himself with the king of England, and they declared war on France. Louis alone was not strong enough to oppose two such powerful adversaries, and in this difficult situation he launched an appeal to all his vassals. With extraordinary speed, the ecclesiastic and feudal contingents joined together; then the communal militias came to lend their support. Eight huge contingents were formed, with their headquarters at Rheims, and branches in Burgundy and Flanders. These combined forces proved so strong that the emperor, arriving at Rheims, turned back without even a fight. France had

The seal of the commune of Meulan under Louis VI the Fat.

been saved by unity and Louis' moral victory
was all the stronger because when the emperor
retreated the contingents from distant regions
such as Brittany and Aquitaine had not actually
arrived on the scene.

There is one more aspect of Louis' character
which will complete the picture of him: he was a
deeply religious king, and it was during his reign
and not that of Pepin that France won the nickname of 'elder daughter of the Church'. It was all
the more easy for Louis to consolidate the ties
between throne and Church because the Empire
was torn by the quarrel over the Investiture, and
the Papacy had a vested interest in supporting
France. The election of a French pope, Pascal II,
made this *rapprochement* even easier. Driven from
his territory by Emperor Henry V, Pascal II took
refuge in France, and the council of Vienna,
brought together by Louis V, proclaimed very
strongly the supremacy of spiritual things,
which constituted a thorough condemnation of
the emperor.

In 1119, Louis VI received yet another French
pope, Calixtus II, who held an important council
in Rheims, but proved very ungrateful for
French hospitality, since he did not take Louis'
side when the Anglo–German coalition of 1124
was formed. After the death of Calixtus II's successor, Honorius II, the Church was torn by
what is known as 'the schism of Anacletus'. Two
popes were elected simultaneously, both legates
in France, Innocent II and Anacletus. Louis the
Fat opted for the latter but Innocent II won.
Louis changed sides so cleverly that the pope,
without ill-feeling, came to visit him at St Denis.

These many aspects of Louis' reign must be
completed by one other which was its
masterpiece. Because of his good relations with
the duke of Aquitaine, the most important feudal
lord, who possessed almost a quarter of France,
Louis VI asked for the hand of his only daughter,
Eleanor, in marriage for his son Louis.

This union seemed to point to an unprecedented territorial expansion, but things did not
turn out as planned. Louis himself was not
present at the downfall of his wise and grandiose
initiative. On his return from Bordeaux, where
he had negotiated the match, he suffered an
attack of dysentery and died on arrival in Paris in
1137, aged only fifty-six, at the end of a reign
which had changed the fate of France.

The court of Louis the Fat. (Fourteenth-century miniature)

✣ LOUIS VII THE YOUNG ✣
(1137–1180)
AND ELEANOR OF AQUITAINE

LOUIS VI LEFT MANY CHILDREN, of which the eldest, Philip, died in a riding accident in which a 'diabolic' boar threw itself at his horse's legs. So it was the younger son, Louis, who was to succeed. The other children were Robert, count of Dreux, Pierre de Courtenay (whose descendants ruled briefly in Constantinople), Henry, a Cistercian bishop of Beauvais and then Rouen, Philip, bishop of Paris in 1159 and finally, Constance, countess of Toulouse.

King Louis VI left behind him a kingdom in which feudal strife had subsided, but Louis VII's great asset was his marriage to Eleanor of Aquitaine, which led to hopes that this huge fief would one day be added to the small royal domain. For the moment the two territories were merely juxtaposed, and everything depended on how the king got on with his wife.

Louis VII was a man of sensitivity, loyal but not particularly intellectual. His religious devotion was of a narrow kind, quite inferior to his father's. Eleanor was a formidable woman, extremely well read, sensual, coquettish, full of vices. From the very beginning, Louis' passionate love for his wife made him her plaything. Fortunately the queen was not interested in affairs of state, and the wise Suger continued as first minister.

The king's very first actions alienated the Church: he clashed with St Bernard about the episcopal seats of Langres and Poitiers. He then crowned these mistakes by falling out with Pope Innocent II about the archepiscopal seat at Bauges, and was excommunicated. All evidence points to the fact that Louis VII's religious policy was dictated by Eleanor.

On top of these early mistakes, he began to make errors in feudal matters also. Louis wanted to revive the claims of the dukes of Aquitaine to the county of Toulouse, where his sister was in power, and this caused friction. He took his wife's side in encouraging Raoul of Vermandois to repudiate his wife. St Bernard intervened and, after the death of Pope Innocent II, persuaded his

successor to lift the excommunication order, but much harm had already been done.

On top of this, an important feudal event took place. Geoffrey the Fair, count of Anjou, married to the heiress to the throne of England, had conquered Normandy, and Louis VII proved incapable of arbitrating a clash of interests from which stemmed many of his later problems.

Attention was diverted from this by events in the Frankish kingdom in the east. St Bernard preached the Crusade at Vézelay, and, in order to be completely reconciled with the Church, Louis decided to take part in it. He set out, accompanied by Eleanor, as he was afraid to leave her alone in Paris because of her amorous nature; but the voyage was not a success.

The king landed in Syria and in March 1148, at Antioch, a scandal broke out in the royal household. Eleanor's relations with her young uncle, Raymond of Poitiers, prince of Antioch, took a worrying turn. A campaign was worked out which involved leaving Eleanor in Antioch. Louis was not in favour of this, and changed his plans; he set out for Jerusalem, with his wife. In the holy city the king conferred with Emperor Conrad and King Baldwin III. The result of this was a useless siege of Damascus and an inglorious return to Jerusalem. Unproved rumour had it that Eleanor meanwhile was bestowing her favours on a handsome Moorish slave.

Suger, concerned about the king's absence, and convinced that he had done enough penance to the Church, was pressing him to return. The king took his advice and returned to France in 1149 via Sicily and Rome, where he visited the pope.

Suger had acted as regent during the king's absence and was delighted to hand power back to him. Louis, whose piety exasperated Eleanor, was seeking ways to dissolve their marriage. Suger dissuaded him, but after this wise minister's death the drama acted itself out, and Louis had his marriage annulled by a reunion of canons in Beaugency on 21 March 1152 under

Louis VII prays for an heir. On his knees, with his wife Alix, he receives his son from the hands of God, in the shape of a small king, the future Philip Augustus. (*Grandes Chroniques de France*)

Louis VII and
Conrad III enter
Constantinople in
1147. (*Grandes
Chroniques de France*)

the pretext that the couple were too closely related. It was an arguable case, but Louis would have done better to consider the interests of France, especially since this annulment was to bring upon him unimaginable misfortune.

As soon as she was free, Eleanor married Henry Plantagenet, count of Anjou, many years younger than herself and heir presumptive to the throne of England. She was to give him many children, who became famous. The effect was not only to produce bad relations with England in the future, but also to give England power of suzerainty over half the territory of France.

Louis VII had two daughters by Eleanor, which did not solve the dynastic problem. He married Constance of Castile but their marriage was childless. After her death, he married Alix of Champagne, who finally in 1165 produced a son who was to become Philip Augustus; he had a hard task in front of him in repairing his father's mistakes.

Henry Plantagenet became king of England under the name of Henry II. He did not deny being the king of France's vassal as regarded the continental possessions, but local conflicts soon broke out to rectify internal frontiers. These were the initial stages of the long struggle which some historians call the first Hundred Years War.

Having said all this about Louis VII, it is only fair to do him justice. Well aware of his mistakes, he attempted to make up for them by pursuing his father's internal policy. He sought to counterbalance Henry II's powerful state, in the fiefs which he controlled, with the general idea that to make France secure he had to create a buffer state between the English possessions and those of the Holy Roman Emperor, who was suzerain of the eastern French territory.

Louis took advantage of his now excellent relations with the Church. With the help of the bishop of Langres he summoned the duke of Burgundy to his court in 1153; he did the same in 1160 with the count of Champagne, Henry the Liberal. In 1166 he secured the defence of Vézelay against Hugh of Nevers, then supported the monks of Cluny against the count of Chalon, whose territory he confiscated.

He then pursued the buffer state idea by forcing the submission of those territories which could serve his purpose. First he received the homage of the Bourbons and Beaujeus, which opened up the way to Auvergne; then he received the vassalic oath of the count of Forez, Guigue III. He neutralized the viscount of Polignac with the support of the bishop of Puy. Then he entered Gévaudan, where he was paid homage by the bishop of Mende. Finally he reached Languedoc, under the pretext of helping his brother-in-law, the count of Toulouse.

The king's arrival in Languedoc gave pause for thought to Henry II, who was about to attack the county of Toulouse. It would seem that as an acknowledgement for this or for his presence, Louis VII claimed the homage of Narbonne. Henry II considered the matter and then proposed to his sons Richard the Lionheart and John Lackland that they should go and pay homage to the king of France. Louis VII then received the sons of the wife he had repudiated. To annoy the king of England he gave asylum to the archbishop of Canterbury, Thomas Becket, with whom the king was in disagreement. And in 1173 the king of France managed to turn Henry II's sons against their own father.

Finally, in conflict with Emperor Frederick Barbarossa, over the Investitures, Louis VII received Pope Alexander III in Sens, and papal intervention prevented the English and Germans joining forces.

Such was Louis' inconsistent reign, which created new foreign threats, but maintained and improved on Louis the Fat's intense anti-feudal struggle. And it was Louis VI who first made the fleur-de-lys into the symbol of French monarchy.

The king died in 1180, after a reign of forty-three years, leaving the sceptre to an unanointed fifteen-year-old adolescent, Philip Augustus, who had an extraordinary future before him.

PHILIP II AUGUSTUS
(1180–1223)
AND ISABELLA OF HAINAULT

EVERYTHING ABOUT PHILIP AUGUSTUS'S forty-three-year reign was extraordinary, both in his private life and in his political actions, which increased by more than forty times the original Capetian fief of Hugh Capet.

Philip had been associated to the throne by his father in 1175. Nicknamed Augustus because he was born in August, Philip ascended the throne on 18 September 1180, and immediately showed signs of independence of spirit, even though he was only fifteen. Little is known of his physical appearance. Chroniclers report that he was:

> ... a 'handsome, well-built man, with a pleasant face, warm, with high colour and a temperament disposed to good food, wine and women.
>
> He was generous with his friends, mean to those he disliked, well versed in science, Catholic by faith, full of foresight and definite in his resolutions. He judged matters quickly and accurately. Fortune's favourite, fearful for his life, easily moved and easily placated, he was hard on great men who resisted him and enjoyed fostering discord among them. But he never caused an adversary to die in prison. He liked to employ lowly people, and established himself as the tamer of proud men, the defender of the faith and feeder of the poor.

(Chronique de Tours, quoted by Luchaire in *Histoire de France* by Lavisse.)

To explain this long and complicated reign it will help to discuss first of all the king's married life. He was married very young to Isabella, daughter of the count of Hainault and niece of the count of Flanders, whose dowry was Amiens and Artois. She produced a son, the future Louis VIII, but died prematurely in 1190.

Being only twenty-five, Philip Augustus decided to remarry, and in 1193 he wed Ingeborg, the king of Denmark's daughter. Then a strange thing happened: during the marriage ceremony the king realized that he felt no desire for his new bride. It is uncertain whether or not the marriage was consummated; what is certain is that he repudiated the new queen and shut her up in a nunnery and then in various prisons, of which one, at Etampes, has been preserved in its original state.

Then the king was struck by passion; he had always been fond of women, and fell desperately in love with a German princess, Agnes of Meran, whose father ruled Merano in the high valley of the Adige. Behaving as if Ingeborg did not exist, he married Agnes; she gave him a son, Philip Hurepel who was virtually considered illegitimate. For the Papacy had taken an interest in this affair, considering it not only as adultery but bigamy, and excommunicated the king. Since he refused to give in, the pope laid an interdict on the kingdom. Against his will, to save the souls of the faithful French, and also because he needed papal support, Philip Augustus had to resign himself to parting with Agnes of Meran and to bring back Ingeborg, with whom his relations remained distant.

Philip Augustus's policy consisted of putting down the feudal lords, as had his father and grandfather before him, and of suppressing as far as possible the Plantagenet empire in France. His success and his ambition gave rise to a European coalition with papal backing, which strongly consolidated his national and international position. Parallel to all this, and of secondary importance to begin with, the drama of the Crusade against the Albigenses was developing. Philip Augustus took no interest in this at first, but placed himself at its head at the right moment to win Languedoc for France.

The early years of the reign were complicated by the rivalry between Flanders and Champagne, provoked by one of the king's first political actions, the signature of a non-aggression pact with Henry II Plantagenet. This pact, signed at Gisors on 28 June 1180, even before the death of Louis VII, strengthened the crown's internal position to such an extent that the feudal lords became alarmed.

The counts of Champagne and Flanders joined forces and gained the support of the great vassals of the north and east. There were a few skirmishes, but mostly intrigue and treachery. These problems were resolved in the treaty of Boves, signed in July 1185. The king became suzerain of Vermandois and won confirmation of the possession of Amiens and Artois, which had been promised as his wife's dowry. Moreover he obtained from Burgundy the concession of Châtillon-sur-Seine. Henceforth his authority over his vassals was uncontested.

Having achieved this, he passed on to the second part of his plan: the attack against the Plantagenets. He began by demanding part of Normandy from Henry II, the part which had made up the dowry of his sister Margaret when she married Henry, son of Henry II, who had just died. He also contested England's vassaldom in Berry and Auvergne. To this end he befriended Geoffrey of Brittany, one of Henry II's sons, and when he died prematurely, befriended another of his sons, Richard the Lionheart.

Then, after strengthening himself by an alliance against England with Emperor Frederick Barbarossa, he crossed the Cher, without declaring war, and seized Issoudun. Henry II, anxious to avoid a war, immediately signed a peace treaty at Châteauroux in 1187.

Richard the Lionheart came to visit the French court; taking the English off guard, the king attacked again and threatened to penetrate into Normandy to reclaim possession of Gisors; this ended in immediate reconciliation. But Philip Augustus went back on this and took advantage of a rising in Aquitaine to attack Berry. The Anglo–French war started again and lasted from July to November 1188.

Henry II, old and tired, offered to negotiate again. Philip Augustus demanded that Richard the Lionheart be immediately proclaimed king of England, and the young prince came to pay homage to the king and fight at his side. The Papacy condemned Philip Augustus for this, but he paid no attention and invaded and subdued Maine. Henry II fled, then surrendered near Azay-le-Rideau. He designated Richard as king of England and died on 6 July at Chinon.

Having made Richard king of England, Philip Augustus expected his future loyalty, but King Richard behaved very differently from Richard, heir presumptive. He took stock of his position and, realizing that he was more powerful than his suzerain, asserted his independence. There would no doubt have been another war had attention not been diverted by the occupation of Jerusalem by the Sultan Saladin, which meant a new Crusade. Richard agreed to take part in it with Philip Augustus; Frederick Barbarossa decided to join them.

Before leaving France, Philip Augustus settled the succession, naming the queen mother eventual regent, but arranging for her power to be restricted.

The French and English kings crossed France together, then split up at Marseilles and took different routes. They reached the shores of Syria only in June 1191. There was trouble straight away, since Richard refused to marry Alix, Philip Augustus's sister. So as not to interrupt the Crusade, the broken engagement was covered by an indemnity.

In addition to this, the rough Philip Augustus soon became irritated with Richard's elegance and ostentation. Relations became strained, and using as a pretext the death of the count of Flanders at Acre, Philip Augustus left the East suddenly in order, in fact, to secure Artois and Vermandois, which had been conceded to him in the treaty of Boves.

Richard, who was becoming suspicious, made Philip Augustus swear not to undertake anything against him until he returned to England. Back in France, Philip perjured himself immediately, and incited John Lackland to rebel in England. Richard the Lionheart rapidly left Palestine and returned to England (1192), but he did not realize that the king of France had an arrangement with Barbarossa's son, Henry VI. While crossing imperial territory, Richard was arrested and imprisoned in the fortress of Trifels, near Landau.

Richard was freed for a ransom and by accepting to be the emperor's vassal. On his return to England he declared war and defeated Philip Augustus at Frétevel on 3 July 1194; among the direr consequences of this battle was the total destruction of the French archives, which were following the army on a wagon. Then, for the defence of Normandy, Richard built the imposing fortress of Château Gaillard. To add to his success, Richard found allies among Philip Augustus's vassals, and an unexpected one in the person of Otto IV, the new emperor, who had spent his youth at the Plantagenet court.

Philip Augustus's military position deteriorated, so much so that in 1198 he sought papal intervention. This was difficult to obtain because he had re-married Agnes of Meran, but Pope Innocent III thought it politic to intervene, and at his instigation a truce was signed at Vernon, followed by a treaty at Péronne, by which the king of France lost all his conquests except Gisors. Had Philip Augustus died at this point he would have been remembered with nothing but scorn. But then chance came to his aid: Richard the Lionheart, who had resumed hostilities in Limousin, was killed by an arrow at the siege of Chalus (1199). The English crown was hotly contested between Arthur of Brittany and John Lackland. Philip Augustus backed the latter, but demanded Anjou and Normandy in return.

With the support of his aged mother, Eleanor of Aquitaine, John pretended to accept, then seized Normandy. Philip Augustus was forced to accept by the treaty of Goulet (22 May 1200), and his position became even worse than in 1198. He was saved by a mistake on the part of John, who entered into conflict with the Lusignan family. They asked their suzerain Philip Augustus to arbitrate, and he summoned John to appear in front of his court in April 1202. John refused to come and was deprived of his rights. As the result of a verdict of forfeiture Philip Augustus took back all his English fiefs.

This was an obvious abuse of power, and the king of France did not have the resources to enter into the possession of such a vast territory. So he decided to occupy Normandy only, and as his vassal in the other territories he placed Arthur of Brittany, who took his position seriously and besieged his own grandmother, Eleanor of Aquitaine, in Mirebeau. Before her death she negotiated the marriage of her granddaughter Blanche of Castile to Prince Louis, Philip Augustus's son.

John rescued his mother, then took Arthur prisoner and had him put to death. But this did not alter Philip Augustus's policy: he laid siege to Château Gaillard. After a long siege the fortress surrendered and Normandy submitted (24 June 1204).

Emperor Henry VI. (A miniature from the *Manessischen Liederhandschrift*)

Taking advantage of this success, the king of France took Anjou, then Poitou. John lost his overseas fiefs, but remained determined to have his revenge. He created a coalition with Emperor Otto IV, with the help of the count of Flanders, the count of Holland and the count of Boulogne. Their plan was to disperse Philip Augustus's forces by attacking on two fronts: Aquitaine and Flanders.

The first of these, at La-Roche-aux-Moines (2 July 1214) proved successful and Prince Louis dispersed the English forces. But in the same crucial month, on 27 July, Philip Augustus defeated the coalition at Bouvines (between Lille and Tournai) and John withdrew from France. He returned, defeated, to London, where his

Simon de Montfort, lord of Ile de France and leader of the crusade against
the Cathars. (Notre Dame de Chartes)

barons imposed upon him the Magna Carta (1215), establishing constitutional monarchy in England. John pretended to submit but appealed to Pope Innocent III. The English barons, outraged, tried to depose their sovereign and to replace him with Philip Augustus's son, Prince Louis, who by his marriage to Blanche of Castile had become Eleanor of Aquitaine's grandson. This plan, very worrying for Philip Augustus, did not lead anywhere because John died in 1216, and the barons recognized his son, the young Henry III, as king. Louis gave up his claims to the throne by the treaty of Lambeth (1217).

While all this was going on, from 1204 to 1214, another drama was being acted out – the famous Albigensian Crusade. This expedition, brought about by feudal ambition, has been wrongly called a 'Crusade' because it was in fact an operation of a religious nature, embarked upon to put a stop to heretical activities.

The Albigenses (also called Cathars) were the distant disciples of an early heretic named Mani. He preached Manichaeism, which distinguished between the two principles of good and evil; the good was spirit, the evil, body. For the élite this meant asceticism, but for the common run of people the prospect of general absolution, the *consolamentum*, led to a life of general depravity. The Papacy had feared this heresy since the Third Lateran Council of 1179, and a missionary offensive, to be called after St Dominic, was begun in Languedoc. But this religious offensive was almost ineffectual, as the Cathars had the support of the count of Toulouse, Raymond VI.

In 1208 the papal legate in Languedoc, Peter of Castelnau, was killed by the heretics as he came out of the abbey church of St-Giles-du-Gard. Despite the heavy honourable amends made by the count of Toulouse in that same church in 1209, Pope Innocent III preached a Crusade against the Cathars, to intimidate them. Remaining faithful to his feudal oath, Philip Augustus refused to wage war on one of his vassals for religious reasons, and what is more, on papal orders. But he could not prevent a section of the nobility from taking part, though the crown maintained a strict neutrality which gave rise to some criticism.

The Crusade was led by a lord of the Ile de France, Simon de Montfort, a man of great tactical ability and tremendous ferocity – people still talk of the massacre of the inhabitants of Béziers in the church of the Madeleine, and of the words attributed to the papal legate, Arnaud Amalric: 'Kill them all. God will recognize his own.'

In the space of a few weeks Simon de Montfort subdued Languedoc and annexed it to his own territory. The count of Toulouse joined forces with King Peter of Aragon to regain his suzerainty; but Simon de Montfort defeated them at Muret in 1213, thus confirming his conquest. The Fourth Lateran Council of 1215 pronounced the defeat of the count of Toulouse and invested Simon de Montfort. The king of France could not accept a foreign investiture in one of his vassal fiefs, and was obliged to intervene through his son Louis.

It was during this conflict that Philip Augustus died in 1223. His reign had been a great one: the history of the royal domain had finally become one with the history of France. The great feudal lords were put in their place. And Paris, as capital, became the definitive administrative centre.

The king occupied the Palace of the Cité, and he established the great crossroads of Paris, two wide paved roads leading towards the four points of the compass. The western entrance to Paris was marked by the tower of the Louvre. The town was surrounded by a wall corresponding to the main line of the great boulevards, which is still called Philippe-Auguste. The university was established on the mount of St Geneviève, and Paris became the capital of learning and intellect.

The splendour of this period is best conveyed by its architectural achievements, the flourishing in Paris and around it of the great Gothic cathedrals whose original style is still called, by art historians, *opus francigenum*.

∽ LOUIS VIII THE LION ∽
(1223–1226)
AND BLANCHE OF CASTILE

BECAUSE OF HIS SHORT REIGN, Philip Augustus's son, Louis VIII the Lion, has not had the place in history he truly deserved, both through his own personal valour and through the merits of his admirable wife Blanche of Castile, Eleanor of Aquitaine's granddaughter, by whom he had eleven children.

Louis VIII, born in 1187, was the son of Isabella of Hainault. He received an early military initiation; his single-handed victory at the battle of La-Roche-aux-Moines in 1214 saved France from invasion in the south and played a big part in the success of the battle of Bouvines.

Then Louis' destiny took an extraordinary turn. The English, after imposing Magna Carta on John, saw that he did not intend to diminish his power and was planning to call on the pope to help him restore the status quo. Feeling that their interest lay in deposing John, they proposed to prince Louis that he should accept the crown of England. This change of dynasty would have affected the whole course of history and the Capetians, as masters of England and France, would have been the principal sovereigns of Europe.

Prince Louis was in fact elected king of England, and as a token of faith twenty-four English barons were sent as hostages to Compiègne to guarantee the election. A French army was raised and on 21 May 1216 Louis' troops landed in England. Prince Louis was received in London with royal honours and prepared to disperse the few troops which had remained loyal to John. There seemed no doubt about the future course of events, when John died on 19 October 1216. His sudden disappearance brought about a revival of English public feeling. Though they despised their dead king, they felt differently towards his heir. A large party formed itself around the young Prince Henry III, who was crowned by the legate of Pope Honorius III, Cardinal Galon. War broke out between Henry and Louis and the new king of England was defeated at Lincoln.

But on 24 August 1217 the French navy confronted the English near Calais; as usual, England won the sea battle and Prince Louis had to give in. Before he departed the English secretly gave him a present of 10,000 golden marks.

Philip Augustus, who disapproved of all this, was glad to see his son back and made use of his help to intervene in Languedoc. The situation was greatly clarified by the death of Simon de Montfort at the siege of Toulouse and his replacement by his mediocre son Amaury.

It is worth noting that Louis VIII was the first Capetian king not designated during the lifetime of his father, who judged the monarchy to be strong enough to take this risk, thus confirming its hereditary nature.

After his coronation, Louis VIII acceded to Pope Honorius III's demands and asked the Papacy for financial assistance in putting down the Cathars. Raymond VII, son of the deceased Raymond VI, was excommunicated. The king bought Amaury of Montfort's rights to the county of Toulouse, which was thus, according to feudal custom, put out of the running.

The siege of Toulouse, which held out for some time, was made easier by the taking of Soignon, about which the emperor voiced no protest, and Louis VIII obtained the complete submission of Languedoc. But these operations were not carried out without considerable violence, and history has retained the painful memory of Marenaude, whose entire population Louis VIII had massacred with no distinction as to age or sex.

In the context of his own life, however, Louis' achievements were considerable. He had subjugated Poitou, Aunis and Saintonge, saved France at La-Roche-aux-Moines, and almost become king of England.

His action in Languedoc was impressive and its consequences propitious, since after his death Blanche of Castile, able politician that she was, was in a position to solve the problem of devolution. By marrying one of her younger sons,

Alphonse, to Raymond VII's daughter, she created the opportunity for the fief to return to France should there be no heir. This occasion arose sooner than expected, since both Alphonse and his wife died in 1271, whereupon Languedoc reverted without question to the crown.

After subjugating Languedoc, Louis made several tentative incursions into Aquitaine, which paved the way for its future annexation. On returning from his excursions in the south, he was taken ill and died of dysentery at Montpensier in 1226. He was only thirty-eight and his death presented the Capetians for the first time with the problem of a regency; it fell upon Blanche of Castile, who performed her difficult task remarkably well.

❧ LOUIS IX OR SAINT LOUIS ❧
(1226–1270)
AND MARGARET OF PROVENCE

LOUIS IX WAS ONLY TWELVE when his father died, and as Louis VIII had designated Blanche of Castile regent she took over without any problems. She kept her husband's ministers, who had also been Philip Augustus's. But however helpful this support, it did not solve the difficulties caused by Philippe Hurepel, son of Philip Augustus and Agnes of Meran, and by Pierre Mauclerc, duke of Brittany; added to this was the justifiable wrath of the count of Toulouse. A first attempt at an uprising took place in 1227, six months after the king's anointing. The regent took up arms and on this occasion, with Philippe Hurepel's support, advanced to London. This manoeuvre brought about the immediate signing of a treaty at Vendôme with Pierre Mauclerc and his ally the count of Marche.

Then Philippe Hurepel changed sides and tried to abduct his nephew, who escaped. Once more, Blanche of Castile broke the coalition, then in 1228 resumed the Crusade in Languedoc and in 1229 signed the treaty of Paris, which guaranteed the future reversion of Languedoc to France. Despite this success, Blanche had more trouble to face. She was accused of too close a friendship, possibly a romantic one, with Count Thibaut of Champagne, and also of over-friendly relations with the papal legate, whose residence was pillaged by Paris students in 1229.

The following year an assembly called by Hurepel and Mauclerc decided to invade Champagne and annihilate Thibaut. Their first objective was Lorraine, whose duke supported Thibaut. Pierre Mauclerc defied the king, saying that he considered himself free from his links as a vassal, and made himself liege man to the king of England. Taking advantage of this, the king of England sailed to St Malo at the head of a powerful army. At that time, Louis IX and Blanche of Castile were in Anjou, where minor hostilities were taking place. However, real battles occurred in Champagne.

The young king and his regent saved the day by letting it be known that they would back Thibaut to the hilt, whereupon Philippe Hurepel abandoned the coalition and came to support his royal nephew. This well-rewarded change of heart disbanded the coalition. Once again the crown maintained its sway over powerful vassals. But since the king of England, Henry III, continued sporadic fighting in the south-west, a three-year truce had to be agreed with him by which the few conquests in Anjou were incorporated into the royal domain. Thus Blanche of Castile's regency ended in complete success. When Philippe Hurepel died in 1234, King Henry III was obliged to conclude another truce, this time for five years.

Louis IX became king at the age of twenty-one, and was soon to surprise his contemporaries by his qualities and his purity of soul. He brought to Capetian royalty a moral authority which it was never to find again. It would be wrong, however, to think that he was patient and meek or that he refused to go to war out of charity.

Louis IX, or Saint Louis.
(Cluny Museum)

Margaret of Provence, wife of Louis IX. (From the door
of the chapel of the Hospice de Quinze-Vingt)

He was a tall, rather thin man with a slight stoop; he wore his fair hair long, and his face, though irregular of features, had an undefinable charm due to his kind expression and naturally gracious manner.

In 1234 Louis ix married Margaret of Provence, the elder daughter of Raymond Bérenger iv, count of Provence, who was later to marry one of his younger daughters to the king's brother, Charles of Anjou. Margaret of Provence was one of France's most interesting queens. The early days of her marriage were not easy, as tradition has it that Blanche of Castile was an authoritarian mother-in-law, who tended to interfere in her son's private life, and Margaret, it seems, resented this. But things changed after the queen's participation in the Crusade, in which she behaved heroically. When she returned to France, Blanche was dead, and henceforth she ruled uncontested over her husband's heart and exercised considerable influence over him, preventing him from abdicating when, at one point, he considered becoming a Dominican. Margaret of Provence survived her husband by nearly a quarter of a century, but far from remaining at court, she retired to a convent, where she died piously in 1295.

Louis ix's first governmental activities were of a military nature. He peacefully completed the conquest of Poitou, which his father had begun. But this conquest displeased the Lusignans who, forgetting their vassaldom, called on the king of England for help. Louis ix was forced to take up arms again.

Henry iii disembarked at Royan on 12 May 1242, bringing with him much gold but few troops. With these reduced capacities he wandered in Saintonge. The French army too was on the march, and one day they found themselves face to face on the banks of the Charente at the bridge of Taillebourg (21 July 1242). Henry iii, outnumbered, struck camp and retreated; this episode has been wrongly called the battle of Taillebourg. Saint Louis pursued and caught up with the English at Saintes, where they were soundly defeated (22 July 1242). The king of England fled and the barons who had hoped for his support were so demoralized that they submitted to Louis ix. The count of Marche and his wife came to throw themselves at the king's feet and beg for his mercy.

Henry iii, still retreating, had set sail at Blaye, as he realized that he could no longer expect any help on the Continent. It seemed that Louis ix's conquests would be definitive, and that English possessions would be reduced to Guyenne alone, that is, the territory between the Dordogne and the Pyrenees.

While the king of France's energies were taken up in his struggle against the English, the count of Toulouse had started a revolt. Louis was all the more determined to put a stop to it because the surviving Cathars had staged a bloody massacre in the little town of Avignonet in Lauraguais. He sent out two armies, one to invade Quercy and the other to watch the passes in the Pyrenees in case the Spaniards made a move.

The defection of Raymond vii, count of Foix, brought about the submission of the count of Toulouse; it was impossible for him to carry on alone, and he asked Blanche of Castile to intercede and threw himself on Louis' mercy. Louis pardoned him and a peace treaty was signed at Lorris in January 1243. To win his pardon, Raymond vii swore to put an end to the Albigensian heresy. His punitive expedition was marked by the famous siege of Monségur and the equally famous burning at the stake of its defenders. But even this did not finish off the Albigenses, who held their other fortress at Queribus for a long time after that.

In 1244, the year of the fall of Monségur, Louis ix fell seriously ill and took a vow to go on a Crusade. Pope Innocent iv, who was in the middle of a conflict with Emperor Frederick ii, disapproved of this project, but Louis carried it out all the same, and on 25 August 1248 a fleet of thirty-eight ships set sail from the port of Aigues-Mortes, the kingdom's only opening on the Mediterranean. Leaving Blanche of Castile as regent, Louis took with him Queen Margaret of Provence and two of his brothers, the counts of Artois and Anjou.

The journey went smoothly as far as Cyprus, where Louis proposed to gather his forces. He was delayed there until 13 May 1249, and took advantage of this to stock up for a long journey. On leaving Cyprus they ran into a storm; part of the fleet had to return to Limassol, and the king's ships did not reach Damietta in Egypt until 4 June; he had chosen this base from which to

The Crusaders attack the Saracens
and (*below*) a game of chess in progress. (*Historia
rerum transmarinarum* by William of Tyre)

attack Palestine by land. The army disembarked
and easily dispersed the few bands of Saracens
who were patrolling the beaches. Scouts were
sent on to Damietta and found that the town had
been deserted by its inhabitants, and so, on 6
June, Louis, dressed as a pilgrim, entered
Damietta. This easy success gave rise to dangerous illusions about the rest of the operation.

Louis made a mistake straight away: instead of
making straight for Cairo, he decided to wait
until the Nile floods were over. Pierre Mauclerc
suggested taking Alexandria but the count of
Artois was for marching on El Mansura. The
crossing of the Nile tributary called Bahr es
Séghir complicated matters further. On 5

February 1250 a crossing place was found. The
count of Artois crossed at the head of his troops
and charged the Egyptian camp; their surprise
was total and the camp was taken. But instead of
stopping there, Robert of Artois led his soldiers
into the streets of El Mansura. The Arab chief
ordered his Mamelukes to charge, and the
French, trapped, were all massacred. Louis, who
had just crossed the Bhar es Seghir, was surrounded by the Muslims and after a heroic six-
hour struggle was taken prisoner. By a miracle
he managed to escape, and for fifty-five days he
clung to his position. But there was an outbreak
of typhus; the king caught the disease, was
forced to take to his bed, and was captured by the
sultan. Threatened with death, the king offered
a ransom: he would give up Damietta and
pay a huge sum of money. He was utterly
defeated.

Margaret of Provence won the admiration of
all at Damietta. While her husband was being
taken prisoner, she gave birth to a son. Before
the delivery she made everyone leave her
chamber apart from an octogenarian knight who
was guarding her and, according to Joinville, she
made him swear to do what she was about to ask
of him. After he had sworn so she said: 'If the
Saracens arrive, behead me before I fall into their
hands.' And the old gentleman nobly replied:
'Madam, I was intending to.'

The queen was saved by the intervention of
the Genoese, to whom she was obliged to pay
considerable sums of money. The king had
trouble paying off his own heavy ransom as the
Knights Templar refused him financial aid.
Joinville saved the day by threatening to smash
open their coffers with an axe. They complied
and Louis IX, saved by this enforced loan,
was set free; on 13 May 1250 he reached St John
of Acre, where he was given a triumphal
welcome.

He began by imposing a public penance on the
Templars, then embarked on negotiations with
the Muslims for the freeing of Jerusalem. He
might well have succeeded, but a messenger
arrived bearing the news of the death of his
mother, Blanche of Castile. His urgent return to
France was necessary, as the regency had not
been free from troubles, and there was a revolt of
the peasants, known as the Pastoureaux.

Louis IX had had one strong reason for

Saint Louis remains in Palestine. He sends his two brothers home to
the queen mother and sets about buying back Christian prisoners
and burying the dead. (*Vie et Miracles de Saint Louis*)

Comment le roy saint loys seiourna en suire vbi. chippre.

Quant le roy saint
loys eut enuoie
en france ses deur
freres pmieuers la royne sa
mer. Il demoura en suire

et y seiourna lespace de ang
ans et œ pendant rachta
moult des prisonniers ypiens
qui estoient encores œ mais
des sarrazins sist fortisser

remaining in the east, and that was that he felt he could not return to France before he had completely repaid his ransom. But this had caused his mother great difficulties, and were it not for her the crown would have been threatened by internal revolt. This state of affairs was to recur with more serious consequences during the captivity of John the Good.

Louis IX cannot be judged by political criteria. His generosity, deep faith and holiness cannot be considered as political virtues, but they greatly increased his moral authority, which gave him a unique position in the world and made him Europe's mediator and the most important figure of the Middle Ages.

The death of Blanche of Castile had fortunate consequences for the king's married life; his relations with his wife became much closer and he put his trust in her to a great extent, which he was later to regret.

The events of the latter years of this reign took a surprising turn. In 1259 he signed a treaty with the king of Aragon at Corbeil, in the form of a compromise: if King James I of Aragon renounced his rights over the counties of Toulouse and Provence, the king of France would give up his suzerainty over Roussillon and Catalonia. More surprising still, considering his desire for equity, was the treaty he signed in the following year with England to settle conclusively the war of 1242. This treaty of Paris, in 1260, surprised the French greatly. Considering the condemnation of John Lackland to be an abuse of power by Philip Augustus, Louis IX felt he could not keep the whole of Plantagenet territory. There was no question of giving up Normandy, Poitou or Anjou, but Louis agreed to restore Saintonge, Périgord, Quercy and a part of Agenais.

Succeeding generations were shocked by this treaty, surprising and exceptional under the usual terms of conquest, as it was one of the causes of the Hundred Years' War. But in Louis' time it was considered an example of strict justice, and the king's prestige grew.

In 1263 he was chosen as mediator by the barons who were revolting against Henry III of England. In 1264, by the 'Mise of Amiens', he decided in favour of Henry, which had the unfortunate consequence of plunging England into civil war.

Another important aspect of Louis' character was his disapproving attitude towards his brother Charles of Anjou. After the death of Frederick II of Hohenstaufen, in the midst of a conflict between the Guelphs and Ghibellines, Charles of Anjou put himself forward to the pope as a candidate for the throne of Sicily. The pope accepted but, to secure his throne, Charles of Anjou resorted to atrocities, including the execution in 1268 of Frederick II's heir, the young Emperor Conradin. Saint Louis could not be associated with such behaviour, but, generous as always, decided to be lenient with his brother. This clemency was to hasten his own end.

After the failure of the Seventh Crusade, Louis' burning desire was to return to the Holy Land; internal problems had kept him in France for the past fifteen years. So in 1270 he set off once again from Aigues-Mortes. But his brother Charles of Anjou, to consolidate his own shaky position in Sicily, advised Louis to stop at Carthage and purge the infidel quarter there. Louis, too weak to refuse, sailed for the Tunisian coast, where his army was decimated by plague. Louis caught the disease and died, lying on a bed of ashes, his arms crossed, on 25 August 1270.

Despite the loss of territories he had not wanted to keep, he left France in an unrivalled moral situation and with a material prosperity the country had never known before. The population had increased considerably, towns had grown up, agriculture had been developed and more land exploited. There was a general rise in prices which proved to be a sign of prosperity because coins were honestly minted. This currency, stable in itself, sometimes saw its buying power wavering.

However, the enrichment of the producers created a great deal of capital, which encouraged commerce. Lending with interest, though condemned by the Church, was morally accepted by the civil powers. And this material prosperity was not without its social repercussions.

The characteristic feature of St Louis' internal administration was a genuine reform of institutions. Louis was the first king to realize that a kingdom as important as that created by his grandfather could not be administered like a private property. Philip Augustus, after the disaster of Fréteval, had realized the necessity of maintaining the archives; it was under Louis that

rer en labaie de saint benoit sur lone ou
il auoit esleu sepulture. Le pmier chap
ple du pmier roy phe coment il saisi la
contee de vouquessin · et comet il fina le
chastel de momehant. Et coment le duc
guille de normdie passa en augletir ⁊ oc
cist le roy et saisi le royaume · Et comt pe
urbain sist croiserie pour aler outre mer·

Philip I and queen Bertrade. (*Grandes Chroniques de France*) 81

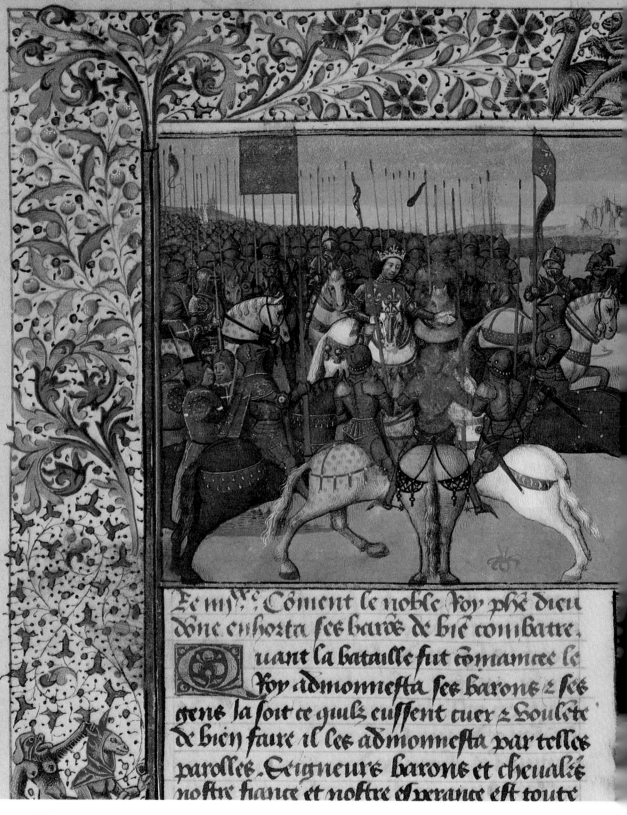

t au plus deuotement quilz poïet. Et
nus rament noient a dieu en oroyson
onneur et la franchise dont see ecïle se sïo
ft ou pouoir du Roy phe. Et dautre part
a honte et le Reprouche quelle seuffre et
souffet par othon et par le Roy iehan
antsleterre. par qui dons et promesses
outes les compaïgnïes qui suret Semes

Comment le Roy print port a dannete. vunn: chappe

la pursin pur   autres dessus nonmes se
le moyen des s   vindrent des contrees des
ambassadeurs   susdittes atout grande
cestassanoyr le patriar   quantite de nes et galees
che de sherusalem et les   en chippre. vindret aussi

the distinction became clear between the king's house and the government itself.

But the terms used then do not apply today. On the one hand there was a particular body with the general name of court (*curia regis*), which met frequently, with the king presiding. It was both a sort of state council and a court of appeal, and people have rightly seen in it the origins of a Parlement. From 1268 onwards, the acts of the Court were noted down in special registers called *Olim*. St Louis could also over-rule this organization and judge a case directly; hence the legendary image of the king dispensing justice under an oak tree at Vincennes.

The other main government body was the treasury, situated at the Temple and adminis-tered by the knights of the order. It gathered the first taxes, such as the poll-tax, and supervised expenditure. The accounts were kept by the *curia in compotis*, ancestor of the Cour des Comptes.

The main areas of expenditure, apart from war and diplomacy, were the subsidies given to the Church, to hospitals, and to good works. These were proof of the king's tireless charity. Local finance was left to the great fiefs, and their cus-toms were respected. The example of the Estates of Languedoc, where the three orders voted on taxation until 1789, was typical of the king's broad-mindedness.

This period was also notable in the fields of art and intellect. It was in St Louis' reign that the great Gothic cathedrals, conceived under Philip Augustus, were built. St Louis' own contribu-tion to this was the magnificent Sainte-Chapelle.

There was a great movement in the field of thought. The legend of the Grail was born, but, parallel with the tales of chivalry such as Lancelot of the Lake, prototype of the French hero, there also arose more original and free-flowing tales such as the famous *Roman de la Rose* by Guillaume de Loris, completed thirty years later in pamphlet form by Jean de Meung.

The historian Jean, Sire de Joinville, remains the precise and ingenuous portrayer of the period of St Louis. Philosophy came to the fore: the writings of Aristotle were discovered, and the intellectual centre was established at Paris, at the university which still bears the name of its master, Pierre de Sorbon. The German Albert the Great and St Thomas Aquinas attempted to reconcile pagan high philosophy with the teach-ings of the Christian Church, and more or less succeeded.

This was the kingdom, in a state of full material and spiritual expansion, which Louis ix bequeathed to a very talented son, who had to handle the difficult situation of succeeding to a saint.

✤ PHILIP III THE BOLD ✤
(1270–1285)
AND MARY OF BRABANT

PHILIP III IS GENERALLY CONSIDERED to have been a mediocre king whose reign affords little of interest. But on closer investigation it becomes clear that his life was far from lacking in interest, that it was full of curious incidents, and that his policies were sound.

Born in 1245, he was, at the age of eighteen, the object of a very strange family manoeuvre. Queen Margaret of Provence, whose influence over her husband had become total, felt the desire to take a hand in government. She there-fore imposed on her son, the heir to the throne,

an oath whereby he swore to obey her until he was thirty, and also never to conclude an alliance with his uncle Charles of Anjou. Louis found out about this oath; he imposed no sanctions on the queen, but asked the pope to free his son from the oath, which was done. It was therefore with-out the slightest hindrance that Philip the Bold was crowned after his father's death.

The voyage to bring back the king's dead body to St Denis took place overland and abounded with drama. At Cosenza Queen Isabella of Aragon died, and was buried in the

Duomo. On 21 and 22 August 1271, Alphonse de Poitiers and his wife died from the rigours of the journey at Savona. These deaths meant the return of Languedoc to the throne, which was a propitious start for the reign.

The inheritance was immense: it consisted of Poitou, Saintonge and Albigeois, the land of Auvergne, and the jurisdiction of Quercy, Agenais, Rouergue, and Comtat-Venaissin, which was part of the Empire. Advised by Pierre

de la Brosse, the king had the succession seized on 9 October 1271 by the seneschal of Carcassonne. In 1273, Philip III thought it wise to concede Comtat-Venaissin to the Holy See, a decision which was soon to have heavy consequences.

The treaty of Paris, signed by St Louis and the king of England in 1260, only came into force as the result of a new treaty signed at Amiens in 1279: the king of France conceded Agenais to

The seal of Philip the Bold.

England, but difficulties remained which were soon to cause a breaking off of relations.

In 1274 Philip III had married Mary of Brabant. Daughter of the duke of Brabant, she was a very innocent girl. Yet in 1276 she was accused by Pierre de la Brosse of having poisoned Louis, the king's eldest son by his first wife. She was in danger of being condemned to death. Fortunately, her brother, John of Brabant, sent a knight to defend her and this emissary proved her innocence in combat. The accuser, unable to substantiate his calumny, was sent to the gibbet. Mary of Brabant, whose story inspired Ancelot, Victor Hugo's rival poet at the Académie, survived her husband and two of his successors, and died only in 1321.

The rest of the reign was marked by a crucial event: the reversion of the appanages. An act of Parliament of 1284 rejected the French claims of Charles of Anjou, unfortunate king of Sicily, by affirming the indivisibility of the territory and the reversion of inheritances to the crown.

Another succession had become open, that of Champagne and Navarre. Philip married the heir to the throne, his second son Philip, to Joan of Navarre. She died in 1305 but, since Navarre was a feminine fief, it was not the queen's husband, Philip IV the Fair, who inherited it, but their elder son, the future Louis X the Head-strong. Champagne later devolved to Joan of Champagne, daughter of Louis X and wife of Philip of Evreux. One of Philip IV's daughters, Isabella, married Edward II of England.

The end of the reign was dominated by a war against Peter III of Aragon, who was contesting the crown of Sicily with Charles of Anjou's son. In a surprising turn of events, in 1284, the crown of Aragon was offered to Charles de Valois, younger brother of Philip the Fair. The king accepted but, in order to effect the change, Peter III of Aragon had to be dethroned. He called on his people to support him and there was war to repel the French invasion. In the midst of manoeuvres Philip III died at Perpignan on 5 October 1285 without having achieved his hopes.

One of France's most imposing pieces of architecture dates from Philip III. No doubt with the eventual intention of resuming the Crusade, he had Aigues-Mortes surrounded by a fortress of walls which, still intact today, is proof of the building skills of the time.

✤ PHILIP IV THE FAIR ✤
(1285–1314)
AND JOAN OF NAVARRE

PHILIP IV WAS THE MOST MYSTERIOUS of the Capetian kings, and even leaving aside the bad reputation which surrounded him, one of the most remarkable. This reputation is due to the most dramatic events of his reign: his conflict with the Papacy, the punishment of the Knights Templar, the bad behaviour of his daughters-in-law, and the issuing of false money. But one must look beyond this to see that on the whole his reign was a favourable one which contributed to the greatness of France.

Little is known of the king's physical appearance: he had fair hair, and a handsome and very expressive face. He is always depicted as sumptuously dressed, in velvet, fur-lined clothes, but it is also known that, under his rich clothes, this pious man normally wore a hair shirt.

His period is often called that of 'Philip the Fair and the lawyers', as he was always surrounded by men of law whose advice he took readily, for example Pierre Flottes, Pierre Dubois and Guillaume de Nogaret. In contrast to this council, which suggests an autocratic style, Philip also showed a democratic side, since by assembling the three orders of the nation in 1302 to gain their support, he was, in theory, the founder of the Estates-General. These contrasts reveal him as one of the most original figures of French history.

His reign was particularly long, with many

problems which often occurred simultaneously. Married to Joan of Navarre, he was the first king of both France and Navarre; but the possession of Navarre remained ephemeral, and the main territorial gains took place elsewhere.

To begin with, judging that his father's war against Aragon was a vain one, he signed a truce with Peter III and gave up the idea of conquering a kingdom for his brother Charles of Valois; a famous saying has it that Charles was son of a king, brother to a king, and father to a king, but never king himself, even though he was on occasion made notable offers, and even proposed himself as a candidate for the Empire.

Pursuing the policy of expansion he attached Quercy to the royal domain in 1289 by a treaty with Henry III in return for a yearly sum. He also acquired the county of Bigorre in 1307 by paying rent, but a smaller one, to the bishop of Puy.

His other acquisitions were paid for outright: Beaugency in 1291, the bishopric of Maguellone and the east side of the town of Montpellier in 1293. In 1301 his possession of Franche-Comté was recognized; the following year he joined to his domain the counties of Marche and Angoulême, and the seigneurie of Forges. In 1313, using felony as a pretext, he confiscated Mortagne and Tournai. After the Flanders war he annexed Lille, Béthune and Douai. These acquisitions often cost a great deal, which explains in part the appalling financial difficulties which obtained throughout the reign.

This financial policy has been much discussed, generally in unfavourable terms. The king used many different means to pay for these acquisitions, to give a reasonable salary to the numerous civil servants he created and to finance several expensive military operations. The first, and the most simple, was spoliation: Jews, and in particular money-lenders, were the first victims. He seized personal treasures and fortunes and reverted debts to the crown. But these were the least of his measures, the culmination of which was the trial of the Knights Templar.

In 1306, short of money, he confiscated the goods of the Lombards, Italian bankers scattered throughout the territory. His most notorious move was the adulteration of the coinage. It was meant to be weighed against gold, but at the mint it was reduced in weight. There was also a discrepancy between real money and nominal money, which made possible very lucrative compensation demands. But it is fair to point out that all this was not operated systematically. Whenever he could, the king had true money minted; but this move was of no benefit to the debtors, who normally outnumbered creditors.

Apart from this, we should consider Philip IV's foreign policy as a whole. Like his predecessors', it was directed against England. Edward I, was summoned to do obeisance as vassal in southern Aquitaine, under pain of confiscation. Anxious for peace, Edward accepted the temporary occupation of strongholds in Guyenne. Once these were occupied by French troops, Philip, his task made easier for him, had the whole territory occupied in three campaigns (1291, 1295, 1296) led by Charles of Valois and Robert of Artois.

In the meantime the king was having a fleet built in the hopes of a landing in England. Edward held out for a long time, then allied himself to the Netherlands and Flanders. The count of Flanders, Guy de Dampierre, also an ill-treated vassal, agreed to help; but the Anglo-Flemish were defeated in 1297 at Vyve-Saint-Bavon.

To facilitate the signing of a treaty, Edward married Marguerite, Philip the Fair's sister, and Philip's daughter Isabella was promised to the future Edward II. From these unions, and in particular, the second, was to stem the Hundred Years' War. But the king could not be expected to see this far ahead, since his three sons assured the succession. The treaty was signed in Paris in 1303; Guyenne was returned to Edward I and the alliance concluded.

The French were now no longer in a position of strength; since the treaty with the English in 1297, they had tried quite simply to annex Flanders, which now revolted and massacred the French on 17 May 1302. Philip IV immediately sent in troops, which were disastrously defeated at Courtrai (11 July 1302). The king then, unsuccessfully, took over the command of his army. The Flemish invaded Artois. A truce was signed in 1303, then hostilities began anew, and a relatively slight French success at Mons-en-Pévèle (18 August 1304) helped to avenge the humiliation of Courtrai. A peace treaty was signed at Athis-sur-Orge in June 1305 and a reconciliation

A Franciscan monk dedicates his book to queen Joan of Navarre.

y commence le
prologue sur
le liure qui est
appelle le mirēr
des dames qui

fist ung frere de lordre de saint
françois par la petiacon et de
māde de noble dame Jehanne
Royne de france & de nauarre a
la louenge de dieu & au salut de
ſõ ame

Edward I of England pays homage to Philip IV the Fair.

was obtained. It was sealed by the annexation of Lille.

If the differences with England and Flanders brought few advantages overall, this was not the case in the east, where the king managed to obtain Franche-Comté, but unfortunately in a rather precarious way, since his son Philip v would have to restore it to the Empire.

But a more memorable aspect of Philip the Fair's reign was his quarrel with the Papacy, in which, it must be said, wrong was by no means entirely on his side. Relations with Popes Honorius iv and Nicholas iv had been excellent. After a difficult conclave at Viterbo the cardinals took the unfortunate initiative of electing a hermit from Mount Majella, Pietro del Murrone, who was not even a priest. He was ordained *per saltum* and, under the name of Celestine v, the new pope made so many mistakes that he had to resign after only six months. He was replaced by the man responsible for his downfall, Cardinal Caetani, who took the name of Boniface viii.

He was a violent, intransigent and authoritarian man. He immediately fell out with Philip the Fair, even though they had been friends for a long time, since Cardinal Caetani had been the pontifical legate to France under Nicholas iv. Trouble began as soon as he was ordained, as Philip, short of money, demanded subsidies from the reluctant clergy, who complained to the pope in 1296. Boniface viii reacted immediately, and by the Bull *Clericis laicos* he excommunicated the king of France, guilty of having taxed the clergy.

This decision was an abuse of power and therefore difficult to enforce; it called for a riposte. The king called an assembly of the clergy and chose two emissaries to discuss matters with the pope. At the same time, he banned the export of gold and silver currency, which deprived the Holy See of the huge resources it drew from the French Church. This brutal retaliation worked, and the pope, by the Bull *Innefabilis amor*, relaxed his sanctions, while still maintaining that the spiritual power excelled the temporal. Since the French clergy had also protested, the pope, by a series of successive Bulls, came finally to renounce altogether the terms of the Bull *Clericis laicos*.

The French king's success made the Italian cardinals contest the validity of Boniface viii.

Fearing an alliance between them and Philip, the pope, by the Bull *Etsi de Stato* canonized King Louis ix. Feeling that he was henceforth on good terms with the king of France, Boniface viii had the treacherous cardinals interned and confiscated their property. They escaped and settled in the region of Narbonne. It would seem that here they got in touch with the bishop of Pamiers, Bernard Saisset, and encouraged him to rebel against the king of France. In 1301, Philip the Fair ordered that the bishop be arrested for treason.

Boniface viii refused to dismiss the prelate and demanded his release, which the king naturally did not grant. This refusal infuriated Boniface who, affirming his power and his right to dictate to princes, called the French bishops to Rome. The Bull *Ausculta fili* was tendentiously abridged by the king's lawyers and published with an interdiction prohibiting the French bishops from going to Rome. A rather dubious tradition has it that the king's text was headed: 'To his fatuity Boniface viii who passes for pope.'

What is surprising is that, to win his offensive against the Holy See, the king first wished to gain the agreement of the French people. And so in 1302, in the cathedral of Notre Dame de Paris, he called the first meeting of the Estates-General. He made them approve a motion, deliberated by the three orders individually, to affirm that since the king was sovereign in his kingdom, the pope had no right to intervene in internal fiscal policies.

Outraged, Boniface viii retaliated with the Bull *Unam sanctam*, excommunicating the king. This coincided with the defeat of Courtrai. Not wanting to lose face a second time, Philip the Fair, who had just witnessed the death of Pierre Flotte, was urged by his successor, Guillaume de Nogaret, descendant of a Cathar, to anticipate the papal threats to place the country under an interdict and to demand the king's deposition.

At the beginning of 1303, Guillaume de Nogaret, bearing royal letters, headed for Italy with the aim of reasoning with Boniface viii. Before he even arrived, the pope renewed the excommunication of Philip the Fair by the Bull *Petri solio excelso* (8 September 1303). By this terrible document, all the treaties with France were annulled, and all provinces attached to the kingdom were freed from their oath of fealty. If

The seal of the Knights Templar.

the pope's threats had been carried out, France would have been completely dismembered.

But all this was to turn out badly for the Papacy. Seconded by part of the Italian nobility, Nogaret, accompanied by Sciarra Colonna, reached the pope's residence at Anagni at the head of a small army. The Caetani palace was attacked, the guards fled and Boniface viii remained alone in his apartments. He put on his papal robes and, when struck by Colonna, simply said: 'Here is my neck, here is my head.'

On 12 September 1303 Nogaret and Colonna transferred the pope to Rome, where he died insane a few days later.

This attack, unprecedented in the history of France, was to have unforeseen consequences. The cardinals elected as Boniface viii's successor a gentle Dominican, Cardinal Boccasini, known as Benedict xi. As a move towards peace he lifted the excommunication order on Philip the Fair, but maintained those on Colonna and Nogaret. He refused to declare Boniface viii a heretic, as the king of France was pressing him to do. After only a few months Benedict xi died at Perugia, after eating figs which may well have been poisoned.

The conclave to elect a successor to Benedict xi lasted a whole year. Under pressure from the French cardinals, it finally elected the archbishop

of Bordeaux, Bertrand de Got, who took the name of Clement v (15 June 1305). This pontiff established the Papacy in the valley of the Rhône, and was unable to refuse Philip the Fair anything. It was during his pontificate that one of the major events of the reign, the trial of the Knights Templar, was to take place. It is quite likely that this trial would not have reached its conclusion if the pope had formally opposed it.

The reasons for it were easy to understand. The Templars were virtually the crown's bankers, and Philip the Fair's financial policy had put him deeply in debt. By neutralizing them he was not only cancelling out the public debt, but also refurbishing the treasury. It was possible to attack the Templars without arousing public hostility because they were unpopular: they were accused, without proof, of unnatural habits, and it was said that their way of swearing an oath was to repudiate the Cross or spit on it.

These more or less slanderous legends made the lawyers' job easy. Under the surveillance of Pierre Dubois and Nogaret, they took the offensive. During the night of 22 September 1307, all the Templars were arrested, in a remarkably well organized raid. Nogaret himself drew up the bill of indictment, paying particular attention to the sacrilegious duties imposed on the Templars and to their obscene habits, and when Pope Clement v felt obliged to make it clear that he did not believe these accusations, Philip the Fair signed a letter, written by Nogaret, which gave the lie to the papal assertion and stated that he was acting with full papal authority.

The trial was a long one; begun in 1307, it only really ended in 1312, on 3 April, when the pope, through the Bull *Vox in excelso*, proclaimed the dissolution of the order. The pope had hesitated for a long time over this decision, but finally yielded to Philip the Fair's demands, and also accepted the results of interrogation under torture. To salve his conscience, he called a council at Vienna before publishing the bull of dissolution.

The trials had been carried out in a revoltingly biased manner; most of the confessions were extracted under protracted torture but retracted immediately it ceased. Nevertheless over fifty Templars were convicted of sodomy and burnt in the Bois de Vincennes. The others, including the grand master of the Order, Jacques de

Molay, and his chief assistant, Geoffroy de Charnay, who had pleaded guilty but whom they could not convict of the sacrilege of sodomy, were put in prison.

While these appalling things were going on, the honour and dignity of the royal family was struck by scandal. Philip the Fair's three sons had married distant cousins of theirs, princesses of Burgundy, who came from a junior branch of the Capetians, which had split away from the main branch at the time of Robert the Pious. The future queen, Margaret, daughter of the duke of Burgundy, was Saint Louis' granddaughter on her mother's side. Her sisters-in-law Joan and Blanche were the daughters of the count of Burgundy, suzerain of Franche-Comté, and the wives respectively of the future Philip v and the future Charles iv.

The adventures of these three royal princesses have been popularized in the stories centred upon the Tour de Nesle. There is a great deal of truth in these stories, and the three sisters-in-law were certainly free in their ways.

Their depravity was brought to light by their other sister-in-law, Philip the Fair's daughter Isabella, wife of Edward ii of England, who has been nicknamed 'the She-wolf of France'. An inquiry was made, and it was discovered that the princesses did indeed have lovers, of whom two were identified as Philippe and Gautier d'Aulnay. The king was merciless, as the purity of the Capetian race was at stake. The two guilty men were arrested and the three princesses put in prison.

When told of the confessions their lovers had made under torture they admitted their crimes, which were all the more serious since Margaret of Burgundy had a daughter. It was no longer clear whether this child was legitimate or not, and this uncertainty was to alter the course of history. The wedding of the future King Louis was annulled. Margaret of Burgundy was imprisoned in Château-Gaillard, where she died of cold, misery and hunger.

The punishment of Blanche, wife of the future Charles iv, was equally severe. Her marriage was dissolved, and then after a long period of imprisonment she was allowed to become a nun at Maubuisson. Philip v, 'luckier' or wiser than his brothers, kept his wife Joan, believing her protestations of innocence. Philippe and Gautier d'Aulnay were castrated before being put to death.

These unfortunate domestic affairs had distracted the king's attention from the trial of the Templars, but he had not forgotten them. On 12 March 1314 he had Jacques de Molay and Geoffroy de Charnay brought out of prison; they were taken to the square of Notre Dame to confess their alleged crimes for the last time and to hear their sentence of life imprisonment read.

But the men, who had been forced to confess under torture, retracted their statements; they insisted on their innocence and on the saintliness of the persecuted order. Reacting with great brutality, Philip the Fair declared that they had relapsed, and that evening had them burnt alive at the corner of the Île de la Cité, on the site of today's Square du Vert-Galant.

As the flames rose, Jacques de Molay is believed to have said: 'Pope Clement, iniquitous judge and cruel executioner, I adjure you to appear in forty days' time before God's tribunal. And you, King of France, will not live to see the end of this year, and Heaven's retribution will strike down your accomplices and destroy your posterity.'

The prophecy (possibly apocryphal) was to be realized point by point.

Forty days after Jacques de Molay's execution, Clement v fell ill, and he died on 20 April 1314.

During the summer Nogaret, from whom Clement had lifted his excommunication order, died in mysterious circumstances.

And Philip the Fair died in the same year after a hunting accident, aged only forty-six (29 November 1314).

This series of deaths announced by Jacques de Molay took on an even more disturbing aspect since Philip the Fair's abundant posterity was to be struck down in its turn, and this would mark the end of the direct line of the Capetians.

THE SONS OF
PHILIP THE FAIR
(1314–1328)

Louis x the Headstrong (Hutin) 1314–1316

BEFORE HE DIED Philip the Fair called his eldest son Louis to his bedside and announced gravely: 'Reflect carefully, Louis, what it means to be king of France.' These words should have been the precursors of a great reign, but this was not the case with Louis x the Headstrong, who reigned for only eighteen months and whose death was the major event of the reign, as it posed a problem of succession unprecedented in the three previous centuries of Capetian rule.

Philip the Fair's death caused strong reactions, coming as it did at the end of a long and very authoritarian reign. There were street fights, riots and general disorder during which Louis won himself the inglorious nickname of Headstrong.

But it is the governmental rather than the civil upheaval which is remembered. The main event was the trial of Enguerrand de Marigny, Philip the Fair's old superintendent of finance. Public opinion was against him, as he was held (rightly) responsible for many of the financial manipulations which had bedevilled the reign.

Shortly after the accession of Louis the Headstrong, Marigny was called before a commission comprising Philip of Poitiers (the future Philip v), Charles of Marche (the future Charles IV) and in particular Charles of Valois, brother of Philip IV. These three princes called on Marigny to justify his financial policy 'as they had found the treasury bare'. The superintendent replied that the empty state of the treasury was due to his having had to pay off the late king's numerous debts.

Not satisfied by this explanation, Louis x had him imprisoned. He was put in the Temple and then appeared at Vincennes before the king himself, assisted by the princes and the *curia regis*. After a highly debatable trial, Marigny was condemned to the gallows and hanged from the gibbet at Montfaucon. A series of further executions decimated Philip the Fair's advisers and civil servants, who had been too recalcitrant in agreeing to the financial demands of the feudal lords.

Attention was then focused on the problem of a new marriage for the king. His adulterous wife had died in prison leaving only a daughter, Joan, whose legitimacy was, perhaps wrongly, in doubt. The king's uncles opted for a princess reputed to be the most beautiful in Europe, Clemence, daughter of King Charles I of Hungary. She was a Capetian of the Anjou-Sicily branch. Chancellor Hugues de Bouville was charged with asking for her hand in marriage and the union was agreed. The future queen made her entry into Paris on 19 August 1315 and less than a week later the newly-weds were crowned at Rheims; it seemed that the future of the dynasty was assured.

The young king began by making a few concessions to the more clamorous of the feudal lords, then attempted to deal with the Flemish question. But his army inopportunely disbanded, a blow softened by the news that Queen Clemence was pregnant.

In May 1316, the king was unwise enough, whilst heated from playing a game of indoor tennis, to drink a tankard of iced wine. He was taken ill, developed a high fever, and died of pneumonia seven days after retiring to bed. The rumour spread that he had been poisoned, and this was often repeated, without proof, by chroniclers of the day. However, since the queen was expecting a baby, it seemed there would be no problem over the succession.

And indeed, during the night of 13–14 November 1316, Queen Clemence gave birth to a son, who was named John.

John I (1316)

TOWARDS THE END of the queen's pregnancy the problem of the regency arose. Philip of Poitiers, who was in Lyons when his brother died, returned hurriedly to Paris. He found there his brother and his uncle who, as brother to Philip IV, claimed the regency. The ambitious Philip did not agree with this, and had himself recognized as regent by the burghers of Paris. His brother and uncle put up some resistance, but Philip defeated them without too much trouble and the oath of allegiance was sworn to him.

However, he began to feel threatened when his sister-in-law gave birth to a son who was obviously the heir to the throne. But his fears were short-lived, since, when he was only five days old, John I the Posthumous died and was buried at Saint Denis.

This death may well not have been a natural one; it was rumoured that the child-king had been killed with a pin by his aunt Mahaut of Artois, mother of Jeanne of Burgundy, Philip's wife.

It was also rumoured that there had been some child-swapping. These rumours are important, as the subsequent story of John I distinctly resembles that of the false dauphins who claimed to be King Louis XVII.

Indeed, forty years later, after the defeat at Poitiers and with the resulting vacancy of the throne, a false John I appeared, supported by the Italian agitator Rienzi. He claimed the crown, and with Rienzi's help raised troops in the Comtat-Venaissin, crossed the Rhône near Orange, and occupied two villages in Languedoc, Chusclan and Codolet, on the exact spot where twentieth-century France erected its first atomic plant, at Marcoule.

The story of the false John I did not upset the crown or the succession in 1357. But the death of the true John certainly did, as it posed an entirely new problem for the Capetian succession.

Philip V the Tall (1316–1322)

THE DEATH OF JOHN I left the throne vacant and it would have seemed logical that it should devolve to Joan, Louis the Headstrong's daughter by Margaret of Burgundy. But now an event took place which was of capital importance for the succession of the kings of France. The regent, Philip V, had himself crowned at the beginning of January 1317 along with his wife Joan, now finally cleared of the charges regarding her adultery.

King Philip V the Tall granting privileges.

This coronation was vigorously debated, as not everyone was in favour of evicting Princess Joan. The king then brought in his lawyers, and on their advice he called a meeting of the Estates-General. These agreed that 'a woman should not succeed to the throne of France' and in support of this they invoked, probably improperly, an old law of the Salian Franks, the 'Salic law', which precluded women from acceding to the throne. It seems that those interested were motivated by far more than just this rather whimsical law: first, Joan's legitimacy was in doubt, and secondly, if she married a foreign prince, the kingdom of France would no longer be ruled by a Frenchman.

Since Joan still had her partisans, Philip was obliged to make concessions. Charles of Valois was given a handsome endowment. Moreover, to keep the Burgundians happy, the king married his daughter Joan to Duke Eudes IV and conceded Franche-Comté to him. Joan, daughter of Philip the Headstrong, was given a rich dowry and married to her cousin Philip of Evreux, grandson of Philip the Bold.

Little is known of Philip V's appearance apart from his height; from this came his nickname, the Tall. He settled down to the duties of king aided by Philip the Fair's lawyers, to whom he made the concession of having Enguerrand de Marigny's body taken down from the gibbet and decently buried.

Ly cõmence les faitz et geftes du
roy phillippe de valoys.
    Le pmier chappitre parle des grãs
queftions ou quel devoit eftre cõmis le
gouvernement du ropaulme.

Pres la mort du roy charles
qui bel fut appelle le quel a
voit laiffe la royne iehanne
fa fême groffe furent affem
blez les barõs z les nobles a traicter du
                                    x.iiij.

During his brief reign Philip V undertook various administrative reforms of which one has survived, namely the autonomy of the Cour des Comptes. He also reformed the king's council and determined the rights of high-placed civil servants. These wise reforms were carried out in a turbulent atmosphere, as a new revolt of the Pastoureaux broke out. Philip V was making ready to re-establish order, and at the same time sought to have weights and measures standardized. He also proposed an income tax of twenty per cent, which gave rise to general indignation.

In the midst of these difficulties the health of the king, who suffered from tuberculosis, suddenly deteriorated and he died on 3 January 1322.

Charles IV the Fair (1322–1328)

PHILIP V LEFT THREE DAUGHTERS, but because of the Salic law his brother Charles IV the Fair was promptly crowned at Rheims by Archbishop Robert of Courtenay (11 February 1322).

To assure his succession, he asked for his marriage to Blanche of Burgundy to be annulled. She was removed from Château-Gaillard, where she was languishing and where, incorrigible, she had had a child by one of her jailers, and was put in a cloister at the abbey of Maubuisson.

The marriage was declared void by an ecclesiastical commission and on 21 September 1322 Charles IV married Mary of Luxemburg, daughter of Emperor Henry VII. He then tried to have himself elected Holy Roman Emperor with the support of Pope John XXII (Jacques Duèse from Cahors).

King Charles IV visited Languedoc where he founded, at Toulouse, the Company of the Seven Troubadours of Toulouse, which was perhaps the predecessor of the Academy of the Jeux Floraux (1323). On returning from the journey to Toulouse, Queen Mary gave birth prematurely to a still-born child in a château near Bourges and died of puerperal fever.

In July 1325, Charles IV, anxious for descendants, married his first cousin Joan, daughter of Louis of Evreux, after obtaining a special dispensation. He then received at his court his sister Isabella of England, who had left her husband King Edward II because of his homosexuality. An arch-intriguer, she tried to have the provinces conceded by England returned to her, and had her son, the future Edward III, invested as duke of Aquitaine. With the help of her lover Edward Mortimer, Isabella had her husband Edward II murdered under the most atrociously cruel circumstances. Charles IV, who had supported her cause, received a reprimand from the Papacy.

By his third wife Charles IV had two daughters of whom only one survived, but there was still hope of a male heir, as the queen was pregnant for a third time. At the beginning of 1328, Charles was struck down by an unidentified illness and died rapidly at Vincennes on 1 February 1328. He had designated his first cousin, Philip of Valois, as regent, until the child was born. But the queen gave birth to a third daughter. The direct line of the Capetians was extinct and there was about to be, if not a change of dynasty, at least a change of line in the person of Philip IV, the first Valois king.

Queen Joan of Evreux, widow of Charles IV the Fair, expecting his baby. But she was to give birth to a third daughter, and this marked the end of the line of the Direct Capetians. (*Grandes Chroniques de France*)

Charles v in his library. His interest in
literature won him the nickname 'the Wise'.

Part Four

THE VALOIS

1328~1589

Hundred Years' War
and Renaissance

THE VALOIS

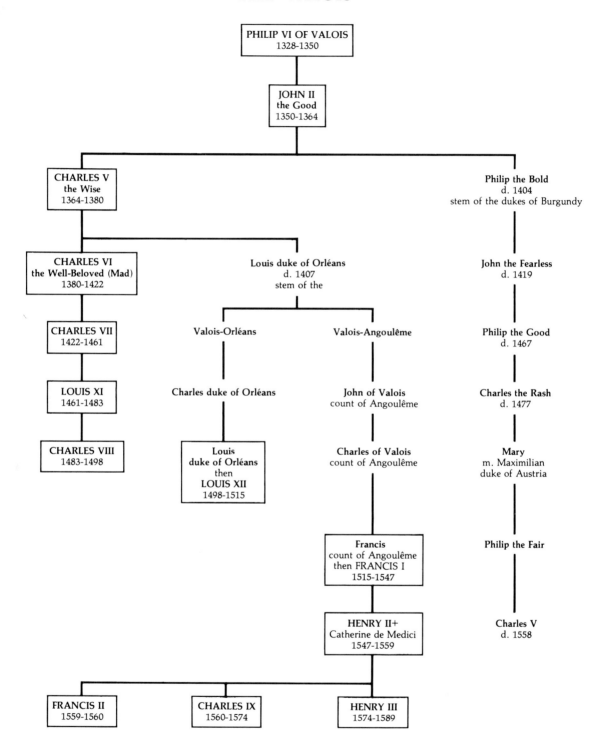

PHILIP VI OF VALOIS
1328-1350

JOHN II
the Good
1350-1364

CHARLES V
the Wise
1364-1380

Philip the Bold
d. 1404
stem of the dukes of Burgundy

CHARLES VI
the Well-Beloved (Mad)
1380-1422

Louis duke of Orléans
d. 1407
stem of the

John the Fearless
d. 1419

CHARLES VII
1422-1461

Valois-Orléans

Valois-Angoulême

Philip the Good
d. 1467

LOUIS XI
1461-1483

Charles duke of Orléans

John of Valois
count of Angoulême

Charles the Rash
d. 1477

CHARLES VIII
1483-1498

Louis
duke of Orléans
then
LOUIS XII
1498-1515

Charles of Valois
count of Angoulême

Mary
m. Maximilian
duke of Austria

Francis
count of Angoulême
then FRANCIS I
1515-1547

Philip the Fair

HENRY II+
Catherine de Medici
1547-1559

Charles V
d. 1558

FRANCIS II
1559-1560

CHARLES IX
1560-1574

HENRY III
1574-1589

PHILIP VI OF VALOIS
(1328–1350)

IT SEEMS QUITE NATURAL to us today that Philip of Valois, who was already regent, and was cousin to three dead kings, should have succeeded to the throne of the fleur-de-lys. But there was also little objection to this in France at the time, since the principle of not allowing descent through the female line had been accepted. This was not the case in England. Queen Isabella, daughter of Philip the Fair, took the view that since her son, by blood, continued the direct line, it was he who should succeed to the throne. The lawyers opposed this claim by maintaining, rightly, that Isabella, because of her sex, could not continue the dynasty, and that because of this she could not transmit to her son a right which she herself did not possess. This was common sense, but the king of England did not accept it, and the change of dynasty in France was to be the cause of a long-lasting conflict between the two nations, which was to be called the Hundred Years War, but which in fact lasted longer, since, with intermissions, the war which began in 1340 ended only in 1453.

Philip VI ultimately left behind him a very mediocre reputation. Nevertheless his accession brought some very important fiefs to the kingdom of France, thus increasing her power. In addition to this, the king was a brilliant horseman. His weak point was his wife, Queen Joan of Burgundy, sister of Margaret, an ambitious and shrewish woman whose influence was generally a bad one.

Fond of ostentation, the new king ordered for his coronation splendid celebrations which took place at Rheims on 28 May 1328. The crown was placed on his head by the archbishop of Rheims, Guillaume de Trie.

The coronation was marred by a slight incident, namely the hesitation of the count of Flanders, who wished to draw the king's attention to the difficulties overwhelming his fief, where the Flemings were in revolt. Philip VI noted this remark, and the first act of his reign was to combat the Flemish revolt.

The Flanders campaign has become something of a legend, in particular the siege of Cassel, at whose gates the inhabitants had placed a huge cockerel bearing the insulting inscription:

Quand ce coq-ci chanté aura
Le roi trouvé y entrera

(When this cockerel crows the *found* king will enter here.) For, faithful to the crown of England, the Flemish contested Philip VI's legitimacy and gave him the nickname 'found king'.

The immediate fall of Cassel, defended by Jacob van Artevelde, was the revenge for Courtrai (23 August 1328). This easy success gave Philip VI military illusions which were later to cost him dear. However, since the new king of England, Edward III, had, at the instigation of the Flemish, proclaimed himself king of France, he had to be dealt with, and Philip VI demanded that he come to pay him a vassal's homage for his fiefs in Guyenne. It took more than two years of discussion to bring this about. Edward III complied, by the letters patent of 28 March 1331, but did so with bad grace, as he refused to render him *hommage-lige* (unrestricted homage), as he had already done at their meeting of 5 June 1329 at Amiens Cathedral.

Philip VI, anxious for peace, contented himself with this half-success. In May 1332 he married his eldest son, John, to Bonne of Luxemburg, daughter of the blind King John of Bohemia; there were sumptuous feasts celebrated at Melun.

This luxurious way of life was very expensive, and royal finances were in grave difficulties from the very beginning of the reign. But Philip's mind was on glory above all, and his reign gave such signs of splendour that in 1333 he was designated by Pope John XXII to lead a crusade. This, in fact, never took place.

In 1336, Philip's glory was so great that the whole of Europe saw him practically as a resurrection of St Louis. On top of this, it was to Philip VI that France owed the acquisition of Dauphiné in 1347 (with the reservation that after the death of the last sovereign of the Viennois the king of France's eldest son would again be called

The Battle of Sluys,
1340, at which the
English destroyed
Philip VI's fleet.
(Froissart's Chronicle)

Quant le roy dan
gleterre z ses ma
reschaulx eurui
ordonnees leurs
batailles et leurs nauires

pou et tournoixtent tant gľz
leuent aleur Woulente. Les
normans qui les Wpient
tourner / semerueilloient
pǒ quoy ilz le faisoient ·z

dauphin), and in 1348 he obtained sovereignty over Montpellier from the kings of Majorca: his reign cannot be said to have been a profitless one.

However, from 1337 the internal situation changed, and this marked the beginning of a series of misfortunes which was in only fifteen years to transform France, rich and prosperous, considered as the leading nation of the Continent, into a wreck of a country, on the brink of misery and ruin.

The first difficulties were caused by the king's brother-in-law, Count Robert of Artois, husband of Joan of Valois. Robert of Artois was litigating about the possession of his county with his aunt Mahaut, mother of the other Joan of Burgundy, widow of Philip V, and he had her summoned by the court of Paris as early as 1329. He claimed to have in his possession four items which proved his rights beyond dispute. Very opportunely Mahaut and then her daughter Joan both died, but the case was carried on by Joan's daughter, the wife of Eudes, count of Burgundy. Robert put forward the four documents to prove his case; expert inspection showed them to be false, and to have been specially fabricated on the orders of an intriguer, Jeanne de Division, who was condemned to be burned at the stake.

Since he was assumed to be the instigator of this, Robert of Artois was summoned to appear before the Court of Peers in 1331; to make sure he appeared Philip VI had his wife and two of his children imprisoned. Robert fled to England. Then, by letters patent of 7 March 1337, Philip declared his brother-in-law an enemy of the state and rejected his demands.

Robert of Artois' reaction was not slow in bearing fruit. In England he had made friends with King Edward III and had been inspiring him with hatred for France and its king. He was listened to with interest, as Edward III, having got rid of his mother and her lover Mortimer, had not forgiven the homage to Philip IV which had been forced on him and was preparing for war.

In the spring of 1337, Robert of Artois, now duke of Richmond, swore to the king of England that he would conquer the land of the fleur-de-lys, and at the end of that year a challenge was sent to the king of France through the bishop of Lincoln. There were skirmishes in Brittany, and Robert of Artois was mortally wounded at the siege of Vannes. He was solemnly buried in St Paul's Cathedral.

The respite was short-lived. Philip VI was equipping his navy with the intention of making a landing in England, but his fleet, badly commanded, was annihilated in 1340 at the battle of Sluys, off the coast of Belgium. Since the treasury was in no state to build a new fleet it became clear that if hostilities began again the battles would be fought on French soil. To strengthen his position, Philip VI took the offensive in the diplomatic field: he won Emperor Louis IV to his side. Artevelde, who had tried to renew the war in Flanders, was assassinated. Edward III tried more skirmishes in Brittany.

In 1345 the situation worsened. Geoffrey of Harcourt, after a quarrel with Philip VI, entered the service of the king of England and brought him the information to effect a successful landing in Normandy. To enable this to be carried out without resistance, Edward III sent troops into Guyenne under the command of the earl of Derby. Philip VI, at the head of his army, went south and laid siege to the town of Aiguillon, and thanks to this unfortunate diversion the king of England was able to land virtually unopposed at Saint-Vaast-la-Hougue in the Cotentin, in the same region as the American troops landed in 1944.

As western France was almost entirely undefended Edward advanced rapidly, pillaging and setting fire to towns and villages. Thus he arrived at Poissy, at the gates of Paris.

Warned of the danger, Philip VI lifted the siege of Aiguillon and headed northward by forced marches. To avoid an encounter, Edward III, whose forces were smaller, retreated to Crécy-en-Ponthieu in Picardy. As he advanced, Philip VI sent on a reconnaissance party led by Captain Le Moine de Bale. The latter, an experienced soldier, advised the king to rest his troops for several days before engaging in a battle of which he sketched the general plan.

But ever since Cassel the French cavalry had been convinced that it was unbeatable, and refused to wait. Badly engaged and badly led, the battle, in which the English for the first time used triple bombardment, turned to disaster for the French. Philip, who fought bravely and had two horses killed under him, saw John the Blind, his son's father-in-law, killed, but was saved

The burghers of Calais give themselves up to Edward III.

from being captured by the count of Hainault, who dragged him away from the battlefield.

At nightfall Philip arrived at the gates of the château of Broyes, where he uttered his famous cry: 'Open the door, Châtelain, I am the unfortunate king of France' (26 August 1346).

But the battle of Crécy did not mark the end of the war. Edward III, free from French pressure, besieged Calais, where the famous episode of the burghers of Calais took place in 1347. A three-year truce was signed. Edward III returned triumphant to England, where he founded the Order of the Garter.

At the same time as this military disaster, France was struck by a far greater one: the Black Death, which killed millions of people, possibly as much as half the population.

But this did not prevent Philip of Valois from resuming his life of festivities. In 1349 both Queen Joan and Bonne of Bohemia died of the plague. Father and son were both widowers and Prince John got engaged to Blanche of Evreux, daughter of the king of Navarre. But Philip took a fancy to her, took her away from his son and married her, though he was old enough to be her father. Prince John consoled himself by marrying Blanche of Boulogne in February 1350.

Philip VI did not withstand the rigours of his new marriage for long, and he died at Nogent-le-Roi during the night of 22–3 August 1350 after solemnly reminding his sons that their house ruled legitimately. This was tantamount to inciting them to renew hostilities against England.

JOHN II THE GOOD
(1350–1364)

IN THE LOUVRE MUSEUM there is a painting of John the Good which is one of the most precise likenesses of the early paintings: it is the picture of a man with tangled hair, bushy eyebrows, heavy eyelids, globular eyes, a heavy jaw. This very unflattering portrait is that of the man who lost the battle of Poitiers, one of France's most calamitous kings, a man cruel and vindictive, totally divorced from reality.

His reign began in difficult circumstances. Calais was lost, the plague had killed off more than half the population and the truce with England was of short duration. Despite these inauspicious beginnings John II continued his life of luxury at court and held constant festivities.

The coronation of the young king and queen took place at Rheims on 26 September 1350. During the ceremony the king knighted his eldest son Charles and his second son Philip, as well as the duke of Burgundy and a large section of his family. They all returned to Paris and celebrated for a week.

Then the wind changed and the atmosphere turned from joy to sorrow. The High Constable, Raoul de Brienne, count of Eu and of Guines, was released by the English after five years of captivity. But, unable to pay his ransom, he planned to give Guines up to the English. King John considered this an act of treason; he had the constable imprisoned at Nesle on 16 November 1350 and three days later had him beheaded, to the general consternation of the nobility.

John named as the count of Eu's successor a foreigner, his own childhood friend La Cerda, grandson of St Louis. He was so much in the king's favour that rumours of homosexuality circulated, but this accusation would appear to be unfounded, since John II also lavished ridiculous favours on other people at court, which shows he had a propensity for surrounding himself with favourites.

To rival the Order of the Garter, which had been highly esteemed right from the start, John the Good created the Order of the Star, of which Froissart talked with an admiration which seems quite excessive.

In February 1352, the king gave his daughter in marriage to the king of Navarre, Charles the Bad, grandson of Louis X the Headstrong. This union was to cause the crown many problems, since Charles the Bad secretly believed that, by his ancestry, he should have inherited the crown. Shortly afterwards Charles the Bad and his brother Philip, with the help of two Norman barons, Harcourt and Graville, assassinated La Cerda. John the Good was desperate with grief; he threatened his son-in-law but was finally reconciled with him. But Harcourt, who refused to pay his taxes, was executed and then, repudiating the reconciliation, the king had Charles the Bad imprisoned.

Simultaneously the war with England began again; the pretext was to obtain the release of Charles the Bad. On 1 September 1355 the king proceeded to a general mobilization and for about ten months he had several quite substantial successes over the Angevins, who were supporting the duke of Lancaster.

A campaign led by the Black Prince, son of Edward III, had ravaged Languedoc from Toulouse to Nîmes. King John judged that he must cut off his retreat and he reached the outskirts of Poitiers just as the Black Prince got there. The legate of Pope Innocent VI, Cardinal Talleyrand-Périgord, attempted to mediate. The English were not ready, but this gave them time to organize themselves. It would have been possible to negotiate and avoid a battle. But John the Good felt that this was a good opportunity to destroy the English army, and he took the offensive as lightly as his father had done at Crécy.

The French army was routed, but John did not want to emulate Philip VI, who had left the battlefield. He carried on fighting courageously, and his son Philip shouted to him: 'Father, look out on the right, look out on the left.' After a desperate struggle, father and son were taken prisoner.

Fortunately the eldest son Charles had got clear in time and made his way to Paris.

This prince, who was to become so famous as Charles V, had still not proved himself, and it appears he did not distinguish himself by his bravery during the battle. He had married the beautiful Joan of Bourbon in 1350, but was not a good husband to her, and wore ostentatiously on his armour the all too obvious arms of his mistress Biette Cassinel (K +*signe* +*aile*).

While King John was taken to captivity in London, Prince Charles, though little was expected of him, was to show exceptional qualities, saving the government from the disaster of the king's captivity. This prince was the first in history to bear the name of dauphin, and he set a fine example for it.

Having arrived in Paris as the lieutenant-general of the kingdom, Charles called a meeting of the Estates-General. This required some courage, as the very same action had landed his father in serious trouble. John the Good had convoked them in 1355 with the aim of obtaining money to finance the war, and the meeting had proved disastrous: the provost of the Paris merchants, Etienne Marcel, had demanded that taxation be controlled by the Estates, and the concept of income tax had been rejected.

There was therefore a great deal to fear from this new assembly, and the worst happened: in the Estates, Etienne Marcel, with the support of the bishop of Laon, Robert le Coq, was about to embark on an unprecedented adventure which was a precursor both of the 1789 Revolution and of the Commune of 1871.

The Estates began by contesting the authority of the king's counsellors, then demanded the release of Charles the Bad, in whom they saw a possible sovereign. Then, after three consecutive sessions, the Estates voted the Grand Ordinance of 1357, whose aim was really to impose a constitution on the crown. Had this been adopted power would have passed to the Estates and France would have embarked on rule by assembly; it was the revolt of the nation against the state, of the Commune against the crown.

Charles the Bad was freed and became the true master of the capital. An attempt was made on the life of the dauphin, lieutenant-general of the kingdom. His two main counsellors, the marshals of Champagne and Normandy, were assassinated in his cabinet before his very eyes. Etienne Marcel, posing as his defender, covered the dauphin's head with his cape, which had on it the arms of Paris.

The battle of Poitiers, 1356, in which John the Good was taken prisoner by the English (Froissart's Chronicle)

Wisely, during the night Charles left Paris in a boat and called the Estates-General to Compiègne with the obvious intention of taking the capital by force. To resist him, Etienne Marcel joined forces with the rebelling peasants, the Jacquerie. At this point, on an old feudal impulse, Charles the Bad changed sides and crushed the rebellious peasants. The dauphin besieged Paris and Etienne Marcel, who had been reduced to asking the English for help, was murdered by his own supporters (31 July 1358).

After this execution, the dauphin entered Paris without difficulty, having saved the internal order of France. Spontaneous resistance rose up in the country and, faced with the intensity of the maquis, Edward III, who was on his way to be crowned king of France at Rheims, decided to sign a treaty instead.

This was all the easier for him since John the Good, in prison, was prepared to make any concessions, even to give up the Atlantic coast of France. The treaty was finally signed at Brétigny in April 1360; the king of England regained Guyenne, augmented by Limousin, Périgord,

In Paris, besieged by the dauphin Charles (the future Charles v), Etienne Marcel is killed by his own partisans, in 1358.

Rouergue, Angoumois and Saintonge. Not only did he keep Calais but he added to it the counties of Montreuil, Guise and Ponthieu. In addition to this, the English sovereign was freed from his feudal oath. A ransom of three million golden écus was demanded, to be paid in six years, and guaranteed by taking the king's sons as hostages.

As a result of this shameful treaty, John the Good returned to France on 8 July 1360. He stayed at Calais for four months until the first instalment of the ransom had been paid. To obtain more money he married his daughter to the heir of the Viscontis. He then bade farewell to the king of England, who took his sons as hostages. On his return to Paris John II plunged once again into the gay life, seeming almost oblivious of the trials of his country which was being ravaged by the *Grandes Compagnies* (or Companies of Mercenaries).

He made another mistake, for which the crown was to pay dearly: remembering Poitiers, he gave Burgundy to his son Philip the Bold. It was to remain outside the kingdom for 117 years, causing serious problems.

Then, when the duke of Anjou, one of his sons, escaped, John decided to go back to England as a prisoner. He did this against the advice of his counsellors, on a false point of honour. His subjects were not sorry to see him go.

On 3 January 1364 John the Good set sail from Boulogne. His entry into London was triumphal and he was sumptuously lodged at the Savoy Palace, where he found his son, the duke of Berry. He remained there for part of the winter 'in a happy and amorous way', according to Froissart. But this good life did not last long. In March 1364 John II fell ill, and he died on 8 April; the king of England gave him a magnificent service and his body was brought back to France.

So ended, finally, one of the most deplorable reigns in history.

⍟ CHARLES V THE WISE ⍟
(1364–1380)

CHARLES V HAS LEFT BEHIND HIM the reputation of a great and good king and his remarkable beginnings as dauphin contributed to this. But one can also say, without disparagement, that his reputation is also due to the contrast of one stable reign between two destructive ones, those of John the Good and Charles VI.

Charles V was at Goulet near Vernon when he heard that his father had died in England and that he was king of France. The new king, matured by his experiences of 1357, was better prepared than anyone else to take up the crown which John's weakness had made so heavy. He was a sensitive and energetic man, with a very strong sense of responsibility. Though by nature he preferred rewarding people, he was nevertheless never afraid to punish, but in a just way. He had, in a word, all the qualities which his father had lacked. He disliked the exploits of chivalry but was liberal and generous. He also disliked festivals and tournaments. On the other hand, he was a cultured man, and was a patron to philosophers, artists and writers; his nickname 'the Wise' stems more from his love of science than from his wisdom.

The poet Christine de Pisan described his physical appearance at the time in rather flattering terms:

A long and well formed trunk, straight, large shoulders, narrow hips, a handsome face, rather long, a large and wide forehead, pleasant, well-placed eyes, chestnut in colour, a rather high nose and not too small a mouth, hair neither blond nor black, pale brown flesh but he had quite pale skin and I think his thinness had come about by accident rather than temperament. He had a wise, reasonable and settled expression at all times, in all states and in all his movements; he was never furious or raging, but moderate in his actions, countenance and behaviour. He had a fine gait, the voice of a gentleman, and yet with all this his words were so well ordered and so pleasant to listen to, with no superfluous discussion, that I believe no rhetorician in the French language could have bettered him.

The strange thing about this description is the mention of the king's 'accidental' thinness; there was a rumour at the time, probably justified, that while he was dauphin Charles had been the victim of an attempted poisoning by his cousin and brother-in-law Charles the Bad; it is a fact that the king's health was always delicate and that he died quite young.

His wife, Joan of Bourbon, was a good-looking, rather plump woman whom he deceived many times, at least before he came to the throne. Once he was king, Charles V felt strongly that God's anointed should steer clear of the pleasures of the flesh and he became a model husband, all the more so since he had never stopped loving his wife.

She gave him nine children, but of their three sons and six daughters, only three survived to adulthood: the dauphin Charles, Louis, count of Beaumont and Valois, and Princess Catherine. All the others died in infancy. Joan of Bourbon owed to her ancestors the seeds of the madness that was later to strike her eldest son. It appears that in the latter stages of her life she too showed definite signs of mental instability. She died on 4 February 1378 after a difficult childbirth which

produced a girl, Isabelle, who lived for only a few weeks.

On the eve of his coronation, Saturday 18 May 1364, Charles V, whom the king of Navarre had challenged, received the news that the French military leader Du Guesclin had defeated the Anglo-Navarre troops at Cocherel. It was a good omen for the rest of the reign. On Trinity Sunday (19 May 1364) the king and queen were anointed at Rheims. Then there was a great feast and celebrations, after which the king returned to Paris, where he was received in great style.

It was now time to turn his attention to government and war. The victory at Cocherel guaranteed control of the Seine from Paris to Rouen. After this, Du Guesclin claimed Brittany from the Montforts, and was for a time imprisoned.

Once freed, he saved France from another threat: some of the mercenaries had not gone home; they had formed small autonomous groups the 'free companies', and were pillaging the country. Charles V decided with Du Guesclin to enrol them and direct their energies towards a different field of operations. He led them to Spain, where he put them at the service of Henry of Transtamara, bastard son of the king of Castile, who was in conflict with his half-brother Peter the Cruel, ally of the English. This was an indirect way of resuming the fight against Edward III, a struggle which permitted Charles V to denounce the treaty of Brétigny.

Things went badly in Spain, and at the battle of Nájera (3 April 1367) Du Guesclin fell into the hands of the Black Prince. The whole of France banded together to pay his ransom and this great soldier resumed his exploits once again.

He led an offensive in Provence; this was an idea of Charles's, who, obliged in 1357 to combat the false John I, had had the dream of annexing Languedoc to Dauphiné by occupying Provence. The operations began brilliantly, with the taking of Tarascon and Arles. They then marched on Aix-en-Provence. Pope Urban V, fearing for the safety of the Comtat Venaissin, excommunicated Du Guesclin. But Charles V, despite this, promoted him to constable in 1370. The new constable continued the sporadic fighting with the English and reconquered the western territories by his victory at Pontvallain,

which won back Poitou and Saintonge for the royal domain.

The reconstruction of the fleet permitted Admiral Jean de Vienne to control the Channel coast, and this facilitated the reconquest of Normandy, of which certain parts belonged to Charles the Bad. Charles did not hesitate to use force to put an end to the king of Navarre's resistance: he seized Charles the Bad's sons, and had those close to him put to death after forcing them to disown their master.

With the aim of annexing Brittany, Charles V confiscated it, under the pretext that its duke, John, was in England. This displeased the Bretons, who revolted. Du Guesclin, a Breton by birth, refused to massacre his compatriots. He preferred to liquidate the remains of the free companies at Gévaudan and died at the siege of Châteauneuf-de-Randon in 1380, at almost the same time as the king.

The military achievement of the reign was most satisfactory, and the offensive operations carried out under Charles V have rightly been called the first reconquest; they had reduced English possessions to Guyenne alone, and generated a peace which adjourned the war with England for nearly forty years.

But unfortunately not everything was running so smoothly.

At the death of John the Good, there existed certain penal taxes, the *fouage* (hearth-tax) and the *gabelle* (salt-tax), which helped to stock the treasury. Thanks to this source of income the reign was spared serious financial difficulty. But the king felt remorse about having taxed his subjects too heavily and, before dying, repealed these taxes which had brought him prosperity. His successor was to pay dearly for this.

The great diplomatic conception of the reign was to prove the cause of a series of catastrophes for France. In 1369 the count of Flanders negotiated the marriage of his only daughter to Edward III's son. Charles V felt that this union posed a great threat to France; he had it stopped, and won the princess's hand for his brother Philip the Bold, duke of Burgundy. To make sure the marriage took place, he willingly handed over to Flanders Philip the Fair's conquests: Lille, Orchies and Douai. He had thus created a kingdom reaching from the Scheldt to the Saône. In doing this, Charles was convinced

King Charles v makes his entry into Paris after his coronation at Rheims. (*Grandes Chroniques de France*)

Charles v entertains emperor Charles iv and his son to a splendid feast to seek his
alliance against England. (*Grandes Chroniques de France*)

that Flanders would become French, but the opposite happened: Burgundy fell under Flemish influence to such an extent that its dukes preferred to live in Bruges rather than Dijon, and for a century France was faced with a rival which several times put the nation in great danger.

It would be fair to object that Charles, not being gifted with second sight, could not know what was going to happen, but unfortunately there were other inconsistencies in his foreign policy. The beginnings of the Great Schism can be attributed to him. He was unable to keep the Papacy at Avignon, and he tried to make up for this mistake by siding with the French cardinals. They elected an anti-pope, Robert of Geneva, who took the name Clement VII and opposed Pope Urban VI, Cardinal Prignano, whom the Italians had elected, and who appeared to be the legitimate heir to the throne of St Peter.

Without the king of France's support, Clement VII would have been deposed; with his help he was able to maintain his position, and for forty years the Church was to be torn between two factions. It seems certain that the king's intentions were of the best in all this, but this only gives one a poorer opinion of his political talents.

One could say the same of the rest of his diplomacy. In 1378 he invited to his court Emperor Charles IV, whose father, the blind King John of Bohemia, had died at Crécy, and he asked him unsuccessfully to give up his alliance with the English. To redeem this failure he began negotiations with King Richard II of England, offering him his daughter in marriage, with a dowry of the reconquered territories. Fortunately these negotiations came to nothing. One must therefore conclude that, despite appreciable successes, he had compromised them by incompetence or weakness.

It is most likely that during these later years Charles V's health was such that he was not able to govern sanely. His medical condition was a sad one. Perhaps he had been the victim of poisoning; his constitution was very weak. With persistent gout as its basis, Charles V's chronic illness made him go bald at a young age. The nails on his hands and feet dried up and fell out. One doctor whom he trusted managed to make the hair and nails grow again, but to do this he had had to open an ulcer in his arm to let the bad humours run out, and ordered that it should not be closed up. So Charles kept this open wound on his arm.

The king probably had scrofula, complicated by slowly developing tuberculosis. When the doctors finally admitted defeat, Charles V went on more pilgrimages and performed more pious acts. But nothing worked: his hands became deformed by gout and the right hand suffered from a chronic oedema which made it difficult for him to hold a pen to sign acts of state.

His grief at the death of his wife finally ruined his health. At the age of forty he could only go out in a litter, having had to give up all the exercise he used to enjoy, particularly hunting. His pain worsened and he began to suffer terribly in his kidneys; finally he died at the age of only forty-three, after sixteen years of a reign of which he could be proud despite his mistakes.

On 13 September 1380 a new reign began, that of the child dauphin Charles, to whom heredity had bequeathed a tragic destiny which almost saw the disappearance of France.

᠅ CHARLES VI THE MAD ᠅
(1380–1422)
AND ISABEAU OF BAVARIA

WHEN CHARLES V DIED, his son had not yet reached the legal age of majority. As the king disapproved of regencies he lowered this age before dying, but this was ignored and the adolescent Charles VI was taken in hand by his uncles the duke of Anjou, the duke of Berry and the duke of Burgundy, and the late queen's brother, the duke of Bourbon.

The battle of
Roosebeke, 1382.
(Froissart's Chronicle)

This oligarchy seized all the important offices, dismissed Charles v's counsellors, and tried to obtain money. They began by raiding the dead king's treasury, then they re-established the *fouage* (hearth-tax) and the *gabelle* (salt-tax). Since public funds were being administered foolishly, they soon had to increase the rate of these taxes. The result was upheaval, often violent, particularly at Montpellier and Puy. These riots, local to begin with, turned into civil war; the most notable groups were the Harelles in Normandy, the Maillotins in Paris and the Tuchins in Languedoc, hordes of brigands who pillaged and terrorized.

Troops had to be armed and when order had been re-established it was decided to use them against the Flemish, who had risen under Jacob van Artevelde's son. These other rebels were defeated at the battle of Roosebeke (27 November 1382).

This success gave Charles vi a certain amount of confidence, but he could not yet get rid of his uncles, who supported him when he took authoritarian measures against the burghers of Paris. In 1385 Philip of Burgundy lost his father-in-law and inherited Flanders; this extra power made him virtually master of the government. Philip of Burgundy (called the Bold) felt the time was right for his nephew to marry, and he thought that a German marriage would suit his own interests; this view, which caused France so many problems, was not incompatible with the last wishes of Charles v. He had tried to form an alliance with the Empire, which, though it was not fully effected, did make a solid truce with Germany.

Learning that Duke Stephen of Bavaria had a fourteen-year-old daughter, Isabeau, Philip intrigued to arrange a marriage between her and Charles vi. The young Isabeau was taken to her aunt the countess of Hainaut, who tutored her niece, and taught her manners and how to dress stylishly. The meeting between the two young people took place at Amiens in July 1385, under the pretext of a pilgrimage to the Virgin of Amiens.

Charles vi had no objections to this interview. Isabeau was led by her chaperones into the king's presence. The young man 'looked at her for a long time; as he looked pleasure and love entered his heart, as she was young and beautiful and he was very desirous to see her and have her. The High Constable of France, Olivier de Clisson, said to the seigneur de Coucy and seigneur de la Rivière: "This lady will remain with us – the king cannot take his eyes off her."'

As a young man Charles vi was very good-looking, and he made a great impression on the young Bavarian girl. After the meeting the two interested parties were consulted and agreed to get married. The wedding was celebrated immediately by the bishop of Amiens, and after a sumptuous dinner the bride was led to the nuptial chamber. The young king arrived, burning with desire. 'You can be sure they had great pleasure together that night', reports the historian Froissart.

The relations between the king and queen were probably only physical to begin with: she did not speak a word of French, nor he of German. The beauty of Isabeau of Bavaria has often been discussed, and it would appear that people were somewhat indulgent; according to descriptions of her, her legs were too short, and her tanned complexion was not appreciated. But she had plenty of sex appeal. Little was known of her character, but she soon turned out to be sensual, greedy, pleasure-seeking, frivolous and a supreme egoist.

We have a description of Charles vi from a prior of St Denis, who wrote:

Without being too tall, he was taller than average; he had robust limbs, a broad chest, a fresh complexion and clear eyes. He had all the fortunate dispositions of youth: he was a skilled archer and javelin-thrower, loved war, was a good horseman, and showed great impatience whenever his enemies provoked him or attacked him. He was so affable that whenever he met even lowly people, he greeted them kindly and called them by their name. From his earliest years he was noted for his liberality; later his generosity went beyond the bounds of moderation and people said he kept nothing for himself but the power to give.

These qualities heralded a great reign; they began with a perfect marriage. Isabeau learnt French quite quickly and was able to converse with her husband elsewhere than in bed. Her maids of honour taught her the rules of the court of France and there was every reason to believe that the king's personal life would be exceptionally happy.

Philip the Bold, whose interests coincided briefly with those of the crown, encouraged his nephew to subdue Flanders by detaching it from its English connections. To achieve this it was planned to wage war on England, to recapture Calais and then attempt a landing. With this in mind a big effort was made to reform the navy, and preparations were made the like of which were never seen again until those of Napoleon at the camp of Boulogne. But these fine plans all came to nothing. The duke of Berry, who had been promoted to High Admiral, never set sail.

However, all these measures had alerted the English. An attempt was then made to negotiate the restitution of Calais. This less aggressive policy succeeded in prolonging the truce due to Charles v's efforts. France accepted as a last concession that the king of England should remain sovereign in Guyenne, on condition that he paid homage as a vassal. King Richard ii, a pacifist by nature, accepted this. He went to Cherbourg and Brest and paid homage, and the possibility was envisaged of his marrying a daughter of Charles vi. This was quite a good beginning, and there was a solid hope of peace.

At this stage in his reign, Charles vi realized that his uncles were placing their interests before those of France; when they had drawn their nephew into a foolish expedition against the duke of Gelderland, who was at odds with the duke of Burgundy, the king, who was now just twenty, carried out a *coup d'état*. He sent his uncles back to their appanages and recalled his father's old counsellors, Olivier de Clisson, Jean de Vienne, Bureau de la Rivière and Juvénal des Ursins, provost of Paris. These wise men, who were sneeringly called the Marmosets,

t pour cefte caufe le
s nocpces et furent

re-established order and formulated a sensible economic policy which made the treasury prosper. But, unfortunately, Charles VI also had a bad counsellor in the person of his own brother, the duke of Touraine, who was soon given the duchy of Orléans as an appanage.

Under the influence of Isabeau of Bavaria, ostentation returned to the court. The king overindulged in pleasures and compromised his health in feasts and celebrations.

In 1392 a series of dramas occurred: the high constable, de Clisson, was seriously wounded by a criminal lord, Pierre de Craon, who to escape his punishment took refuge with the duke of Brittany. Although Charles VI's health was giving cause for concern, he was determined to set out on a punitive expedition. He called together a huge army, which headed west. As they were crossing the forest of Le Mans, in very hot weather, a decrepit old man, probably a leper, dashed out from the bushes, seized the bridle of the king's horse and cried out that he had been betrayed.

Charles VI suddenly went out of his mind, attacked his men-at-arms with his axe and killed four of them. He had to be bound and pinioned (4 August 1392). In the midst of general distress he was taken to Le Mans, and then to the château of the Val d'Oise, where it was hoped the fresh air would restore him to health. The doctors who were consulted diagnosed hereditary insanity passed on from his mother Joan of Bourbon, who had more or less lost her senses in her later years. Fortunately the king recovered, and when he heard that he had killed four men he wept and said he could never be consoled.

Since he appeared to have recovered he continued in government and resumed his intemperate way of life. On 28 January 1393 there was a ball at the hôtel de Saint-Paul. In the middle of the evening six 'wild men' came in dressed only in feathers and bits of cotton. Louis of Orléans, to get a better look at them, unwisely brought a torch too near to one of the dancers, and the 'wild men' were transformed into fireballs as their costumes burst into flames. A cry went up of 'Save the king', as some people realized that he was one of the dancers.

Isabeau of Bavaria fainted in terror, as the spectacle was too horrific to contemplate, and the smell of the burning bodies was particularly

The 'Bal des Ardents'. On the left, a cloak is thrown over Charles VI to save him from burning. (Froissart's Chronicle)

gruesome. Then, suddenly, there was a respite and Charles VI appeared. He had been saved by his aunt, the duchess of Berry, who, by throwing her cloak over him, rescued him from a horrible death. This tragedy set off a riot known as the 'Bal des Ardents', and shortly afterwards the king's reason again failed. Henceforth, to the end of his life, which was a long one, he was to be plagued by repeated periods of insanity. He was aware of his condition, and burst into tears each time he felt a new attack coming on. During these attacks he felt that he was made of glass and repeated that he was going to break.

Queen Isabeau was deeply afflicted by her husband's state; he would no longer sleep with her. From this time on this sensual queen began to stray. She became the mistress of her brother-in-law the duke of Orléans, and then, when he had been assassinated, led a thoroughly debauched life. But in Charles's periods of sanity he took to her again, and she became pregnant several times, although there was permanent doubt about her children's legitimacy.

To keep Charles VI occupied a favourite was found for him, the gentle Odette de Champdivers, who gave him a daughter and who took devoted care of him until his death.

Needless to say, during the king's bouts of madness disorder grew within the government. At first a policy of peace with England was pursued, and, according to plan, Richard II married one of Charles VI's daughters in 1396. But this token of peace soon proved useless. The prolonging for twenty-five years of the truce between the two nations was to provoke a revolution in England. Feeling himself to be in a strong position as the king of France's son-in-law, Richard II began to play at being an absolute ruler, and when his cousin Lancaster died he confiscated his inheritance.

Lancaster's heir rebelled. He plotted, landed in England, threw Richard II in prison and had himself elected king as Henry IV. This adventure, which rather strangely foreshadows the accession of Louis-Philippe to the throne, did not leave the new king's hands entirely free: realizing that he owed his crown to the nobles, to the Church and to Parlement, he felt obliged to gratify all three parties – that is, he did nothing. It was only after his death that his son, Henry V, could think of resuming the war against France.

The first cause of this war was the ambition of the duke of Orléans. Married to Valentina Visconti, John the Good's granddaughter, he wanted to set Louis II firmly on the throne of Naples and then build up a powerful kingdom in Italy. Through his wife he held the county of Asti, and he used his influence in Italy to have Charles VI named lord of Genoa, with the ultimate intention of adding it to his own possessions. He was strongly supported in these aims by the duke of Burgundy, Philip the Bold, who was co-regent with him during the king's periods of insanity.

These ideas were not unopposed by the Papacy in Rome since, like Charles V, the duke of Orléans supported the new antipope at Avignon, Pedro de Luna, alias Benedict XIII; they were also at odds with those of the duke of Burgundy, who was a supporter of the Roman popes, first Boniface IX and then Innocent VII. From 1402 onwards their differences grew, as the duke of Orléans acquired Luxemburg, which foiled Philip the Bold's Lotharingian plans; but when the duke of Burgundy died in 1404, the duke of Orléans found himself sole regent.

Philip the Bold was succeeded by his son John, nicknamed the Fearless because of his conduct against the Turks at the battle of Nicopolis (1396), a sort of crusade. John the Fearless immediately took on the duke of Orléans, and by 1407 the discord was so great that the duke of Burgundy had his rival put to death.

The duke of Orléans left a son, Charles, later to gain fame as a poet. He was married to the daughter of Count Bernard VII of Armagnac, a name which his partisans were to take, while those of John the Fearless were called Burgundians. John the Fearless, after daring to justify his crime, neutralized Charles of Orléans, aged seventeen, by a peace signed at Chartres, then allied himself to Queen Isabeau of Bavaria. She helped him repel all the princes of the blood, in particular the dukes of Berry and Bourbon, who signed treaties with Charles of Orléans at Gien and Poitiers, both in 1410.

The western and central counties and Languedoc allied themselves to the Armagnacs, and the rest of the country fell under the sway of the Burgundians. Now split in two, France was ripe for civil war. The other issues at stake were the confessional consideration of the Great Schism, and the nationalist considerations which arose when war with England began again, and the Burgundians took the side of the English.

The struggle did not begin immediately. In 1413 the Estates-General were assembled. The debates were dominated by the Burgundian party. A plan was adopted rather similar to the Grand Ordinance of 1357, which had never been applied.

The duke of Burgundy was put in charge of organizing the defence of the state against the English threat. But John the Fearless, soon overwhelmed by the extremists led by the agitator Caboche, had an illusory policy of reform adopted, the *ordonnance cabochienne* (27 May 1413). Despite John the Fearless's opposition, the moderate Paris party negotiated a treaty of alliance with the Armagnacs at Pontoise (4 September 1414). By this treaty, the duke of Burgundy gave up any English alliance. This clause was in his interest, since Henry v, who had just succeeded his father, was loudly asserting his claim to the French crown.

Given moral assurance of Burgundian support, the king of England and his troops landed at Cap de la Hève on 12 August 1415. So began the second phase of the Hundred Years War. Henry v seized Harfleur on 22 September and headed for Picardy, by a manoeuvre which repeated Crécy blow for blow. The battle took place at Agincourt on 25 October 1415; it was a disaster for the French army. Charles of Orléans, leader of the Armagnacs, was taken prisoner. The king of England seemed surprised at his victory and announced out loud that God had wanted to punish the French.

King Henry v, whose success had made him virtually master of Paris, did not rush to get there, and contented himself with occupying Normandy, of which he was completely master in 1417.

French resistance was personified by Bernard of Armagnac, who had taken over from his imprisoned son-in-law. But the Burgundians seized Paris, where he had entrenched himself, and he was massacred with his companions. The dauphin Charles, the future Charles vii, aged only fifteen, managed to escape. Paris was given over to rioting and massacre, and John the Fearless and Isabeau of Bavaria, masters of the government and of the person of Charles vi, made their entry into the capital recaptured by the Burgundians, where they were received by Capeluche, instigator of the massacres.

A few sensible people felt that to regulate the situation and save the country from English occupation a meeting between the dauphin and the duke of Burgundy was necessary. The meeting took place at Montereau on 10 September 1419. It was a tragic one – the dauphin's knights assassinated John the Fearless, in revenge for the murder of the duke of Orléans.

This odious crime proved quite pointless. Isabeau extorted from her mad husband the order to transmit the dead man's authority to his son, the duke of Burgundy, Philip the Good, and Philip's first act was to negotiate the convention of Arras (2 December 1419) with the English. This convention suspended hostilities. It held the seed of the treaty of Troyes, which was signed by Isabeau of Bavaria on 22 May 1420.

By this treaty the queen concluded the marriage of her daughter Catherine of France to Henry v. At the death of the mad king, the king of England or his heir would become rightful king of France and would bring together the two crowns. A collaborationist party supported by the University of Paris, seeing in this treaty the possibility of permanent peace, did everything it could to have it adopted.

Henry v became regent, and the dauphin Charles was deprived of his rights and fled to Bourges. He was still master of a territory stretching from the Loire to the Pyrenees, with the exception of the Atlantic coast. It seemed likely that the English would later succeed in occupying the whole of France.

Henry v died at Vincennes on 31 August 1422, and Charles vi shortly afterwards. Before the open tomb at St Denis the duke of Berry pronounced the ritual words: 'Lord have mercy on the soul of the most high and excellent prince Charles, king of France, sixth of that name, our natural and sovereign lord.' Then, after a minute's silence, he said: 'Long live King Henry, by the grace of God king of France and of England.'

It was all over. Isabeau of Bavaria's treason had run its full course. There was no longer a king of France, and the future seemed hopeless.

However, by an unprecedented reversal, it was England which was to be defeated, and France would rise triumphant from her shame.

CHARLES VII THE WELL-SERVED
(1422–1461)
AND MARY OF ANJOU

THE REIGN OF CHARLES VII was one of the most interesting in the history of France, and it was marked by an event of a supernatural nature, the advent of Joan of Arc, which transformed the course of history.

The future king was the penultimate of Charles VI's twelve children; born in 1403, he bore the titles successively of count of Ponthieu and duke of Touraine.

'He was a man of good stature and healthy living, of sanguine complexion, humble, gentle and debonair, liberal without being over-generous. He was a solitary man, sober, but was given to mirth. He liked women in the most decorous of ways, and honoured all women. His favourite games were chess and crossbow shooting; he got up betimes in the mornings and did not shirk his work.'

His early years, needless to say, had been seriously disturbed by France's troubles; added to this were his dynastic fears since, when he realized the life his mother had led, he often wondered whether he were legitimate. This anxiety cast a shadow over the early part of his reign. Forced to flee Paris because of the troubles there, deserted by his father, on difficult terms with his mother, the dauphin seems to have had a morose youth. He established himself at Bourges with a small court of debatable merits, and chose his advisers fairly badly. It was they who in 1419 advised him to have John the Fearless assassinated, a crime for which he felt remorse all his life.

His marriage to Mary of Anjou was a good one, less because of his wife's character than that of her mother, Yolande of Aragon, a fine woman who kept up her son-in-law's morale and played an important though ill-documented political role.

From Bourges, the dauphin, perhaps influenced by his mother-in-law, made an attempt during his father's lifetime to repel the English. Shortly after the treaty of Troyes, his armies under Marshal de la Fayette gained a substantial victory at Baugé. Unfortunately this offensive was not followed up.

Charles VI died and the dauphin learned the news at the château of Mehun-sur-Yèvre, where he was residing. Since he was the dauphin, he naturally became king, but Rheims was occupied by the English and there was no question of going there to be crowned. The idea did occur to him, and he tried to open up the road to Rheims, but his troops were twice repelled by the English, once at Cravant in 1423 and once at Verneuil in 1424.

Between these two defeats there was one source of joy: in 1423 Mary of Anjou gave birth to a son, the dauphin, the future Louis XI. But joy was mingled with anxiety: while Charles VII was at a meeting at La Rochelle, the floor collapsed. Though he was miraculously spared, many people were killed, and this catastrophe worsened his hypochondria. The court at Bourges was achieving very little and it became clear that this passivity was likely to cost them dear.

Henry V, at his death, had left in the person of Henry VI a mere babe in arms. Since he could not be crowned, it was necessary to organize a regency; this had been put in the hands of the duke of Bedford, Henry V's brother. He was a man of great courage, a good administrator, with sound ideas. His first thought was that the most important thing for his ward was to become master of all the territory which was attributed to him, in other words the non-occupied part of France, from the Loire to the Pyrenees.

Since the battles of Cravant and Verneuil had proved the superiority of the English army, Bedford took the offensive and tried to open up the road to Bourges. To get there he had to take the key town of Orléans. Bedford laid siege to the town during the year 1428, and by 12 October the English troops had the place partly encircled. The resistance of Orléans, defended by a bastard son of the duke of Orléans, Dunois,

OPPOSITE Charles VI (the Mad), reclining on his bed, converses with Jean Salmon.
(*From a 15th century manuscript*)

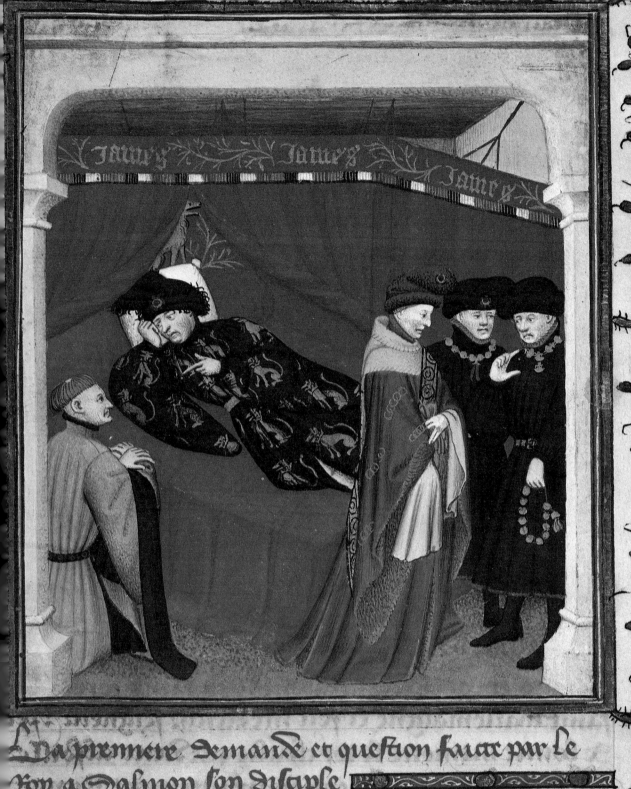

Cy la premiere demande et question faicte par le
Roy a Salmon son disciple

Salmon comme par vraie experience de fait
Auons maintesfoiz apperceu le grant desir
et la bonne voulente que vous auez au bien
de nous z de nostre royaume Tant par les

Charles VII, by Fouquet.

was heroic, and the town was still holding out after six months. But the risks were still great, and to avoid them Charles VII had left Bourges and taken shelter in the Château de Chinon.

It was in this castle that on 25 February 1429 an extraordinary event took place. A young girl asked to be granted an audience; she was well-built, dressed as a man, and said her name was Joan of Arc.

The dauphin then had the strange idea of disguising himself and, dressed as a commoner, he had the girl ushered in, having given his own clothes to a courtier who took his place. To everyone's great surprise, the girl ignored the false dauphin, searched around in the crowd, and approached the dauphin, whom she had identified by a true gift of insight, and she said to him: 'Gentle dauphin, I tell you on behalf of God my master that you are the true heir to the throne of France.'

These words had a magical effect on Charles VII. Having always doubted his legitimacy, he listened to Joan's voice and he believed in her because she forced him to believe in himself. There was a prophecy in the kingdom that it would be lost by a woman and saved by a maid; Joan's words seemed to be the fulfilment of this. (It is worth noting that Isabeau of Bavaria was still alive when Joan appeared, and she would be a witness of her actions, since she died only in 1436, abandoned by everyone and in misery.)

However, Charles VII, probably perturbed by the claims of this seventeen-year-old girl, who said she had been sent by God, thought it wise to have her examined by an ecclesiastical commission which took place at Poitiers. Joan explained that for several years she had seen apparitions while watching over her flocks near her village of Domrémy in Lorraine. These apparitions, in the form of the saints and of the archangel Michael, had ordered her to go and deliver Orléans and to save France, and they had kept repeating to her: 'Go, daughter of God, go.' A gentleman who lived near Domrémy, Robert de Baudricourt, had taken the risk of escorting Joan to Chinon, in a near-miraculous crossing of occupied territory, and she had recognized the dauphin despite his disguise.

This strange story would normally have been greeted with scepticism by the ecclesiastical commission. But even though she was only seventeen, she managed to convince her examiners of her supernatural mission. Charles VII then decided to put Joan in charge of an army which included some of the most famous captains of the day, and this army, about seven thousand men strong, set out for Orléans. Before leaving, Joan gave the English an ultimatum: 'King of England and you, Duke of Bedford who call yourself regent of France, surrender to the Maid, sent by God, the keys of all the good towns you have seized and violated in France. If you do not do this, king of England, I am in command, and wherever I find your people in France I will make them leave, whether they like it or not.'

The English did not reply, and Joan went into action. She arrived at Orléans on 29 April, and managed to enter the town in a boat thanks to an unexpected flood of the Loire. She inspired the defenders with courage and, when the reinforcements arrived, raised the blockade.

In the early part of May she took part of her troops across the Loire and successfully attacked the English fortresses on the left bank. On 7 May 1429, during the assault on the fortress of Toutelles, she was shot through the neck by an arrow; she bravely removed the arrow, confessed her sins, encouraged her wavering troops to renew the assault, and took the fortress. The next day, 8 May, the English forces lifted the siege and Orléans was miraculously delivered.

During the next few days she cleared the area around the town and won memorable victories at Jargeau and Beaugency. The operations were crowned by a decisive victory at Patay (18 June) against the most famous of the English generals, Talbot.

Then, accompanied by the dauphin, Joan set off for Rheims; the subjugated towns opened their doors without resistance and on 17 July 1429, in Rheims Cathedral, Charles VII was crowned by Archbishop Regnault of Chartres.

Joan stood at the king's side, carrying her banner which bore the words 'Jhesus Maria'. In the course of five months the shepherdess from Lorraine had accomplished her mission – she had given back to France its rightful territory; she had done her duty towards God; she could now withdraw. 'I would hope,' she said sadly in the evening of this day of triumph, 'that it might please God, my creator, to allow me now to give up my weapons and go and serve my father and mother, and watch over their flocks with my sisters and brothers, who would be glad to see me again.'

But heaven did not grant her this humble prayer. For Joan's mission to achieve its full meaning, she had to become a martyr.

New military ventures were undertaken and they began successfully; Laon, Soissons, Château-Thierry, Senlis and Compiègne had surrendered. Now Joan besieged Paris, but here she was betrayed. Charles VII's own advisers, La Trémoille and Regnault of Chartres, had an understanding with the Burgundians, who held the town, and they caused the assault on the St Honoré gate to fail. Joan was once more wounded by an arrow from a crossbow.

Joan's and the king's armies retreated to Sully-sur-Loire. The king's entourage led Joan into an absurd venture, the siege of Charité-sur-Loire. But the Maid reverted to her original plan of liberating Paris. First of all she wanted to free Compiègne, which had already been re-occupied by the Burgundians. She fell into their hands on 24 May 1430 and they sold her to the English. Her fall satisfied the intriguers who surrounded Charles VII and it is a fact that he did nothing to save the girl who had saved him.

The English were careful not to conduct Joan of Arc's trial themselves. Bedford, like a good lawyer, preferred to leave the odium to those who had collaborated with the occupying forces. It was into the hands of the Church, allied to the English, that he committed the fate of his prisoner. Since Compiègne was a dependency of the bishopric of Beauvais, it was the bishop of this town, Pierre Cauchon, who took charge of the trial.

The actual course of the trial, in Rouen, followed normal procedure, but it was obvious that the outcome would be influenced by the occupying forces. However, Joan's answers to her prosecutors were so well judged that they did not dare condemn her to death, but only to life imprisonment 'on the bread of suffering and the water of anguish'.

Joan, who had been forced to wear woman's clothing again, was imprisoned under the guard of English soldiers, who stole her dress and tried to take liberties with her. To keep her modesty, she resumed her male dress. Using this futile pretext, and in order to satisfy the English, who

had reproached him for sparing the life of 'the sorceress', Cauchon declared her relapsed, which was in effect to condemn her to be burnt at the stake without further trial.

On 30 May 1431, in the Old Market Square at Rouen, Joan was burnt alive. Her last words, as the flames reached her, were that her voices came from God and had not deceived her. This death made a great impression on the English, one of whom cried out: 'We are lost, we have burnt a saint.'

Charles VII, who had not taken any action to save God's messenger, later atoned for this by having a rehabilitation trial opened in 1457, which the saint's mother was able to attend. By then Joan's work had been achieved and France was freed from the English yoke.

After Joan's death things did not happen as fast as when she was in charge. In 1430 the boy king Henry VI had been installed at Rouen, the new capital, and after Joan's death he was crowned king of France. King Charles VII had once again fallen under the influence of his bad counsellors; the duke of Burgundy, in close contact with them, sued for a two-year truce, which was signed at Chinon in December 1431. Then the atmosphere eased a little under the good influence of the high constable de Richemont, an experienced warrior and a man of duty, who did not hesitate to suppress La Trémoille and eject the assassins of John the Fearless.

Philip the Good, not daring to break with the English completely, had a meeting at Nevers with de Richemont and negotiated. He went so far as to consider a general peace which would have perpetuated the territorial division, and would have recognized that Charles was Henry VI's vassal. Negotiations with the English on this basis were abandoned. They then continued between France and Burgundy, and, in the hope of safeguarding national unity, Charles VII accepted Philip the Good's very harsh conditions.

Bedford died, and this weakened the English resistance. The war began again, this time successfully. Richemont occupied Normandy and made a triumphal entry into Paris on 13 April 1436. Two years later the reconquest of Guyenne was undertaken, and the English asked for a truce. A marriage between Henry VI and Mary of Anjou was suggested, and a peace

Joan of Arc in armour.

conference was even held in London (1444), though unsuccessfully.

In 1347, the English resumed hostilities in Normandy. They were defeated at Formigny in 1450, and the whole of Normandy was conquered. Emboldened by this success, the French army under Dunois subdued Bordeaux and Aquitaine in 1451, but the population of Aquitaine was angered by the clumsy dealings of the French officials there and called on the English for help. An army under Talbot, who had been defeated at Patay, recaptured Bordeaux and the whole province. In the summer of 1453 Charles VII retaliated by surrounding Guyenne. On 16 July there was a decisive battle at Castillon, in which Talbot was killed.

France was completely free of British occupation, apart from Calais, and a truce was made. It was twenty years before it was transformed into a peace treaty, under Louis XI.

But this king, who did so much for France, was an intractable dauphin. Though he supported his father, who had to put down a feudal revolt known as the Praguerie, he also quarrelled with him and made Dauphiné rise against him. Then, fearing military intervention from Charles VII, he took refuge with the duke of Burgundy, who installed him at the château of Genappe, in Brabant. There he remained until he came to the throne. 'My cousin of Burgundy is nourishing a fox which will eat his chickens,' the old king declared philosophically.

To complete the picture of Charles VII we must deal with his private life and his immense achievement in domestic policy.

The king's private life was determined by his meeting, in about 1443, with a maid of honour of the queen of Sicily, the wife of King René of Anjou. This young girl was called Agnès Sorel, and she is remembered as the 'dame de Beauté', because the king gave her the royal palace of this name. Three daughters were born of this adulterous relationship, Marie, Charlotte and Jeanne. Suitable husbands were found for them by Louis, who was secretly very good to his half-sisters.

Charles VII, who was well over forty, was transformed by this love affair, into which he threw himself with frenzy. The role of queen seemed to have passed from Mary of Anjou to Agnès Sorel. Never before Charles VII's time

had a king of France behaved so blatantly; nothing was too beautiful, or too expensive, to satisfy Agnès Sorel. It is only fair to admit that this favourite had many qualities: she was particularly generous, was a patron of the arts and mixed with the writers of the day.

Queen Mary was very upset by this relationship, which caused her a great deal of suffering; she complained bitterly. But the liaison ended tragically in 1449. The 'dame de Beauté', who had followed her lover to Normandy, died of dysentery; she may well have been poisoned. The favourite died at peace with God and received the last sacraments piously. Charles VII was sadly afflicted by her death, and he never forgot his beautiful mistress, even though he had deceived her during her lifetime with her cousin, and had other minor adventures.

Setting aside these sensual irregularities, it is worth paying tribute to him as an administrator, one of the best France has ever known. It was Charles VII who rebuilt the state after the exhaustions of the Hundred Years War. Though his immediate circle had been such a bad one in his early years, it changed considerably when he reached middle age; it was this which earned him the nickname 'Well Served'. The most famous of his devoted servants was Jacques Coeur, who restored the financial situation, and who was rewarded, like Joan of Arc, with base ingratitude.

The last twenty years of the reign saw tremendous achievements in the military, financial and administrative fields. Out of these reforms was born a new social order which was to remain, broadly speaking, intact up to the 1789 Revolution.

The final successes of the Hundred Years' War were due to military reforms. Before Charles VII there was no permanent army, which made any long-term strategy impossible. In 1445 a national army was created for the first time in France; made up of fifteen companies *d'ordonnance* (of noble volunteers), it became a professional body, distant precursor of the *gendarmerie royale*. To this cavalry the king added infantry, the Compagnie des Francs-Archers, a kind of militia, made up of one fiftieth of the male population. Finally the artillery, created by the grand master Bessoneau and developed by the Bureau brothers, proved in time to be the best in Europe.

Agnès Sorel, mistress of Charles VII.
(French school, sixteenth century)

The death of Charles VII. (*Chroniques de Charles VII*)

Since the formation of a regular army meant a permanent financial commitment, the king took the measures necessary to cover it. Before Charles VII's time the Estates would vote temporary subsidies called *extraordinaire des guerres*. They kept this palliative title, but were made permanent.

All this had begun in 1436 by increasing indirect taxation and making it permanent. The surprising thing is that the king managed in 1439 to extract the same terms for the '*extraordinaire*' from the Estates of Languedoîl. The Estates of Languedoc were the only ones to keep the right to assess themselves and collect and donate of their own free choice. They owed this immense privilege, it would seem, to their fidelity to the king at Bourges, when he would have been lost without their support.

The extraordinary taxes were of three kinds: the *gabelle*, or salt-tax, the *taille*, or tax on commoners' property, and the *aides*, or tax on consumer goods. It is interesting to note that this

taxation principle still exists in the twentieth century: the *aides* are called VAT, the tax on goods is both land-tax and income-tax, and the *gabelle* has been replaced by monopolies such as tobacco. These taxes had the disadvantage of being badly distributed, which brought about great inequalities; moreover they were collected by agents who would one day become the Farmers General, and take too big a cut.

Charles VII's administrative reforms were as important as his fiscal ones. A body of civil servants was formed, and decentralization became the order of the day.

Because the kingdom had so suddenly increased in size, the Paris Parlement was no longer big enough to hear appeals. Charles VII therefore created parlements in the provinces – this was the object of the great ordinance of Montils-les-Tours in 1454, which legalized the Toulouse parlement and founded those of Grenoble and Bordeaux. The famous *Cours des aides* of Montpellier and Rouen were created in the same spirit. Those newly charged with these responsibilities acceded to the nobility; this was the *noblesse des charges*, which soon rivalled the old hereditary nobility, a remnant of feudal times.

Finally we must mention Charles VII's religious policy. In 1438 he had formulated the Pragmatic Sanction of Bourges, following the principles of the Conciliary fathers of Basle, who had just elected the antipope Felix V of Savoy. The aim of the Pragmatic Sanction was to make the French episcopal seats elective and free from the advice of Rome, which would merely invest whoever was elected. This meant the establishment of a Gallican Church, and it provoked such serious protestations from Rome that Louis XI had to modify it considerably.

Charles VII could be proud of his reign, which had seen one of the greatest military recoveries in history, and one of the most important internal reforms. In 1458 he developed a cancerous wound on his leg; he was also suffering from general tuberculosis. In 1461 he suffered a dental inflammation so severe that he could no longer eat, and he died on 21 July, aged fifty-eight, after reigning for nearly forty years.

✥ LOUIS XI ✥
AND CHARLOTTE OF SAVOY
(1461–1483)

LOUIS XI WAS THE STRANGEST OF ALL THE VALOIS, and he is still an enigma, as he aroused the most contradictory opinions, generally unfavourable to the man himself but full of praise for his achievements, which, by a series of fortunate circumstances, were substantial.

When Charles VII died, the dauphin was living in the Château de Genappe, which belonged to the duke of Burgundy. Scarcely able to conceal his joy at being king, he set off immediately for Paris. Halfway there, at Avesnes, he ran into an important delegation of ministerial and administrative officials, accompanying the greatest lords of the kingdom. They were all on their way to pay homage to their sovereign in the hopes of consolidating their positions and privileges. But they knew little of their new king: he received their homage, and, to let them know who was master, dismissed them all from favour. He then took to serve him all those who had been dismissed by Charles VII.

Louis had a funeral service held for his father which many considered rather stingy. Then he went to Rheims to be crowned, with his wife, on 15 August 1461.

It is worth while commenting here on the king's personal life: according to the chronicler Thomas Basin, Louis XI at first meeting had nothing handsome or pleasant about him. Worse than this: 'If you ran into him without knowing who he was you would have taken him for a buffoon or a drunkard, at any rate for a man of low condition rather than a person of distinction.' It is a fact that, judging from the paintings of him, he was not a prepossessing man: his pallid face has a sly expression which suggests the double-dealing which went on throughout his reign. He is poorly dressed, and his personal avarice was much remarked on by his contemporaries, who were used to Charles VII's ostentatiousness, and even more to that of the duke of Burgundy.

A desperately restless man, the king spent nearly half his reign wandering about the kingdom, which did not make court life any easier.

His first marriage was to a Stuart princess who died prematurely. He then reigned with Charlotte of Savoy who, unlike him, was fond of luxury. Although she had many children by him, he spent little time living with her, and confined her to the Château d'Amboise or to Tours during the entire second half of his reign. He had a favourite, Marguerite de Sassenage; she gave him two daughters of whom one, Marie, who married a Saint-Vallier, was the grandmother of Diane of Poitiers, favourite of Henry

II; there was therefore a certain continuity in these matters.

The queen appears to have accepted this liaison, for which he made up by being as generous to his wife as he was mean with himself: at Amboise, Charlotte of Savoy had fifteen maids of honour, twelve ladies of the bedchamber, fifty formal dresses and 175 pairs of shoes.

She gave her husband seven children: the eldest, Anne, a remarkable woman, married a Bourbon, Pierre de Beaujeu, and we will come across her again soon, as well as the second, Joan, a hunchback and with a limp, whom he forced his cousin, the duke of Orléans, to marry in the hope of extinguishing his line. Of the other children only one survived, the future Charles VIII.

King Louis XI has a great reputation for cruelty, and he is often depicted as paying ironic visits to his prisoners, who were locked up in iron cages; he even threw one of his ministers, Cardinal Balue, into one of these.

If his ferocity in this field has been somewhat exaggerated, the rumours about his entourage seem to have been justified: though he did not despise the nobility and though he founded the order of the knights of St Michael, of which he was the grand master, he took pleasure in the company of very humble people, notably his doctor, Coictier, the provost Tristan l'Hermite, and his barber, Olivier le Daim, who were to the end of his life his favourite companions.

Pious by nature, though he held the evangelical principles in little respect, Louis XI in his maturity became very devout, went on numerous pilgrimages, and in his last days was attended by St Francis of Paula. His first major political act was to make contact with Pope Pius II (Sylvius Aeneas Piccolomini); he was interested in the pontiff's idea of starting a crusade to rid Constantinople of the Turks, who had established themselves there in 1453. Louis XI liked the idea of a crusade, and, to get on good terms with the Papacy, he agreed to abolish the Pragmatic Sanction which Charles VII had promulgated in 1438. This gesture was then followed by the signing of an agreement with Sixtus IV (1474), which alienated the sympathies of the French clergy.

But before embarking on a crusade (which never took place) Louis XI had to deal with serious internal difficulties, as his brutal ways of purging the political personnel had won him some irreconcilable enemies. Moreover the king increased taxation, as he had great plans for the nation. He wanted to be free of the influence of Philip of Burgundy, and so, taking advantage of his senility, he seized the northern towns agreed upon in the treaty of Arras against a payment of 400,000 golden écus, to be covered by the collection of new taxes.

These various measures made him most unpopular, and the great feudal lords joined together to defeat him. A coalition was formed called the League of the Public Weal, headed in theory by Charles of Berry, the king's younger brother. Its true leader was in fact the son of Philip the Good, the future heir of Burgundy, Charles the Bold. Obliged to find allies to defend himself, Louis XI turned to the usurper of the throne of Milan, Francesco Sforza, and also to the inhabitants of Liége, Charles the Bold's subjects. The meeting of the armies took place at Montlhéry on 16 July 1465. The outcome of the battle was so close that the king, by the treaties of Conflans and Saint-Maur, was forced to make large concessions: he restored, without compensation, the northern towns he had seized from Philip the Good and was forced to give Normandy to his brother as an apanage and to name the commander-in-chief of the coalition, Saint-Pol, high constable.

This humiliation put its mark on the king's character, and for the rest of his reign he set his mind on regaining his lost prestige. To this end he employed intrigue and guile, which won him the nickname of 'universal spider'. In 1468 he called together the Estates-General, who agreed to free him from the engagements he had made with Burgundy. But Charles the Bold, who had succeeded his father in the previous year, would not agree to this. So the other confederates had to make concessions; the Estates took away the duke of Berry's Norman appanage and the duke of Brittany was defeated at the battle of Ancenis (September 1468).

While surreptitiously inciting the Liégeois to rebel against Charles the Bold, Louis XI proposed to him a conciliation conference which took place at Péronne in October 1468. In the course of the negotiations Charles learned about the revolt of the inhabitants of Liége. He took the

Louis XI and the knights of the Order of Saint Michael. (Statutes of the Order of Saint Michael)

king prisoner, and released him only after having obtained the execution of the treaties of Conflans and Saint-Maur and the promise that the duke of Berry would receive Champagne instead of Normandy, as this territory would make communications easier for the duke of Burgundy between his possessions. Louis XI not only had to accept these humiliating conditions, but was forced to witness the repression of Liége with Charles the Bold, and to accept the duke's marriage (his third) to Elizabeth of York, and also his purchase of Breisgau and Alsace.

When Louis XI finally regained his freedom of action he had lost all credit; France was now threatened from two fronts, as it had been under Charles VII. If Louis had died at that point history would have considered him a second-rate king. The interesting part of the rest of his reign is precisely the fact that he managed to extricate himself from a seemingly impossible situation and that during the next fifteen years he was to augment French territory and power in an impressive way.

In 1470 he once again assembled the Estates-

General to make them vote that it was impossible to alienate a territory. They denounced the concessions made to Charles the Bold and, to be rid of the duke of Berry, sent him to govern Guyenne instead of Champagne.

The king then launched into foreign affairs. In 1461, King Henry VI, who in his youth had lost France, lost England in his old age. He was dethroned, with the help of Warwick, by his cousin of the elder branch, the duke of York, who took the name of Edward IV. Louis XI rapidly bribed Warwick to replace Henry VI on the throne. Then, having secured his English position, he attacked Burgundy and occupied all the towns of the Somme which had been wrested from Philip the Good (1470).

His success was resounding, but was once again put in peril as Warwick, living up to his name the Kingmaker, got rid of Henry VI a second time and re-established the house of York, which the Lancastrians had dethroned under Richard II. Then, following the same logic, King Edward IV of England, priding himself on his lawful right, claimed the throne of France, as Edward III had done. Since his sister had married Charles the Bold, he prepared to help the duke to crush the Valois.

Once again Louis XI's intrigues were going wrong, and France was again threatened by the dangers of the Hundred Years' War. But Louis' anxieties were about to be allayed, and luck was to turn his way.

While waiting for the help brought by the English landing, Burgundy stuck to local actions, of which the most famous was the siege of Beauvais, famous for the heroism of Jeanne Hachette (1472). The English army took three years to arrive. Louis XI had established a defensive league on the Somme, but was in danger of being taken from the rear by the Burgundian troops. But this never occurred, because Charles the Bold committed the huge mistake of besieging the town of Neuss, whose inhabitants had revolted against their suzerain, the archbishop of Cologne. Louis XI, with an admirable eye for the main chance, took advantage of this situation. Instead of directing his troops against the English army he asked for a meeting with Edward IV and proposed a negotiation. The king of England, whose finances were in a terrible state, saw in the French king's proposition a

chance to improve them. He offered to sell his neutrality: 75,000 golden écus as down-payment and a yearly payment of 50,000 more.

This was not just a simple truce: the king of England, at the treaty of Picquigny (29 August 1475), accepted the peace which Charles VII had been unable to obtain after the victory at Castillon. The treaty put an end to the Hundred Years' War; Louis XI had skilfully achieved the peace which his father had initiated.

But, if the king of England was neutralized, there was still the duke of Burgundy to deal with. To achieve this Louis XI formed a coalition with the Swiss and the Lorrainers. It was the turn of Charles the Bold to be caught between two fires.

Judging that the Swiss were weaker than the French, Charles attacked them first, but soon realized that he had underestimated them. The defeats at Grandson (2 March 1476) and Morat (22 June 1476) were the beginning of the end for him. Having failed to defeat the Swiss he attacked Lorraine, possession of which would have enabled him to attach Burgundy to Flanders and put together the new Lotharingia which was his dream. At Nancy he was defeated for a third time, on 5 January 1477. After the battle his body was found on a frozen mere, half-eaten by wolves.

This was a total success for Louis; not only was he rid of his main rival, but by the law of apanages, since the Burgundian line was now extinct in the masculine line, the Burgundian fief reverted to the crown of France.

But Louis XI did not content himself with this little deserved success; he wanted to go too far. Burgundy, as a Capetian fief, did indeed return to the crown, as well as Picardy. But the rest of Charles the Bold's heritage went to his daughter Mary. This remainder was considerable. It consisted of Flanders, Brabant, Hainaut, Luxemburg, Artois, Franche-Comté, Alsace and Breisgau. Totally ignoring this basic distinction, Louis XI had Franche-Comté occupied and tried to appropriate the whole heritage. To this end he gave severe instructions to the occupying forces, and this proved a deplorable move. The harshness of the occupiers, the clumsy displacing of the population, made the Burgundians regret that they were not being ruled by the daughter of Charles the Bold.

Being of marriageable age, Mary found a defender in the person of the son of the Emperor Frederick III, Maximilian of Habsburg, and married him. This had the long-term consequence of establishing the Habsburgs in the Netherlands, a source of conflict which was to plague three centuries of French history. The war for the possession of Burgundy lasted five years; it took up a large part of the end of the reign, and put the royal finances in difficulties.

In 1482 the situation was partly resolved when Mary of Burgundy fell from her horse and died. At the treaty of Arras Louis XI negotiated with Maximilian: his daughter, Margaret of Austria, would marry the dauphin Charles and would bring him as dowry Artois and Franche-Comté; the rest of the heritage would return to the dead woman's son, Philip the Fair.

No one could have envisaged at that stage the complications and the dangers which were to stem from this arrangement. The English, judging that Calais was being threatened, considered that the treaty of Picquigny had lapsed. The only way to resolve this problem in consequence was to break the dauphin's engagement, which meant losing Artois and Franche-Comté once again. Louis XI's diplomacy had therefore been checked, and it was unfortunately to suffer setbacks on other points too.

In Spain he compromised French interests by pointlessly disputing the succession of Navarre, alienating Castile without taking advantage of the weakness of King Henry IV the Powerless. The result of these clumsy interventions was that Castile was reconciled with Aragon. The marriage of Isabella of Castile to Ferdinand of Aragon sealed the reconciliation. This exceptional match was to assure the reconquest of Spain and unify the nation. Henceforth France would have a powerful and dangerous neighbour in the south. Add to this the fact that Ferdinand and Isabella's only daughter, Joan the Mad, was to marry Mary of Burgundy's son Philip the Fair, and that they were to produce the future Emperor Charles V, and one can only moderately admire certain aspects of Louis XI's foreign policy.

There are other dubious points too, notably his friendship with the Sforzas to the detriment of the rights of the Viscontis, and his indifference to the rights of the house of Anjou over the kingdom of Naples, which paved the way for the future wars in Italy through which France was to acquire a great deal of military prestige, but would also suffer much political vexation.

But Louis' mistakes were overshadowed during his lifetime by very impressive territorial gains. In 1482 he definitely annexed Burgundy, and put an option on Artois and Franche-Comté. Other equally important successes came to him from different areas. To begin with, the death of his brother, the duke of Berry, allowed Guyenne to revert definitively to the crown, and the balance of the struggle in Spain allowed an occupation of Roussillon.

The most important success came from elsewhere, however. King René of Anjou, descendant of a younger branch of the Valois, died in 1480 without a male heir. His kingdom therefore reverted to the crown, which was now able to annex not only Maine and Anjou but also Provence, which had been an imperial fief.

These huge territorial gains were on the whole to be maintained, and give a particular brilliance to Louis XI's reign, putting him in the category of the great builders of the nation.

His domestic policy completed the work undertaken by Charles VII. Personal power was established, the revenue from taxation had quadrupled since 1450, the permanent army had been organized, and the artillery had become the first in Europe.

The end of the Hundred Years' War brought peace to the country and produced great progress in agriculture and the development of commerce. These advantages brought about a lowering of agricultural prices, an increase in the price of industrial products and a substantial increase in salaries. However, since France was lacking in precious metals, its economy was lagging behind that of the rest of Europe.

However, King Louis XI could be pleased with the balance of his reign. But he does not seem to have profited from his successes. Ill, afraid of death, ensconced in his château of Plessis-les-Tours surrounded by his intimates, who had been joined by the historian Commines, former chamberlain of Charles the Bold, he died, attended by Saint Francis of Paula, on 30 August 1483. Since his son Charles was still a minor he confided the regency before dying to his daughter Anne of Beaujeu.

Charles VIII. (A painting on wood, inserted into the binding of a book)

ᘒ CHARLES VIII ᘒ
(1483–1498)
AND ANNE OF BRITTANY

CHARLES VIII WAS BARELY THIRTEEN when Louis XI died. He had a rather unfortunate physical appearance: an enormous head, globular eyes, flat lips and a large hook nose which almost touched his upper lip. His body was equally ill-favoured: he was short, but perched on legs that were too long and too thin. Added to this unfortunate physique, made worse by a difficult adolescence, was an alarming intellectual backwardness. One can well see why, although he was legally of age to rule, Charles VIII was given a regent, his sister Anne, nine years older than him, who was married to Pierre of Bourbon, lord of Beaujeu.

This nomination for the regency seriously antagonized the duke of Orléans, the king's closest cousin, heir presumptive to the throne and also Louis XI's son-in-law by his marriage to the unfortunate Joan of France. Annoyed at being superseded by his sister-in-law, Louis of Orléans demanded a meeting of the Estates-General in the hopes of getting from them full power, part of which he already held as lieutenant-general of the kingdom.

These Estates, assembled at Tours in 1484, took on a particular importance because they were the first whose deliberations have been recorded. The members of this assembly had taken the liberty of presenting *cahiers de doléances* (books of complaints), and the debates revealed a desire to put a curb on absolute power. Philippe Pot, lord of La Roche, made a moving appeal for political equality and demanded that taxes should be agreed by all contributing parties. The deputies of the clergy demanded a return to the Pragmatic Sanction. The envoys of the third estate (commonalty) complained about the heavy taxes and demanded a reduction in them.

However, agreement was reached on certain points, such as independence for tribunals, improving the means of communication and reducing tolls. On the other hand the Estates unanimously agreed not to allow any manifestations of revolt against absolute power; but the agitation was so worrying that the Beaujeus were inclined to make concessions. The *taille* was reduced, and some of Louis XI's advisers fell from grace.

Louis of Orléans tried to have his marriage dissolved because of his wife's physical defects. He had always dreamed of marrying Anne of Beaujeu, and it is possible that she was secretly in love with him. Disappointment in love sometimes explains harsh behaviour. When Louis spoke too much about it, Anne had his palace surrounded, and issued the order for his arrest. Louis was warned in time and took refuge with the duke of Brittany – a serious act, as the new king of England, Henry VII, had allied himself to the duke of Brittany and was counting on his help to renew the war in France.

Several important feudal lords had grouped themselves around the duke of Orléans. Maximilian of Austria was asked to join them, and the great French seigneurs demanded the programme of the League of the Public Weal. Anne of Beaujeu put down the revolt, known as the 'guerre folle', the 'mad war'. Under the leadership of Louis de la Trémoille an army of twelve thousand men defeated the rebels at Saint-Aubin-du-Cormier (14 July 1488).

Louis of Orléans was taken prisoner and imprisoned in the château of Lusignan on dry bread and water, without regard for his position as heir presumptive to the throne. Joan of France intervened on behalf of her imprisoned husband, but he remained in captivity for three years. It was only in 1491 that Charles VIII, who had only just become king, sent for his cousin and had him reconciled with the Beaujeus.

Louis of Orléans proposed to have Brittany joined to France again by negotiating the marriage of Charles VIII with Princess Anne, who was to inherit the duchy. This plan presented two problems. First, Charles VIII had been engaged by Louis XI to marry Margaret of Austria, daughter of Maximilian, and he, since Mary of Burgundy had died, was to marry Anne of Brittany. This marriage threatened to place France between two lines of fire, and it was thought politic to prevent it. So Charles VIII's engagement had to be broken and the dowry given up, i.e. Franche-Comté and Artois (treaty of Senlis, January 1493). Secondly, the French had to buy the withdrawal of Henry VII Tudor's troops from Calais at the treaty of Etaples, 1493.

There still remained the problem of the marriage between Charles and Anne, which was celebrated at the Château de Langeais. The contract still contained one problem, which was that since Brittany was a female fief, of which Anne remained sovereign, it would be necessary, in order for the province to return to France, for the queen, if she became a widow, to marry the new king. One can guess the complications brought about by this clause, which nevertheless worked out; for Anne of Brittany, a unique phenomenon in French history, was twice queen, loved both her husbands, and was loved in return, even though she was not particularly beautiful and had a slight limp. But it was Brittany, even more than the duchess, that they were marrying.

Maximilian of Austria, doubly offended by the rejection of his daughter and the theft of his fiancée, took his revenge by inciting France's neighbouring kings to take up arms against her. He had succeeded with Henry Tudor and this had cost him dear. He repeated his mistake with Ferdinand the Catholic to whom, by the treaty of Barcelona, he was obliged to give up Cerdagne and Roussillon.

Louis XI had had the idea of demanding the rights he held over Naples through his mother, Mary of Anjou, but preoccupied by other things, he had not followed up his intentions. Charles VIII found this plan attractive. He was very fond of chivalrous tales, and dreamed of war while surveying the objects in his collection: the swords of Charlemagne and St Louis, Du Guesclin's axe, Joan of Arc's coat of armour.

Charles VIII was certainly haunted by the idea of a crusade against the Turks. A base in Italy would be the obvious way of doing this successfully. By conquering Italy the king would achieve two of his aims in one. Moreover the French army was the best in Europe, and soldiers are difficult to control in peacetime. And so Charles VIII crossed the Alps at the head of thirty thousand men and set out on his adventure.

He expected a serious war, and his advance was very much in the style of a triumphal march: prepared by long and skilful diplomacy, the Italians were almost looking forward to the arrival of the French. Savoy was conquered without a blow being struck; the same went for the marquisate of Saluzzo and Montferrat. The only reticence Charles VIII encountered was in Milan, where his ally, Lodovico Sforza, seemed less than pleased with his success.

In Florence events took a surprising turn. A visionary monk, Savonarola, had ousted Piero de Medici and held power over the town. He had prophesied that the Florentines' love of luxury and debauchery would be punished by a foreign invasion. His dearest wishes were therefore fulfilled by the approach of the French. He was ready to collaborate with the invading force. Piero de Medici fled and Savonarola came to the king of France in person to present him with the keys to the Tuscan capital.

Assuming that his rear was secure, Charles VIII pressed forward. At Siena the inhabitants took down the town gates as a sign of respect, and the French advanced towards Rome (31 December 1494). Pope Alexander VI Borgia was not happy at the arrival of the French. Cardinal della Rovere, the future Julius II, suggested that Charles VIII should depose the pope, but this proposition was rejected. But during his stay in the Palazzo Venezia, he made the pope hand over to him a distinguished Turkish prisoner, Prince Djem, brother of the Sultan Bajazet, to be used as a possible hostage during the crusade.

Then the king of France went on to take possession of Naples, where he made his entry on 22 February 1495. He installed himself in the Villa Poggio Reale and fulfilled his dream, with constant festivities; he even went so far at one ball as to appear dressed as the Emperor of the Orient. His troops were making reconnaissance raids as far as Calabria, and it appeared that henceforth Italy was entirely subjugated.

But alas this was only an illusion. The sovereigns of Europe, whose neutrality Charles VIII had unwisely paid for in advance, had only one idea in mind, to unite in order to maroon the king in the middle of his conquests, which would leave France defenceless against their attack.

Lodovico Sforza, whose daughter had just

married Maximilian, had been in charge of the whole operation. Philippe de Commines got wind of this, and warned Charles VIII in time. The king had to head for home immediately, and while coming down from the Appenines in the valley of the Taro he met the coalition forces near Fornovo. His own troops charged and the coalition, under the marquis of Mantua, was routed (6 July 1495). Charles VIII crossed the Alps with the rest of his troops. He returned to France fired with enthusiasm for Italian art, and opened the way for the Renaissance. He was determined to try again.

But his time was short. In 1498, at his favourite residence, the Château d'Amboise, he went one day to play a game of real tennis. He cracked his head on the lintel of a low door, collapsed, and died almost immediately, aged only twenty-eight. All the three sons he had had by Anne of Brittany had died in infancy; the elder branch of the Valois became extinct; the throne was vacant.

The heir was the duke of Orléans, the rebel of Saint-Aubin-du-Cormier, brother-in-law to the dead king by Joan of Valois. He was his cousin by blood and, though already married, was bound by law to marry Anne of Brittany, Charles VIII's widow.

The tomb of the children of Charles VIII and Anne of Brittany, who died in infancy, at Tours.
After them the elder branch of the Valois died out, and the duke of Orléans became king.

This branch of Valois-Orléans only provided France with one sovereign, Louis XII, whose reign, despite a few mistakes, remains a remarkable one.

⊗ LOUIS XII ⊗
(1498–1515)
SAINT JOAN OF VALOIS
AND ANNE OF BRITTANY

THE NEW KING was the great-grandson of Charles V; his grandfather had been assassinated in 1407, and his father was the delicate poet Charles of Orléans. He was born of his father's third marriage to Anne of Cleves in 1462, shortly before his father's death (Charles of Orléans was sixty-seven when his son was born).

First prince of the blood, he had been nominated lieutenant-general at the death of Louis XI. We have described how he rebelled against Anne of Beaujeu, and had been imprisoned in tough conditions for three years, then pardoned in 1491

by Charles VIII. He had become reconciled with the Beaujeus, and was now so much their friend that they supported him with constancy. But envious courtiers persuaded Charles VIII that the duke of Orléans was trying to bring about the secession of Normandy, of which he had been named governor. An inquiry was opened on royal orders, and Louis of Orléans felt the situation to be so dangerous that he left Rouen and went to earth in his castle of Montils-les-Blois.

One spring day in 1498 Louis heard the sound of cavalry in the courtyard and saw it filled with

Joan of France, repudiated by Louis XII, obtains permission
from the Pope to found the Order of the Annunciation.

armed men. His breath was quite taken away, as
he was convinced that they had come to arrest
him, until a man entered, clasped the duke by the
knees and said simply: 'The king is dead.' And he
told Louis of the king's accident and subsequent
death.

Though still suspecting a trap, the duke of
Orléans set off at great speed for Amboise, and as
soon as he appeared all the courtiers bowed to
him. The first in line was La Trémoille, the victor of Saint-Aubin-du-Cormier. The king took
him aside, told him that he would retain all his
posts, and begged him 'to be as loyal to him as he
had been to his predecessor'.

A few days later he granted an audience to the
burghers of Orléans; they were very anxious, as

they had disowned him when he was disgraced.
His famous reply to them was: 'It would not be
seemly for a king of France to avenge the injury
done to a duke of Orléans.' This behaviour was
the sign of a generous nature and corresponded
well with the king's physical appearance: he was
a handsome man, full-faced, with a Joan of Arc
hairstyle, and a pleasant smile.

Nevertheless the reign was to begin with a
cruel act, the repudiation of Joan of Valois. In
fact the marriage had not been consummated,
but Joan did not realize this, having been very
innocent when she married. Moreover, a terrible
letter written by Louis XI was produced for official purposes, which read: 'I have decided to
marry my small daughter Joan to the small duc

OPPOSITE Louis XII, by Jean Perréal.

Et roy ferrand darrago estoit ra partp de gapete:
monte en mer pᵒ sen reuenir en espargne ⁊ passer
par sauone ce⁻ auoit mande au roy de quop le pape adᵼ
sen alla a lostie ung port de mer terre deglize sur la passe
dud roy darrago ⁊ la fist faire grandes prisions ⁊ gre⁻
parceil pᵒ le euder illecq̄ recueillir ⁊ treter mais sanch⁻
lors celuy roy darrago q̄ le pape nauoit en a gre le prop

of Orléans because it seems to me that the children they might have would not cost much to feed . . .'

Although it was difficult to annul the marriage on the basis of this evidence, which was rather defamatory to the memory of Louis XI, the ecclesiastical tribunal under the archbishop of Albi, Louis d'Amboise, invoked the clause of non-consummation. The marriage was declared void on 17 December 1499 and Joan, after governing the duchy of Berry for a while, founded a cloistered order called the Annonciade. She died in 1505 and was soon canonized.

This severe but justified sentence made it possible to save Brittany, since Louis XII could now marry Anne of Brittany without committing bigamy. Louis was thirty-six, and much better looking than Charles VIII; Anne was twenty-three, and not insensitive to considerations of love. The marriage, made for political reasons, was an excellent match. Anne of Brittany, twice queen, had a marked influence on the country even though, a true Breton at heart, she twice put the country in danger. She founded the order of the Cordelière and supported her husband in a dignified manner. She gave him a daughter, Claude, but died quite young, on 9 January 1514.

The characteristic feature of Louis XII's reign was not only the resumption of the war with Italy, to whose crown Louis, through his mother Valentina Visconti, had a greater claim than his predecessor, but in particular the fact that this was about the only time that the French declared themselves content with their government.

His first act of foreign policy was to bring to heel Lodovico Sforza, who had fomented the coalition against Charles VIII and was usurping the throne of Milan to the detriment of the Viscontis. Before beginning his operations against Milan, he made sure of the neutrality of Henry VII Tudor and Emperor Maximilian, as well as of Spain, Florence, Ferrara and Mantua. He then contracted an alliance with Venice and with the Holy See.

Since he owned the county of Asti, Louis was present for the preparations. An army of twenty-four thousand men and fifty-eight cannons was put under the command of the condottiere Trivulzio, and Arezzo was occupied, thus isolating the Milan area from the south. Lodovico Sforza fled to Austria. Louis XII

arrived after the fall of Milan. On 2 October 1499 he made his entry into Pavia, and then resumed possession of Milan amidst general enthusiasm.

Trivulzio was made marshal of France and was given the government of Milan, but he made so many mistakes that Lodovico Sforza was able to recapture Milan. Then La Trémoille brought reinforcements, and Lodovico the Moor was handed over by the Swiss guards who were in his pay. Louis XII had him imprisoned in the fortress of Lys-Saint-Georges in Berry, where he died in 1508.

Milan was annexed and placed under the governorship of Cardinal d'Amboise, then the reconquest was moved on to Naples. Louis XII thought it wise to share the kingdom of Naples with Ferdinand of Aragon, whose benevolent neutrality he bought, but this sharing-out caused friction as soon as it had been carried out. Maximilian's son Philip the Fair offered to mediate, but in vain. The Spanish attacked, and the French were defeated at Cerignola (1503) and Seminara. The exploits of Bayard at Garigliano bridge slightly softened the blow of these defeats, which had the effect of detaching Venice from the coalition.

To punish Ferdinand of Aragon, the king attacked in Roussillon and laid siege to Salses, but in vain: he had to lift the siege and, since Ferdinand had attacked Narbonne, sign a truce. Negotiations were begun with Spain, but just as they started Louis XII fell so seriously ill that it seemed he would die. Anne of Brittany took it upon herself to sign a treaty at Blois whose consequences could have been tragic, since it allowed for the marriage of the young Claude of France to the son of Philip the Fair and Joan the Mad, the future Emperor Charles V. This unfortunate act almost places Anne of Brittany on a par with Isabeau of Bavaria.

But fortunately Louis XII, unlike Charles VI, was not insane; when he had recovered his health he did not wish publicly to disavow his wife, but to save Brittany from the risk of falling into the hands of a foreign prince, he submitted the treaty to the Estates-General. They met at Tours on 14 May 1506, and the deputies demanded the annulment of this dangerous marriage project and suggested that Claude of France should be engaged to one of the king's nephews, the count of Angoulême, heir presumptive to the crown –

The meeting of Louis XII and Ferdinand of Aragon.
(*Chroniques de Louis XII*)

'Monsieur Françoys qui est tout français' (Monsieur François who is all French). Naturally Louis XII agreed to this, thus cancelling out Anne of Brittany's mistake.

At that point one of the deputies from Paris, Thomas Briart, whom the assembly had elected their spokesman, spoke the following words, which are virtually unique in the history of France: 'Because he has suppressed the licence of the men of war so that there are no longer any bold enough to take something without paying, because he has granted back to the people a quarter of the *taille*, because he has reformed the legal system and appointed good judges everywhere, for all these reasons the sovereign shall be called Louis the Twelfth, father of the people.'

This unequalled eulogy is still astounding today for, with hindsight, though Louis XII was of an exceptionally generous nature, his administration and his policies cannot remain uncriticized. Certainly the *taille* was reduced, but at what price? The *gabelle* had to be increased and the system of putting official posts up for sale was restored, which was ultimately to do the monarchy a great deal of harm. But it must be noted, to the king's credit, that the income from these taxes was faithfully used to maintain the roads, that an effort was made to develop mining in the country, and that construction was encouraged.

These feeble successes do not however make up for the rest of his policies, which were singularly adventurous.

The breaking of Claude of France's engagement coincided with the death of Isabella the Catholic, and Ferdinand of Aragon was replaced in Castile by his son-in-law. In this predicament, Ferdinand did not object to the broken engagement. On the contrary, he met Louis XII at Savona in 1507 and agreed to marry Germaine de Foix, the king of France's niece. The two sovereigns agreed to restore order in Milan, where agitators were trying to place on the throne the son of Lodovico Sforza, who was still in prison.

Louis XII's energetic intervention in Milan infuriated Emperor Maximilian, who prepared an expedition to expel the French from northern Italy, but the republic of Venice refused to let the emperor's troops through. Louis XII sent Trivulzio to support the Venetians; they took advantage of his help to seize Fiume, Trieste and Görz, and then, carried away by their success, they signed a truce with Maximilian without telling the French.

Louis XII, feeling that this constituted real treason, declared war on Venice and sought an alliance with Pope Julius II. This pontiff, a shrewd but unscrupulous politician, agreed in principle and signed, with Louis XII, the alliance of the League of Cambrai, which was negotiated by Cardinal d'Amboise (10 December 1508). The Venetians, under Bartolommeo d'Alviano, were crushed by Louis at the battle of Agnadello (10 December 1508). The king of France was now master of all the territory from Lake Gard to the River Brenta. He came within sight of Venice and bombarded the lagoon, but the town did not surrender.

But Louis XII now held too much territory in northern Italy for the Italians to rest easy. Pope Julius II was the first to realize this. He did not want to see the republic of Venice destroyed, merely to put a curb on her ambition. He therefore formed an alliance with the Most Serene Republic, which broke his alliance with France. This coalition, called the Holy League, put France in a dangerous position in Italy, particularly since Julius II had gone so far as to propose to Henry VII Tudor that he should claim the throne of France, reviving the danger of a war on two fronts. There was no alternative but to fight the Holy League.

The pious Anne of Brittany would have nothing to do with this, however, and went so far as to release the Breton bishops from their oath of fidelity to the king of France. The rest of the French clergy swung the other way, and a general assembly of bishops in Tours authorized war, by stating that Julius II was not fighting as head of the Church, but only in his capacity as a temporal sovereign.

The war began, but the French army contented itself with occupying the frontier of the Papal States. Once in position, the king of France tried to negotiate with Julius II. The pontiff, more and more intransigent, convoked a Lateran Council which opposed any kind of settlement.

Having exhausted the negotiations, Louis XII attacked. The Italian campaign led by the king's nephew, Gaston de Foix, became something of an epic. The young general seized Brescia and then Bologna with a masterliness which heralded Bonaparte's successes in the same field. But alas Gaston de Foix was killed at Ravenna and Bayard, in tears, stood vigil over his body (1512). The situation was reversed by his death and became unfavourable to the French. Although the alliance with Venice had been restored, they were unable to prevent the son of Lodovico the Moor from seizing Milan.

Louis XII hastily sent reinforcements under La Trémoille. But this army was crushed at Novara on 6 June 1513 and Milan was lost; the French had to make a rapid retreat across the Alps to France, where they were faced with new dangers.

Taking advantage of France's difficulties Ferdinand attacked Roussillon, while Henry VII landed his troops at Calais and had a success at Guinegate. Moreover, the Swiss were threatening Dijon. This deplorable situation was resolved by the death of Julius II who had been underhandedly inciting everyone against France.

A truce was signed with Spain early in 1514, and a matrimonial solution was found to the English problem. Since Anne of Brittany had died at the beginning of 1514, Henry VIII, Henry VII's successor, demanded as a condition for a truce that the king of France should marry his sister Mary. Easily consoled, Louis · XII accepted all the more readily because the young English princess was beautiful and charming. But she was only sixteen and he was fifty-three.

The marriage took place in October 1514, and Louis XII went the same way as his ancestor Philip VI of Valois. Too anxious to please his young wife, he not only excelled too much as a husband, but wanted to stun her with sumptuous feasts. His health did not hold out for long and he died suddenly during the night in 1515.

Although his reign had ended with a series of stalemates, Louis XII was universally mourned, probably because during his reign financial life had been easy and France had prospered. Since the king had no son the crown went to his son-in-law and nephew Francis of Angoulême, great-grandson of Duke Louis of Orléans, who became the head of the house of Valois.

His was to be one of the most brilliant reigns in the whole history of France.

᪥ FRANCIS I ᪥
(1515–1547)
CLAUDE OF FRANCE
AND ELEANOR OF AUSTRIA

WHEN FRANCIS, DUKE OF ANGOULÊME, WAS BORN in 1494, the son of Charles of Angoulême (Charles V's great-grandson) and Louise of Savoy, nothing seemed to indicate him for the throne. Charles VIII was young and married to Anne of Brittany, and in the event of the absence of a male heir the crown would go to the duke of Orléans.

This was what did happen, in fact, but the duke of Orléans, as Louis XII, had only daughters by Anne of Brittany. By popular demand he married his daughter Claude to Francis of Angoulême, who became heir presumptive. As the late king's son-in-law, Francis of Angoulême took the throne uncontested as Francis I.

The new king was just twenty-one. He was a giant, over two metres tall, and had the marked acromegalic features of long arms and legs and huge hands and feet. His face is well known to us from paintings: he had a large hook nose, low forehead, bulbous eyes; the chin is made thinner by a pointed beard. The magnificence of his clothes, the close-fitting doublets, tight at the waist and with large skirts, with slashed sleeves, the tights and extravagant shoes, the feathered hats, drew the crowd's notice to his physical appearance, which was possibly ill-favoured, but made appealing by a certain languor in his expression and a great affability.

Queen Claude, whom he loved deeply and who gave him several children, was also fairly

OPPOSITE Claude of France on the lap of Anne of Brittany.

RIGHT The golden seal made for Francis I by Benvenuto Cellini.

good-looking, but she played a minor role since she was dominated by her mother-in-law, the famous Louise of Savoy. Moreover she died in 1524 in the prime of life.

The reign of Francis I represents a period during which the arts flourished tremendously in France; he had the château de Chambord built, continued the work on the château of Blois, and created Saint-Germain. He was the patron and friend of artists, and it was in his arms that the great Leonardo da Vinci died.

At the time of Louis XII's violent death, Francis I was in a very difficult political situation. France

was being threatened from three sides, by the king of England, Henry VIII, by the emperor Maximilian, and by Ferdinand of Aragon. And still greater dangers threatened, since Charles of Austria was to become the heir to both Spain and Austria. Francis I judged that his prime duty was to impose himself by a coup d'état; as heir to the last of the Viscontis, he decided to recapture the duchy of Milan.

To be sure of succeeding in this bold plan, he secured Henry VIII's neutrality, and proposed that Charles of Austria marry the sister of queen Claude, Renée. He also tried to neutralize

Emperor Charles v by Titian.

Francis I (from the studio of
Clouet), and (below) his wife,
Claude of France.

the Swiss, who rejected his offers. He gathered his armies in the valley of the Durance, and took their head, together with the constable of Bourbon, and the three marshals of France Lautrec, Trivulce and La Palice. They had a force of twelve thousand horse, thirty thousand men, seventy-two pieces of heavy artillery and three hundred light cannon.

The crossing of the col of Larche by this artillery was truly miraculous. They descended into Piedmont after making sure of the neutrality of the duke of Savoie. Operations began with a victorious battle at Villa-franca which forced the Swiss to double back towards Milan. Before continuing the war, Francis I attempted a negotiation with the Swiss which would have brought them great advantages. But, under the influence of the cardinal de Sion, papal legate of Leo x, they refused to listen. There was nothing for it but to attack. The battle took place at Marignano and the fighting went on for two days (13–14 September 1515). It was a dazzling victory for the French, during which Francis was made a knight by Bayard.

When the Swiss were in his power, the king offered them the same conditions as before the battle, and signed with them a treaty of perpetual peace, the peace of Fribourg, the only one in history which has never been broken. He then made a treaty with the son of Lodovico the Moor, who gave him the duchy of Milan against considerable holdings in France.

Finally he sought an agreement with the pope, who up to that point had been hostile to him. With Leo x, who was a good diplomat, he signed the treaty of Viterbo, after a sumptuous meeting at Bologna. It was from this treaty that the Concordat of 1516 was to arise, of which the terms were settled for France by chancellor Duprat, the great minister of the reign. Charles VII's Pragmatic Sanction was definitively abolished. The right to raise subsidies in France was given back to the pope on condition that the king should propose bishops to him and that he would make the nominations for ecclesiastical benefices. This was an instrument of financial power for the crown which it was to use and even abuse to the extent of provoking the Revolution of 1789. The French clergy were not pleased with this Concordat, and in order to apply it Francis had to use the procedure of the *lit de justice*.

The double success of the victory at Marignano was completed at the treaty of Cambrai (1517) by an arrangement with Henry VIII whereby the two kings mutually guaranteed each other's respective possessions.

Just when peace seemed certain, an upheaval occurred with the death of Ferdinand of Aragon, followed by that of emperor Maximilian. The heir to the two crowns, Charles v, became the true master of Europe, and France was caught, surrounded by his different possessions. This was the greatest danger France had ever been in, and the policy adopted to counter it has been called that of the 'balance of Europe'.

It was obvious that Charles v's first move would be to propose himself as a candidate for the Empire. Since it was out of the question to support Henry VIII against him, which would have provoked similar dangers, Francis proposed himself as candidate. He conducted his campaign with extraordinary naïvety, and paid the electors in advance. Charles v, wiser than he, offered them bonds which would be payable after the election. They had little trouble in reaching their decision.

Henceforth the true arbiter of the situation was the king of England, the only person capable of making the balance of power in arms shift in favour of his ally. Francis I realized this perfectly well, and, when he heard that Henry VIII had received his nephew Charles v at Canterbury, he invited the king of England to France.

Henry VIII had promised Charles v nothing; he wanted first to make contact with the king of France. The meeting of the two sovereigns took place between Ardres and Guines at the famous Field of the Cloth of Gold. Francis I laid on too sumptuous a reception, won several games against Henry VIII, and his manner so antagonized the king of England, who still wished to become king of France, that no agreement was reached. And indeed Henry VIII, on returning to England, allied himself to Charles v, forcing France into war, caught between her two most powerful enemies.

To complete the picture of the period, it is necessary to mention the unwise papal policy: to finance the building of the basilica of St Peter's, the traffic in Indulgences was organized, in which the archbishop of Mayen, Albert of Brandenburg, was scandalously involved. Some

of the funds collected went to paying the electors of Charles v.

At this point a monk of Wittenburg, Martin Luther, revolted by these events, raised a protest which was to have tremendous repercussions. The pope ordered him to retract it, and when he refused, Luther was excommunicated by the Bull *Decet romanus Pontificus* (3 January 1521).

Charles v called Luther before the Diet of Worms to explain himself. In front of the

emperor, the monk defended his doctrines and insisted that the pope was wrong. It is quite likely that this attitude would have led Luther to the stake had he not been removed by the greater power of the most powerful German prince, Frederic the Wise, the elector of Saxony, who was the only possible opponent to Charles v.

To anger the emperor, some of the German princes adopted the new religion which arose from the Reformation, and made their subjects

ABOVE Martin Luther preaching.
(From the church at Wittenberg)

LEFT Henry VIII of England and
Francis I meet at the Field of
the Cloth of Gold in 1520.

do likewise. This religious upheaval in Europe was also a political one, as a game of allegiances was to arise naturally from these religious differences. And because Henry VIII, for personal reasons, was causing the English church to break away and refuse allegiance to Rome, Europe was entering a dangerous period during which the struggles were to arise which have been called the Wars of Religion. But this did not figure in the war which from 1521 was to oppose France to the European coalition.

When mediation with England failed, the fighting began; despite local successes on the northern front at Hesdin, and the taking of Fuentarabia, Lautrec's disaster at the battle of La Bicoque lost him the duchy of Milan. This French defeat had the effect of adding to Francis' enemies the papacy, the republic of Venice and finally Henry VIII, who up till then had been playing a waiting game.

Francis I planned to recapture Milan; but as he was setting out to do so terrible news was brought to him. His cousin, the constable of Bourbon, supreme head of the French army, was going over to the enemy as the result of a quarrel over inheritance, in which he was not altogether in the wrong. His defection opened up to the enemy his territories in France, i.e. the Dombes, Beaujolais, Bourbonnais, the Marche and Auvergne. This treason put France in great danger. After trying in vain to conciliate, Francis I gave the order to seize the constable who, warned of this, went over to the enemy.

France was invaded on three fronts. The English and the imperial forces advanced to less than fifty kilometres away from Paris. Bayard managed to contain the invasion in the north, then went to help Bonnivet, who lost northern Italy in the battle of la Sesia. It was here that the famous scene took place in which Bayard, mortally wounded, said to the constable of Bourbon, who came to comfort him; 'Do not pity me, Monseigneur: it is I who pity you for serving against your prince, your country and your oath.' (1524.)

The defeat of la Sesia opened up the road to Provence, to which the constable of Bourbon rushed, but his siege of Marseilles was unsuccessful and he headed back for Liguria. At this point, Francis I, who was descending towards Italy from the cols of Mont-Genèvre with a strong army, had only to head for Genoa, and Bourbon would have been caught. But instead of doing this, the king recaptured Milan and laid siege to Pavia.

The constable, his troops reformed, came to attack him at the very walls of the city. A badly-led battle ensued. Francis I was wounded, and his horse killed under him; he was captured. He refused to hand over his sword to Bourbon, and wrote to his mother, Louise de Savoie, the famous phrase: 'All is lost except honour.'

After such a promising start, the king of France found himself in the same deplorable state as John the Good at Poitiers; but France, energetically led by the regent Louise of Savoie and by chancellor Duprat, avoided internal strife.

Charles V made Francis I his prisoner in Madrid, and his captivity was a harsh one. Remembering that he was the heir of Charles the Rash, the emperor claimed Burgundy and intended to restore western France from Normandy to Guyenne to the king of England; moreover he proposed to return the constable of Bourbon's fiefs to him, and to add Dauphiné to them. Francis I flatly refused. In Paris, acting on Duprat's advice, the regent bought the king of England off for two million écus. Feeling that he had been abandoned by Henry VIII, Charles V moderated his ambitions, freed Francis I against the giving up of Burgundy and demanded as hostages the dauphin Francis and his brother, the future Henry II (1526).

The king of France, who had no intention of carrying out the terms of the treaty, had very cleverly taken his precautions by handing his ring to the sultan Suleiman the Magnificent as a pledge of alliance. The Turks marched on Hungary and won a victory at Mohacs (1526), which convinced Charles V that he could not fight on two fronts.

As soon as he returned to France, Francis I had himself freed from the clauses of the treaty of Madrid by an assembly of notables gathered at Cognac. The delegates from the Estates of Burgundy opposed any alienation of the French territory. Europe felt that Charles V had abused his power and Henry VIII offered an alliance, together with the republic of Venice and the Swiss, with the intention of freeing Italy from imperial clutches.

This new war was marked by the sacking of Rome, where the constable of Bourbon was killed (1527), by the reconquest of the kingdom of Naples by Lautrec, and by the siege of Vienna. Charles was therefore forced to sue for peace. By this peace, called Peace of the Ladies (1529), Francis I gave up the duchy of Milan, the hostage princes were released for a ransom of two million golden écus, and Francis I married Charles V's sister Eleanor.

As soon as he returned to Paris, Francis I dealt with the internal problems: the constable of Bourbon's possessions were brought back to the crown, and the controller-general of finances, Jacques de Beaune, baron of Semblancay, was hanged for fraud. This was the end of territorial and financial feudalism.

The hostage princes returned to France, but the dauphin Francis died, possibly poisoned. His younger brother, Henry, became dauphin. He had just been married, for diplomatic reasons, to pope Clement VII's niece Catherine de Medici. This queen, the most interesting in the history of France, was to dominate the scene for nearly 50 years.

Preoccupied with the problem of the European balance, Francis I, whose alliance with the Turks had been a successful one, established an embassy in Constantinople and signed with the Sultan the treaty called of the Capitulations, which was a real alliance (1536). Henceforth the Turkish fleet, with the help of the Berbers of North Africa, were to police the Mediterranean for France.

Moreover, to counterbalance the power of Charles V, Francis I was obliged to ally himself to the league of Smalkalde, which had been formed by all the German protestant princes (1531). But this alliance did not bring freedom to the French protestants, who were gradually establishing themselves, and for whom the king's sister, Margaret, showed sympathy: some heretics were burned at the stake. But on the whole they were not too badly repressed during the reign.

By this policy, so bold in the religious field with its alliances with infidels and protestants, Francis ran the risk of making Charles V the defender of the Catholic faith and the moral head of Europe. And so the last years of the reign were taken up by a long war with intermissions, for, though the German princes had decided to help the king of France against the emperor, they still intended to benefit from the emperor's help in defending central Europe against the Ottoman invasion.

Before discussing this war it is worth pointing out that Francis I, enamoured of Renaissance art, was also a man of his time. During his captivity in Spain he became interested in her possessions in America, and wanted to acquire some for France. In 1517 he founded the port of Le Havre and encouraged exploration. In 1523 Verrano was to discover the site of New York. Ango was to establish commercial channels with India, and then from 1534 to 1541 Jacques Cartier, leaving from Saint-Malo, was to explore Canada and found Montreal.

Internal achievements were equally important: the system of justice was centralized by the ordinance of Villers-Cotterets (1539), the use of French made compulsory in official documents, and in 1535 the Collège de France was founded.

The end of the feudal age brought about a social revolution: the nobility was in greater and greater material difficulties because of the depreciation of the ground-rent and was obliged to draw nearer to the throne to obtain favours. Money moved into the hands of a bourgeoisie which was keen to link itself with the nobility.

The financial situation was persistently unstable; taxes had to be constantly increased, and when this failed a system of loans had to be implemented; the creation of bonds on the Hôtel de Ville was the basis for the principle of public debt, which was to become heavier and heavier.

Wars proved very expensive. Hostilities were resumed in 1536 with increased resources which made possible the conquest of Savoy, Bresse, Bugey and finally of Piedmont.

Duprat's successor Montmorency recommended a truce, which was signed at Nice. As a result of this Francis I met his brother-in-law Charles V at Aigues-Mortes (1538). But the entente did not last long. Charles wanted to make his brother king of the Romans and hostilities were resumed as a result of the assassination of the French ambassador Rincon by the emperor's supporters.

Charles V once again sought the help of Henry VIII. France was attacked in Roussillon, and Italy was lost again despite a success at Ceresole (1544). Francis I launched his troops against the Empire once again, and, faced with so many dangers, Charles V agreed to a treaty. By the peace signed at Crépy in Laonnois in 1544 France gave up Italy, but Charles V also abandoned his claims to Burgundy. Henry VIII, worried at the prospect of a landing, sold Boulogne to France by the Peace of Ardres (1546).

The reign was nearing its end. Francis had led a dissolute private life; of his mistresses Anne de Pisseleu, duchess of Etampes, and Madame de Chateaubriant were famous. There was also much talk about La Belle Ferronnière, through whom her jealous husband was reputed to have infected the king, which supposedly hastened his end.

This brilliant reign ended in 1547 in a twilight threatened by religious and also by political problems, since Charles V, now more powerful than ever, had not ceased his aggressions.

HENRY II

(1547–1559)

AND CATHERINE DE MEDICI

HENRY II WAS FRANCIS I'S SECOND SON, and he had been married to Catherine de Medici before becoming dauphin. With his brother's death in 1536 he became heir to the throne and his Florentine bride became the future queen of France.

A fascinating queen, she far outshone her rather dull husband. He was tall, with very broad shoulders, a sad face and a bitter mouth; his virtual hypochondria was attributed to his years of captivity in Madrid. He was unintelligent, devoid of intellectual curiosity, uncultured, and interested only in physical exercise.

His emotional life was a strange one: he loved his wife, but their marriage was fruitless for nine years during which Henry II, after fathering several bastards by ladies-in-waiting, fell madly in love with the widow of the seneschal of Brézé, Diane of Poitiers; she was thirty-eight, he was only twenty-nine. She was to dominate the king morally and sensually, and in his way he was faithful to her. She had the châteaux of Anet, Chenonceaux and Chaumont built, and is remembered in the arts and in heraldry, since she was made duchess of Valentinois.

Despite this astonishing relationship Henry II was a devoted husband, and fond of his wife, who after her sterile years gave him ten children. Of these three became kings of France, as had happened at the time of the extinction of the direct Capetian line.

Catherine de Medici was a figure of prime importance; she was brought to France at the age of fourteen, married in the presence of Francis I and Pope Clement VII, and adored her husband despite his infidelities. She was not really attractive and lost her figure through child-bearing. She was portly, with a large head and forehead; she had auburn hair which curled around her temples, a fat face, clear, wide eyes, a large, hooked nose, sensual lips, a short, receding chin, a large bust, a sanguine temperament, a tremendous capacity for resistance, and a good appetite.

Never happy, Catherine showed true states-manlike qualities, but made mistakes through fear, violence, and perhaps also through cruelty. She is among those who have changed the course of history, but not always for the better, and posterity has generally been critical of her. Though she became queen after her husband's death, she played virtually no part as such during his lifetime, since he was dominated by Diane of Poitiers and by his first minister, the high constable Montmorency.

Montmorency, Francis I's creature, had been virtually in disgrace since 1540. But as soon as Henry II came to the throne he summoned him and placed his absolute trust in him, as he admired him unreservedly. Despite this Montmorency appears to have been a very ordinary man, a mediocre strategist and second-rate politician. Through the king's favour he became the first duke and peer of France, and assumed a role and an importance far beyond his capacities.

The financial situation in the early years of the reign was a difficult one, since in the last months of his life Francis I had let things slide. Taxes were not being properly collected, and tax riots broke out. Montmorency did what Henry II would not have dared – he used force, going so far as to bombard the town of Bordeaux, killing several of its inhabitants.

His brutal methods were compared unfavourably by the French people with the skill of the man who was pacifying Saintonge, the duke of Guise, who was soon to become famous. He was the queen of Scotland's brother, and was to negotiate the marriage of his niece Mary Stuart to the dauphin against the wishes of England. This match was to have serious consequences for domestic politics.

Things abroad were no better than at home. At the battle of Mühlberg in 1547 Charles V had succeeded in putting down the resistance of the Protestant Schmalkaldic League, and he was on the way to becoming the federator of Germany, which renewed the threat to the European balance.

Henry II. (Musée de Condé, Chantilly)

Diane de Poitiers. (School of Fontainebleau)

Remembering the harsh terms of the treaty of Madrid, Henry II hated Charles V, and his attitude towards him was to be adopted by his successors: 'Keep the affairs of Germany in hand, and cause them as much difficulty as possible.' The means had to be found to implement this policy, and Henry II hovered between several possibilities; finally he decided to invite Charles V to his coronation in his capacity as vassal of Flanders. The emperor, taking this as an insult, replied that if he took the trouble to come it would be at the head of a large army.

Montmorency and his Andelot nephews (of whom the most prominent was the future Admiral de Coligny) suggested negotiation. But the Guise clan were for reconquering the

Catherine de Medici by Clouet.

kingdom of Naples. They were supported by Catherine de Medici's Italian entourage, known as the *fuorusciti*.

To gain support the alliance with the Turks was strengthened; approaches were made to the Protestant princes of Germany; and military aid was given to Scotland in its struggle against England.

This Scottish intervention had a romantic outcome: the duke of Somerset, protector of England during the early reign of Edward VI, wanted to kidnap Mary Stuart to marry her to the future king of England, which would have brought about a true alliance between Scotland and England. But the success of the French troops in Scotland produced the opposite effect:

the heiress to the throne of Scotland was brought to France to continue her education, and, to satisfy the wishes of her Guise uncles, was engaged to the dauphin; the indemnity allowed for buying back Boulogne was reduced by half.

To strengthen defences to the east the alliance with the Swiss cantons was reinforced. The only danger now lay on the north-eastern frontiers, and it was to Henry II's credit that he provided for this. He had Maurice of Saxony conduct negotiations with the German princes to have him recognized as Vicar of the Empire. The result, which was confirmed at the treaty of Chambord (1552), was that the three bishoprics of Toul, Metz and Verdun were placed under the king of France's protection. Under the pretext that he was going to visit these towns, he handed over power to Catherine de Medici and set off for the Rhine at the head of an army.

The French king was well received in Lorraine, where Charles V was unpopular, and organized a regency in Nancy, where he arranged for the marriage of one of his daughters to the duke of Lorraine, who was still a minor. Then after travelling in the Rhine valley he returned to France without having fought a battle.

The centre of operations was elsewhere: Maurice of Saxony, at the head of the Protestant forces, crossed the Bavarian Alps and marched on Innsbruck, Charles V's seat. The emperor fled to avoid being taken prisoner by his vassal, and by the treaty of Passau he confirmed German liberties.

Henry II thought he had won, but he was deluding himself. Determined to take revenge for his humiliation, Charles V marched on Metz, where Francis of Guise immured himself. Montmorency established a second line of defence simultaneously in Champagne and in Picardy. Charles V conducted the siege of Metz in person, but Francis of Guise's heroic defence saved the place and won him an authority which he was soon to exercise.

But the emperor was not discouraged by his defeat at Metz, and he now took the offensive and defeated the French at Thérouanne in 1553. A front had been opened in Italy, and the defence of Siena has been immortalized by Montluc's *Commentaires*. The marshal of Termes, aided by the Berbers, occupied Corsica, while the marshal of Brissac seized Piedmont. All this confirmed

Charles V in his determination to retire from the world and to divide his estates.

Under the pressure of an English mediation Henry II signed a truce at Vaucelles in 1555; through it France kept Piedmont, her conquests in Montserrat and in Tuscany, and, most important, the three bishoprics.

Before retiring to the monastery of Yuste, Charles V took certain precautions: he handed over Austria to his brother Ferdinand, together with Bohemia and Hungary. His son Philip II, who had Spain, Flanders, the Netherlands and Franche-Comté, now posed an even greater threat to France because he had married the queen of England, Mary Tudor, which re-created, perhaps even more seriously, the dangers of the Hundred Years' War.

Moreover, the election of Cardinal Carafa as pope, under the name of Paul IV, made it clear that Italy would soon demand to be liberated; France was to be obliged to play a major role in this, and to wage war on one more front.

Since one party in France favoured war, a secret treaty was signed with the Holy See on the instigation of Francis of Guise, who still hoped to obtain the kingdom of Naples and to add to this the papal tiara for his brother Cardinal de Lorraine (1556).

Spain took the offensive on the Italian front: from Naples the duke of Alba occupied Anagni, and then Tivoli, right next to Rome.

Henry II had sent the duke of Guise to Italy with twelve thousand men; with such poor forces he was forced to retreat, but his troops made an impression in the sector in which Philip II was hoping to make his main effort. With fifty thousand men, swelled by an English contingent provided by Mary Tudor, Philip II instructed the duke of Savoy to lay siege to Saint-Quentin. Coligny managed to gain entry to organize the defence, and Montmorency tried to raise the blockade on the town from the south. On 10 August 1557, Montmorency clashed with the Spaniards and was taken prisoner. His troops scattered, leaving the road to Paris open. To commemorate this victory Philip II had the palace-monastery of the Escorial built.

But Philip II's army did not take advantage of its success. Henry II organized the defence of Paris, and while the Spaniards were wasting time with local victories, the king ordered the duke of

Guise to recapture Calais. The mission was a success and on 8 January 1558 the town of Calais, lost for 211 years, was returned to France. To mark this victory, which destroyed the last English enclave in France, Henry II ordered a solemn celebration of the marriage of the dauphin Francis to Mary Stuart.

While the war pursued its course, Charles V and Mary Tudor died, within days of each other. These two deaths hastened the peace, which was signed on 2 April 1559 at Cateau-Cambrésis. In order to keep the three bishoprics, France gave up all her conquests in Italy; and Elizabeth of France, Henry II's daughter, married the widower Philip II.

To celebrate this peace, Henry II organized a succession of festivals, and while watching a tournament he had his eye put out by Gabriel de Montgomery's lance. He died after ten days of terrible suffering, aged forty-one, and leaving France on the brink of a crisis in which she nearly perished.

ᖚᕝ FRANCIS II ᖚᕝ
(1559–1560)
AND MARY STUART

FRANCIS II'S REIGN was one of the shortest and most deplorable in the history of France. Henry II's death did not give rise to a regency, since Francis was fifteen at the time. But the new king seemed incapable of ruling. He was feeble in spirit, and had never shown any inclination to study because of his lack of concentration. He suffered constantly from the most atrocious headaches, and he probably had tuberculosis.

This sort of illness tends to excite sexual appetites, and there is no doubt that the new queen, the charming Mary Stuart, was a very sensual person. They had a frenzied sexual relationship which overwhelmed the king and hastened his early death.

Catherine de Medici would have liked to have a hand in the government, but Mary Stuart's domination of her husband made this impossible.

Under the queen's influence, Francis had Montmorency eliminated and replaced by her uncle Francis of Guise, and his brother Cardinal de Lorraine. Claiming that they were descended from Charlemagne, they considered themselves more worthy to exercise royal power.

The domestic situation had become very difficult as the result of religious strife. During the last days of Henry II's reign, the parliamentary adviser Anne du Bourg had dared to criticize the persecution of the Protestants. The king had him declared a heretic and con-demned him to be burnt at the stake. The cruelty of this treatment of a man of obvious probity was attributed, perhaps wrongly, to the Guises, who had opposed the leniency which would have been a wise political move.

There was general discontent, and a meeting of the Estates-General was called for in the hope that they would get rid of the Guises and hand over power to the princes of the blood, which would have pleased Catherine de Medici greatly. The candidate for the opposition was the prince of Condé, younger brother of Antoine, head of the house of Bourbon, who had become king of Navarre by his marriage to Joan d'Albret.

But the Estates-General were not called, and a conspiracy arose, led by an adventurer from Périgord, the Protestant La Renaudie. Having rounded up a fairly strong contingent of men, he was to seize Blois on 15 March 1560 and to impose the wishes of the conspirators on the king. But he was betrayed: one month before the date appointed, the Guises found out about the plot. Although they refused to take it seriously, they made the king leave Blois and installed him at the impregnable Château d'Amboise.

La Renaudie's lieutenants were foiled by a clever plot. Nevertheless there was an assault on the Château d'Amboise on 16 and 17 March 1560. The Guises used their artillery and the conspirators' forces scattered. La Renaudie was killed on 19 March, and many of the conspirators

The coronation of Francis II in 1559.

had their throats cut on the spot. The others, taken prisoner and given summary trials, were hanged from the castle battlements. It is said that Francis and Mary Stuart, together with the members of the court, took pleasure in gazing on the hanged men by torchlight.

In the king's eyes the most guilty party was the prince of Condé, whom he saw as the instigator of the plot. Despite this the prince had come to Amboise to insist that he had had nothing to do with it; then, realizing that they did not believe him, he fled. Catherine de Medici, sensing how unpopular the Guises were, had Michel de l'Hospital named chancellor,

which proved to be a good choice.

The chancellor and the queen agreed to call a meeting of the Estates-General, which had not met since Louis XII's time in 1506. The king called the meeting in the town of Orléans. Navarre and Condé were invited, and, despite the risks, they accepted. They had an icy reception from Francis II.

As king of Navarre, Antoine of Bourbon was inviolate. But the same did not go for his brother, and, on the instigation of the Guises, who hated the Bourbons, he was arrested in the middle of a session of the Estates. On the king's order he was tried and sentenced to death. But

Michel de l'Hospital, judging that the execution of a prince of the blood would be a tremendous risk, took advantage of the king's illness to repeal the execution.

The king's condition suddenly worsened; on 16 November 1560 he fainted and his headaches became so intolerable that he began to scream uninterruptedly. The doctors could do nothing for him, and on 5 December Francis II died of meningitis, following a suppurating inflamma-tion of his left ear, allied to adenoidal growths. His death seemed destined to overthrow the Guises, and opened the way for Catherine de Medici's regency, since the heir to the throne, the duke of Anjou, who was later to become Charles IX, had not yet reached the age of majority.

Condé escaped death and was set free, and Mary Stuart was taken back across the sea to meet her tragic destiny.

❧ CHARLES IX ❧
(1560–1574)

WHEN CHARLES IX BECAME KING he was only ten years old. The Venetian ambassador Michiele wrote that he was:

> ... an admirable child. He has ardour, generosity and goodness. He has a handsome face and particularly beautiful eyes, but a weak constitution. He eats and drinks little. He loves physical exercise, such as games of royal tennis and dressage, which are, no doubt, princely exercises, but far too violent for him. After the least exertion he has to rest for a long time. He takes no pleasure in studying; nevertheless he does it to please his mother.

Alas, the handsome youth depicted by the ambassador was destined to become one of France's most tragic kings, and his love for his mother, together with his own weakness, was to lead him to the most terrible actions.

The problem of the regency gave rise to a compromise: it could have been said to belong to the first prince of the blood, Antoine of Bourbon, king of Navarre, but the precedent of Blanche of Castile had been set. Catherine de Medici demanded the regency, but had to name Antoine of Bourbon lieutenant of the kingdom. The Catholic and Protestant factions were affronted from the start, and from this was to stem the bloody struggle which took the name of 'Wars of Religion'.

At first Catherine de Medici tried to reconcile the two religions. Some of the representatives of the Estates-General, which were still meeting, envisaged peace. By the Ordinance of Orléans (31 January 1561) the religious persecutions laid down by Henry II and expressed in the death of Anne du Bourg were stopped; and to confirm this the Protestant prisoners were set free.

Catherine de Medici and Michel de l'Hospital wanted to go further, and they organized a meeting of Protestant and Catholic theologians. This famous meeting was called the 'Colloquy of Poissy' (September–October 1561). The doctors of theology could only note with regret the differences between their religions, and they parted without reaching any agreement; but the Protestants profited from the meeting. This became evident at the Edict of Saint-Germain (17 January 1562) which confirmed the acquittal and gave the Protestants freedom of worship on certain conditions. These had been demanded by l'Hospital, who hoped thereby to disarm them. He reinforced his benevolent attitude by reducing the military budget, which was to deprive him of the necessary forces when trouble broke out.

The Catholics felt that too much had been granted to the Protestants, and the duke of Guise made preparations in the event of a civil war. The pretext for this was a massacre of Protestants who were worshipping at Vassy, perpetrated by men of the duke of Guise, who were travelling through the town (1 March 1562). The Protestants took this massacre for a declaration of war; they called on Queen Elizabeth I of England for help, and she signed a treaty with

leaders, since the duke of Guise was dead.
Catherine de Medici offered peace to Condé and
granted the Protestants freedom of worship, but
only in private. And then by the treaty of Troyes
(12 April 1564) they made peace with Elizabeth
of England.

Charles IX, who had become king in 1561,
now reached the age of legal majority. Accompanied
by his mother, he visited his kingdom,
taking with him the young Henry of Navarre,
Antoine of Bourbon's son. During this journey
the Edict of Roussillon was proclaimed, fixing
the beginning of the year at 1 January, and a
meeting took place in Bayonne with the queen of
Spain, the young king's sister.

This meeting sparked off religious strife again.
Civil war broke out anew as the result of a Protestant
plot called the 'tumult of Meaux', during
which the Protestants tried to kidnap the king.
He managed to escape in time, but the Protestant
forces tried to lay siege to Paris. The blockade
was lifted by the battle of Saint-Denis, in which
Montmorency was killed. A peace treaty was
signed at Longjumeau (23 March 1568). Michel
de l'Hospital, who had realized the Protestant
threat too late, resigned.

Shortly afterwards a third war broke out in
the west of France which was to last for two
years. The duke of Anjou, the future Henry III,
Charles IX's younger brother, showed great skill
as a soldier and won two important victories
during the year 1569, at Jarnac and Moncontour.
Condé, taken prisoner at Jarnac, was savagely
murdered by one of the duke of Anjou's captains
of the guard.

Coligny, now at the head of the troops, had
doubled back to La Rochelle, where he was
receiving reinforcements and subsidies from
England. Since he could obviously hold out for a
long time, Catherine de Medici offered him the
peace called the Queen's Peace, and it was signed
at Saint-Germain in 1570. This very liberal peace
treaty showed a general wish for reconciliation.
Charles IX, who had nothing against the Protestants,
granted them freedom of conscience and
of worship, and four strongholds. It has since
been considered that he created a bad precedent
by treating with rebels. He did more: he called
his cousin, the young Henry of Navarre, to court
with the intention of marrying him to his sister
Margaret of Valois, the future Queen Margot.

Charles IX. (French school, sixteenth century)

Condé and Coligny at Hampton Court on 20
September 1562, promising them troops and
subsidies in return for the transfer of Le Havre
and Calais. The Guises in turn asked Philip II for
help.

Civil war raged all over the country. The clash
of the troops led by the two chiefs took place at
Dreux on 19 December 1562. Condé and
Coligny were utterly defeated by Francis of
Guise, who then laid siege to Orléans, where he
was assassinated by a Protestant fanatic, Poltrot
de Méré. The lieutenant-general of the kingdom,
Antoine of Bourbon, had placed himself at the
head of the Protestant troops who were besieging
Rouen, but he was killed by an arrow from a
crossbow, and this deprived both parties of their

Charles IX had just married the charming Elizabeth of Austria and he hoped to marry his last brother, the duke of Alençon, to Queen Elizabeth Tudor. The queen only gave him a daughter, but Charles IX had an official favourite, Marie Touchet, by whom he had a bastard, the future count of Auvergne.

Leniency towards the Protestants went so far that Coligny returned to court. He soon became the sovereign's adviser and tried to impose his own policies on him. This caused serious complications. The naval victory of Lepanto (1571), in which Archduke John of Austria crushed the Turkish fleet, was a direct blow to French prestige, since France was the traditional ally of the Sublime Porte. Since he could not attack Austria, Coligny planned to attack Spain through the Netherlands, which were being racked by an atrocious religious persecution conducted by the duke of Alba. The feeble Charles IX let himself be persuaded by the Admiral, who assured him that this operation would appease his co-religionists, who he felt were on the brink of starting a fourth civil war. The Admiral expressed this point of view at the council of ministers in terms which greatly irritated Catherine de Medici.

This event took place in the first fortnight of August 1572, on the eve of the marriage of Henry of Navarre to Margaret of Valois. The wedding was celebrated on 18 August in the square of Notre Dame, because of the differences in their religions.

Then a council of ministers was held during which Catherine de Medici openly declared to Coligny that she preferred the risk of civil war to that of a foreign war. The Guises, informed of this, intervened personally. Under the pretext of avenging their father's death, they hired a paid assassin, Maurevert, to kill Coligny. On 20 August 1572, Maurevert shot at Coligny with a crossbow and wounded him in the arm, cutting off one of his fingers. Coligny took to his bed.

Charles IX was informed of this attack and visited Coligny. The Admiral explained the situation to him. Catherine de Medici, very worried about this interview, questioned her son about it. He admitted to his mother that Coligny had advised him to rule single-handed.

A fanatical power-seeker, the queen saw that she was lost. She used her maternal influence and

Elizabeth of Austria, wife of Charles IX, by Clouet.

her power over her weak son to convince him that the Huguenots were determined to overthrow the monarchy and that a plot was about to break out. Her logic was admirable: to get rid of Coligny, she had to side with the Catholics. But her methods were deplorable, since to achieve her aim she advised her son to have all the Protestants massacred.

The king took several hours to make up his mind, but finally yielded in the atmosphere of panic brought about by his mother's insistence. When it came to giving the order he hesitated. 'Are you afraid?' asked Catherine. And Charles IX made this famous and terrible reply: 'Kill them all, so that not one will be left to reproach me for it.'

The massacre of Saint Bartholomew's Day (24 August 1572), in which nearly 15,000 Protestants died.

The killing began at once under the order of Henry of Guise, Francis' brother. Admiral Coligny was attacked in his home, run through with swords and thrown out of the window.

The number of people massacred on this occasion is still disputed; it took the name of the day on which it took place, Saint Bartholomew (24 August 1572). It is generally agreed that during the massacre, which went on all over the country, at least fifteen thousand people were killed. The Catholic nations were not shocked, and Pope Gregory XIII sent his congratulations to the king of France.

The Massacre of Saint Bartholomew's Day sparked off a fourth religious war which consisted only of the sieges of La Rochelle and of Sancerre. The duke of Anjou, in charge of operations, was then elected king of Poland, in preference to Ivan the Terrible, and went to his new kingdom.

Since the Massacre, the king of Navarre had been practically a prisoner at court. He tried to escape with the help of La Môle and Coconnas, but the plot was discovered and its leaders beheaded. Charles IX acted with great cruelty in this affair: it seemed that since Saint Bartholomew's Day he had acquired a taste for blood.

The king's health now deteriorated rapidly. It was said that a mysterious illness 'made his body produce a constant, red perspiration'. He repeated to the old Huguenot nurse who watched by his bedside: 'Nurse, nurse, so much blood all around me! Is it that which I have shed?' This has led people to say that he died of remorse. But it seems that it was in fact tuberculosis which killed him on 31 May 1574.

ᘒ HENRY III ᘒ
(1574–1589)

HENRY III WAS ONE OF FRANCE'S STRANGEST SOVEREIGNS. His morals gave rise to much discussion and because he occasionally appeared in official ceremonies dressed as a woman he was nicknamed 'the king of Sodom'. Nevertheless he had several affairs with women and he was an excellent husband to Louise de Vaudemont. But his pampered physical appearance, his earrings and his entourage of attractive men called 'mignons' have left a blot on his memory.

He was a clever, brave man, and a good politician; he was also a man of culture, which he owed to his tutor, the famous Jacques Amyot. His taste for literature manifested itself in the founding of an academy, his love of bestowing honours by the creation in 1578 of the famous French order of chivalry, the Order of the Saint-Esprit. Very given to pomp, he laid down a strict etiquette which forbade anyone to approach him too closely. The only time he made an exception to this rule it proved fatal for him.

He had shown a taste for military matters at an early age, and he was only twenty at the victories of Jarnac and Moncontour. Elected king of Poland in 1573 in preference to Ivan the Terrible, he went to his new kingdom and there gained brief but useful political experience. He was informed of his brother's death on 15 June 1574 by a message from Catherine de Medici. Keeping the news a secret, he fled in the night of 15–16 June and headed for Vienna, where the emperor gave him a magnificent reception.

Even more splendid was the reception he received in Venice, where Henry III spent a week in dazzling festivals, and then, crossing Piedmont, he conceded to the duke of Savoy Pinerolo and Savigliano, fortresses which had been saved at Cateau-Cambrésis. These concessions, dictated by considerations of foreign policy, immediately made him unpopular, and this was made worse by the modifications in the order of precedence included in his reform of etiquette.

On 13 and 14 February the king was crowned and married. When the crown was placed on his head he complained that it hurt him, which was considered a bad omen.

The kingdom was not in a peaceful state, even though Catherine de Medici, changing direction

A celebration given by Henry III and Louise of Lorraine. (Flemish tapestry)

once again, had implemented a more tolerant religious policy. Even so a fifth war broke out under the direction of the prince of Condé, whose father had been assassinated at Jarnac. Having promised the three bishoprics to the German princes, he obtained twenty thousand mercenaries from them, which Henry of Guise dispersed at Dorinass, where he received the wound which won him his father's nickname of 'the Scarred'.

The duke of Alençon proposed himself as mediator, and the treaty which was completed by the Edict of Beaulieu was called the Peace of Monsieur (5 May 1576). This edict put a check on the Catholic party, since the Protestants were given back freedom of worship, their strongholds, and *chambres mi-parties* (i.e. special courts, composed of Catholic and Protestant judges, to judge cases involving Protestants). It seemed that the policies leading to the Saint Bartholomew's Day Massacre were being disavowed.

Henry III had to concede a great deal because he did not have the money to pay his troops. On the advice of the Guises he assembled the Estates-General at Blois. At this assembly a Catholic faction was constituted, the Holy League. And to prevent this League from posing a threat to royal authority, Henry III placed himself at its head at the opening of the Estates on 6 December 1576.

The meeting of the Estates was a stormy one, and its conclusion was the Edict of Poitiers, which was a financial decision fixing the course of the golden écu at three pounds and that of the silver franc at one pound; this stabilization remained in force until the end of the sixteenth century.

But since nothing had been decided on religious matters a sixth war broke out, limited to the Languedoc area. It was brought to an end by Damville, one of the Montmorencys, and concluded by the Peace of Bergerac (27 September 1557), which limited the concessions made by the Edict of Beaulieu.

As head of the League Henry III regained his authority. But he had new difficulties to face in the form of the escape of Henry of Navarre, who had managed to leave court in 1575, and, with the help of Agrippa d'Aubigné and Rosny, future duke of Sully, had reached first Saumur then Niort, a Protestant citadel. There he

renounced Catholicism, which he had been forced to embrace during the Saint Bartholomew's Day troubles, and became the true head of the Protestant faction.

He established himself at Nérac, and a truce seemed to have been established, but to consolidate his position as leader of the Protestants, Henry of Navarre went into action and took the head of operations in the seventh war of religion, which was known as the *Guerre des Amoureux*; it consisted only of the siege of Cahors, and of the establishment of a few Protestant strongholds: Sommières, Lunel and Aigues-Mortes. Condé, who had tried to rouse the north of France, had to flee to Germany.

Once again, Monsieur, the ex-duke of Alençon, who had become duke of Anjou, offered to mediate, and the peace signed at Fleix (26 November 1580) established a six-year truce, during which time there were no more wars. The duke of Anjou, who had fought his brother Henry III countless times, ended up by serving him and fought an operation for the king in the Netherlands, where he fell ill and died on 19 June 1584.

His death caused a serious dynastic crisis: Henry III had no children by Louise de Vaudémont and it seemed unlikely that he ever would have; in this case the crown would go to his cousin twenty times removed, who was also his brother-in-law, Henry of Navarre. Since it seemed impossible that France, a Catholic nation, should be ruled by a Protestant king, the duke of Guise put himself forward as pretender. In order to placate him, Henry III had to make concessions to the Catholics, and he ordered the dissolution of all the Protestant leagues by the Treaty of Nemours.

Pope Sixtus V, on his side, proclaimed by a virulent Bull the nullification of Henry of Navarre's rights to the throne since he was a Protestant. With this support, Henry of Guise also negotiated with Spain, to be sure of its help in securing the throne of France for himself at Henry III's death.

The execution of Mary Stuart by Elizabeth of England was used as the excuse for another war of religion, the eighth, which has been called the war of the three Henrys: Henry III, Henry of Guise, and Henry of Navarre. This war, which resembled in some ways the conflict between the

Henry de Guise.

Armagnacs and the Burgundians, was also that of the League against the Protestants and of Spain against England, since these states respectively supported the two parties.

The League, which had obtained strongholds from the king and had constituted itself as a state within a state, received a bloody defeat at Coutras (15 October 1587), where Henry of Navarre defeated one of its leaders, the duc de Joyeuse. On the other hand, Henry of Guise, fighting the eastern armies, had two important victories at Vimory and Auneau.

Though Henry III could see clearly that his successor would have to be Henry of Navarre, the League took over Paris, which placed the king in a tragic situation.

The duke of Guise, strengthened by his victories, invited the king to ally himself more

actively to the League and to confiscate all Protestants goods; the king did not take up this offer, and the League concluded from this that Henry III was in agreement with Henry of Navarre. Henceforth the League's only idea was to depose Henry III. To minimize this risk, the king forbade the duke of Guise from coming to Paris. But Henry of Guise braved this interdict, and on 9 May 1558 he made his entry into Paris, where he was received with enthusiasm. He went to the Louvre, where Henry III hurled reproaches at him. To protect himself the king brought a Swiss regiment and French guards to Paris. The League accused him of abusing his power, and barricades went up around the Louvre (12 May 1588). Henry III managed to escape and hid at Chartres.

But the war abroad was taking a new turn: the presence of Philip II's Invincible Armada around the French coast gave the League such support that the king felt some concessions would be necessary. He made these by the Edict of Alençon (19 July 1588), by which he stated that his successor would have to be a Catholic, and named the duke of Guise lieutenant-general of the kingdom.

The defeat of the Armada, which neutralized the threat from abroad, did not restore calm in France. The king resigned himself to calling a meeting of the Estates-General. It opened at the Château de Blois, and the deputies, led by the president of the nobility, Cossé-Brissac, made the king's unpopularity quite clear and demanded Huguenot blood. They were urged on by the duke of Guise, whose position as lieutenant-general had given him a dangerous authority. Henry III could see no way out but to eliminate such a dangerous rival. Unable to use legal means, he resorted to assassination.

On 23 December 1588 Henry of Guise, who had been summoned to the council, was struck down in a room in the Château de Blois by Henry III's personal guard. Contemplating his opponent's dead body the king is reputed to have said: 'He is even greater in death than he was in life.' And Catherine de Medici is supposed to have said: 'Well cut, my son, now you must sew it together again.' It was the last statement uttered by this terrible queen, who died a few days later on 5 January.

Henry of Guise's place was taken by his

brother, the duke of Mayenne, who, in collusion with the League, raised troops which caused a rising in part of France. Cardinal de Bourbon was proclaimed king under the name of Charles X, and the pope excommunicated Henry III for the murder of Cardinal de Lorraine, Henry of Guise's brother.

Like Charles VII before him, the king now only held the central and southern territories. At this point Henry III called on Henry of Navarre. At a conference held at Plessis-les-Tours on 2 April 1589, the two brothers-in-law embraced each other and joined forces to recapture Paris and subdue the north of the country. They laid siege to Paris and took up headquarters at Saint-Cloud.

The members of the League saw that they were lost. They delegated a fanatical monk, Jacques Clément, who, having received absolution in advance, asked for an audience with Henry III. Forgetting to stick to his own rules of etiquette, the king let the monk into his dressing room, and he was stabbed in the stomach (1 August 1589).

Jacques Clément was thrown out of the window, and his true motives remain shrouded in mystery.

On 2 August, the dying king sent for Henry of Navarre, begged him to become a Catholic, and said: 'My brother, I can feel clearly that it is for you to possess the right which I have worked for, to preserve for you what God has given you.' ('Mon frère, je le sens bien, c'est à vous de posséder le droit auquel j'ai travaillé pour vous conserver ce que Dieu vous a donné.') Then, exhausted by this final effort, Henry III died. With him expired the house of Valois, which had ruled France for 261 years.

The crown was to pass, not without difficulty, to Henry of Navarre, who was to place on the throne the dynasty of the Bourbons.

The meeting of the armies of Henry III and Henry of Navarre in 1558.

Henry IV. (Musée Condé, Chantilly)

Part Five

THE BOURBONS

1589~1792

Apogee of the nation

THE BOURBONS

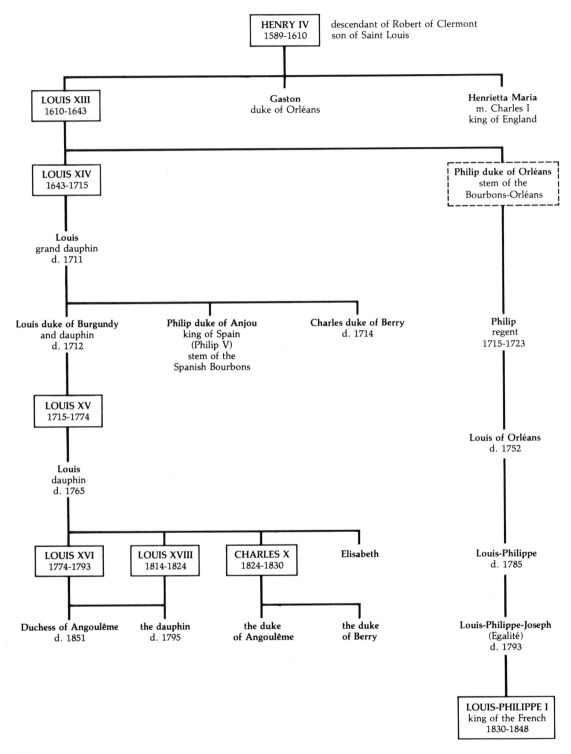

❧ HENRY IV ❧
(1589–1610)
MARGARET OF VALOIS
AND MARIA DE MEDICI

HENRY IV, 'THE ONLY KING REMEMBERED BY THE POOR', is the most popular figure in French history. He owes this partly to an extraordinary destiny which made him the restorer of unity in a France torn apart by religious wars, and to a private life so stormy that it earned him the nickname of 'Vert-Galant'.

He was born at Pau on 12 December 1553, the son of Antoine of Bourbon, head of the house of Bourbon, and of Joan d'Albret, the daughter of Henry II d'Albret (1517–55) and Margaret of Valois, sister of Francis I and heiress to the throne of Navarre. Nothing at his birth seemed to indicate that he would become king: Catherine de Medici and Henry II had four sons, and it seemed that the throne of France was secure for a long time to come.

It is worth, however, noting one curious dynastic particularity: if the Salic law had not been enforced at the death of John I, the young Henry of Navarre, descendant of Joan of Evreux, would have been more certainly heir to the throne of France by primogeniture than he was by his distant Bourbon descent, which made him a cousin of Henry III on the male side to only the twentieth degree. But the fact that they were also close cousins through the first Margaret of Valois, and brothers-in-law through Henry's marriage to Margaret of Valois, daughter of Catherine de Medici, certainly brought Henry closer to the kings and to life at court.

Henry IV's youth has become a legend: at the Château de Pau one can still see the huge tortoise-shell which was his cradle, and his peasant upbringing at the Château de Coaraze is famous. But it is not often mentioned that because his father, Antoine of Bourbon, was lieutenant-general of the kingdom at the death of Francis II, Henry came to Paris at an early age, and that Queen Catherine de Medici, perhaps with foresight, took him with her on her journey around France in 1564 and presented him to the famous visionary Nostradamus, who predicted that he would become king and that the queen mother's sons would not perpetuate their line.

The future king's adolescence was marked by religious rivalries, because his mother having started off as a Catholic, changed sides, became a proselyte of the Reformation, and made her husband and son join her in this.

To bring the king of Navarre closer to her own sons and to calm religious strife, Catherine de Medici arranged his marriage to her daughter Margaret of Valois, nicknamed 'Queen Margot' by posterity. Their wedding, as we have seen, was celebrated in the square of Notre-Dame, on the eve of the Massacre of Saint Bartholomew's Day. Henry of Navarre narrowly escaped the Massacre, was forced to renounce Protestantism and was held at court as a prisoner with his wife.

Their marriage was not a happy one. The future Henry IV was quite a handsome man, well-built, with square shoulders and a beard which was to acquire massive proportions. But he was slovenly in his appearance, rarely washed, and smelled strongly of goat. Margot on the contrary was very meticulous of her person, took great pains over her dress, was sensitive to smells, and loved court life. Moreover, she was in love with Henry of Guise and was probably his mistress. So the marriage soon fell apart, and both partners had affairs, of which the most famous were Margot's with La Môle, and the sharing of Madame de Sauves between Henry of Navarre and Henry of Guise.

Though she was frequently unfaithful to her husband, as he was to her, Margot was devoted to Henry and organized his flight in February 1576; he reached Saumur on the 26th, and then on 13 June 1576, at Niort, he solemnly renounced Catholicism, a gesture which was to have a profound effect not only on his own life, but on the history of France.

Being both king of Navarre and governor of Guyenne, Henry of Navarre established his court at Nérac, where Queen Margot joined him. Cohabitation did not prevent them from being unfaithful to each other, and Henry had notorious affairs with La Fosseuse and with Corisande d'Andouins, countess of Gramont.

These adventures were intermingled with the civil wars, of which one, called *des Amoureux*, was led by Henry of Navarre in person. He laid siege to Cahors on 29 May 1580 and revealed great military qualities there. The peace signed at Fleix in 1580 put an end to hostilities and there was peace for six years.

Pope Sixtus v contested this by a Bull saying that a Protestant could not become king of France.

This was also the opinion of Henry of Guise, who presented himself as pretender, as a descendant of the Carolingians. He roused Catholic support and the League promised the throne to Cardinal de Bourbon in the event of Henry III's death. The ensuing war proved successful for Henry of Navarre, who defeated the League led by the duc de Joyeuse at Coutras (15 October 1587). This was the first major Protestant victory over the League.

The chapter on Henry III has described the sequence of events, namely the barricades, the king's flight, the assassination of the duke of Guise, the reconciliation with Henry III at Plessis-les-Tours, and Henry III's tragic end at Saint-Cloud.

Henry IV's reign began on the day of Henry III's death, amid unprecedented difficulties, since France did not want a Protestant king. The problem of the succession, though solved on the dynastic level, was pursued on the religious level, and war broke out again.

This was a necessary war: Henry IV was the only man who could keep France together, and had he given up the country was in danger of being torn apart at the death of the puppet king Cardinal de Bourbon, or Charles X. Philip II of Spain was claiming the throne of France for his daughter Isabella, granddaughter of Henry II; the duke of Savoy, grandson of Francis I, was proposing himself as a candidate; and the house of Lorraine entered the running in the person of the duc de Mayenne, Henry of Guise's brother.

The only possible solution was for Henry to renounce Protestantism straight away. He felt it ran contrary to his honour and to his religion to do so immediately, but on 4 August 1589 he proclaimed liberty of conscience, which only won to his side three provinces: Champagne, Picardy, and the Île de France, Paris excepted.

The reconquest of the kingdom was to take place on two levels: militarily on national territory, and diplomatically by international agreements. Being an absolute believer in unity, Henry IV was determined to become master of the whole territory.

Because of his Protestant connections with Queen Elizabeth of England, it seemed logical to

Henry IV at the battle of Ivry, 1590.

But in June 1584 the duke of Anjou died, and this was to have great importance for the destiny of the king of Navarre. If Henry III died childless, which seemed almost certain, Henry of Navarre necessarily became heir to the throne.

ally himself to her, which implied conquering a port in the north. This explains why the first battle took place near Dieppe, where he defeated the duke of Mayenne at Arques on 21 September 1589. Taking advantage of this, and supplied with reinforcements by the English, he marched on Paris and seized the faubourgs of the left bank. Then, faced by a renewed offensive from Mayenne, he retired and went to make sure of the Loire provinces which offered him their allegiance.

Thus refortified he fought Mayenne and his Spanish troops at Ivry near Evreux on 13 and 14 February 1590. It was during this famous battle that he pronounced the words, 'Follow my white plumes, you will always see them on the road to honour.' He also added the famous comment to his faithful friend, the brave Crillon: 'Go and hang yourself, we have had a battle and you weren't there.'

Having opened the road to Paris by this battle, Henry IV laid siege to the capital for a second time. Famine had almost overcome the resistance, when the troops of the duke of Parma, Alexander Farnese, managed to break the blockade on the town. Henry IV was forced to lift the siege, though never losing sight of the fact that without Paris there was no possessing France.

In 1591, the king proclaimed the Edict of Mantes, which repealed all measures of intolerance. The death of Cardinal de Bourbon and the risk of dismembering the country were causing many Catholics to think twice: they did not want the duke of Mayenne as king, and they were prepared to rally round the legitimate heir to the throne if he returned to the Catholic faith.

The prevailing regime in Paris, the Committee of Sixteen, in effect a partisan oligarchy, ruled by terror and indulged in such excesses that Mayenne carried out a sort of coup d'état and hanged its principal members. But the capital kept a Spanish garrison, which grated against the latent patriotism. To get out of this impasse, the League called a meeting of the Estates-General with the mission of electing a king.

At this point, Farnese died and Henry IV seized Rouen. In this strong position, he seized the opportunity offered to him by the meeting of the Estates-General. At the conference of Suresnes on 16 May 1593, the king proclaimed his rights and declared himself ready to be converted, a declaration which aroused a deep-seated movement of public approval. The Parlement came to its senses and bravely indicated to Mayenne that the kingdom could no longer be occupied by foreigners.

To save time, Henry IV opened negotiations with the episcopacy: for appearances' sake he wanted to receive instruction in the Catholic religion before officially adopting it. He was hastily given lessons in the catechism, and on 25 July 1593, in the basilica of Saint-Denis, he officially renounced Protestantism. Legend has it that at that moment he said to his mistress of the day, the beautiful Gabrielle d'Estrées: 'Paris is surely worth a Mass.'

The League did not submit immediately but Henry IV, who had been crowned at Chartres on 15 February 1594, took a firm line, since he was now king in every respect. Harsh negotiations were opened with the League, which split into factions. The more intransigent retired with Mayenne, while those who had conceded under pressure from the governor, Cossé-Brissac, opened the gates of the capital, into which the king made his solemn entry on 22 March 1594, while the Spanish garrison withdrew in good order.

The immense success symbolized by the submission of Paris did not put an immediate end to the war. There was a military confrontation with the Spaniards at Fontaine-Française on 5 June 1595. Although Henry IV won an uncontested victory there, there were still three years of hostilities and varying fortunes ahead, before peace with Spain was agreed by the treaty of Vervins on 2 May 1598. The terms of this treaty were similar to those of the treaty of Cateau-Cambrésis, but Holland was separated from the Netherlands, which seemed to diminish the threat from the northern frontier.

It was a regrettable fact that forty years of civil war had caused a stagnation of France's foreign policy and interrupted its growth. But internal peace, in consequence of Henry IV's conversion, had become possible, and it was to be the king's task and the glory of his reign.

The first thing to deal with was to provide a statute by which religious persecution would be definitively ended. Reconciliation with both Catholics and Protestants was necessary to achieve this, since Henry IV, though converted,

The proclamation of the Edict of Nantes, 23 February 1598.

had become somewhat suspect to both sides because of his numerous abjurations.

Of the two, reconciliation with the Catholics was the easier to obtain. The Papacy, which saw in France an excellent ally, almost took the first steps towards it. On 17 September 1595 Pope Clement VIII, at the request of Cardinals d'Ossat and du Perron, lifted the excommunication on Henry IV.

The heads of the League, who no longer had any valid excuse not to ally themselves to him, submitted, following the example of Mayenne, whom the king received with open arms, remembering that the last of the Guises had also fought for the unity of the territory. Following their leader's example, the last members of the League gradually submitted; the last to do so was the duke of Mercoeur, who, as a token of faith, agreed to marry his daughter to César de Vendôme, bastard son of Henry IV and Gabrielle d'Estrées.

Agreement with the Protestants was much harder to reach, as the Catholics remained on the defensive about them.

In 1595 Henry IV made a memorable speech before the Assembly of notables at Rouen, where, with great skill, he proclaimed himself to be the liberator and restorer of France, asking his faithful subjects to help him to accomplish his immense task, and going as far as asking for their advice in order to achieve this. Despite this it took a long time to achieve religious peace, and there was sporadic local skirmishing. Conferences were organized for representatives of the two religions; the most important of these took place at Loudun in 1596 and at Chatellerault in 1597.

As a result of these conferences it was realized that the only solution was the recognition of a Protestant state within an officially Catholic France. But in order for this difficult recognition to be made, it was vital that the Protestant faction should remain an associate of the Catholic faction.

But though Henry IV realized this perfectly well, he was wise enough not to make it explicit for fear of starting another civil war. The Edict of Nantes (13 April 1598), which gave an

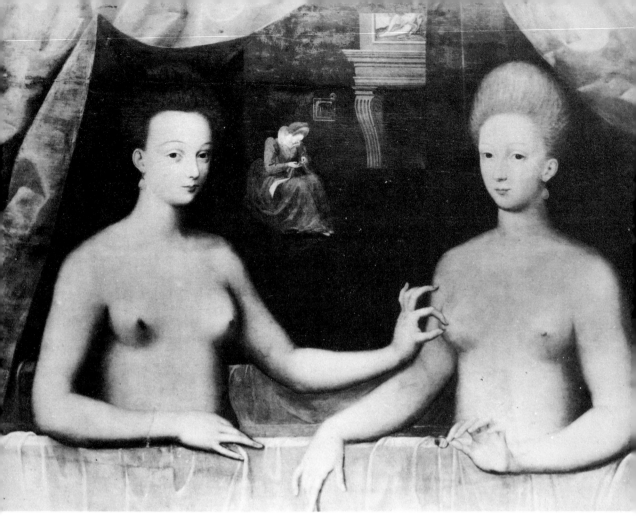

Gabrielle d'Estrées and her sister, the Marquise de Villars.
(School of Fontainebleau, about 1594)

apparently severe ruling on the Protestants, in fact conceded to them many advantages: freedom of worship, strongholds, *chambres-mi-parties*. Fully aware of this subterfuge, the Parlement held back from registering the edict, but Henry IV held firm and insisted on being obeyed.

With the religious problem solved, another arose, the dynastic problem. Though Henry IV already had several bastards, he had no legitimate heir. His marriage with Queen Margot had not been dissolved: she lived at the Château d'Usson in Auvergne, and consoled herself over being abandoned by having numerous adventures.

Henry IV, who was living with his beautiful mistress Gabrielle d'Estrées as man and wife, hoped to legitimize their son, the duke of Vendôme, and decided to ask the pope to annul his marriage so that he could marry Gabrielle. Pope Clement VIII, who would have agreed had it been a question of state, refused for a mere sexual whim. Henry IV was furious, and even more so because Gabrielle was pregnant for a second time.

Preparations were made for their wedding; the king placed a large diamond ring on her finger and she dared say in public: 'Only God or the king's death can put an end to my good luck.' A few days after tempting fate in this way, Gabrielle suffered an attack of eclampsia and gave birth to a still-born son. The following day, 10 April 1599, she died in terrible pain.

Henry IV was deeply grieved, especially since there was a rumour, probably a true one, that she had been poisoned. The king's wise minister Sully judged that the time was ripe to make the king marry again; and he had his sights fixed on a Florentine princess, Maria de Medici. Although the king had already found new mistresses, he did not object to this plan, and the pope was asked to pronounce the annulment of his marriage to Queen Margot.

Before the annulment was pronounced the king had fallen under the spell of a very dangerous woman, Henriette de Balzac d'Entragues, the daughter of Marie Touchet, ex-mistress of Charles IX. She was a twenty-year-old brunette 'beautiful enough to bring damnation to men'. She yielded to the king for 100,000 écus, and managed to obtain from him a written promise of marriage. Sully tore up this contract, but the king wrote it again.

While this shameful farce was going on, an embassy sent to Rome under Sillery was obtaining the annulment of the king's marriage to Queen Margot, for reasons of state (17 December 1599). Sully held out for the Florentine marriage, and the king resigned himself to it, but he did not give up his mistress, by whom he had children at the same time as with the queen. He was also unfaithful to both of them, filling the court with bastards by various women, whom he brought up with his own children. Subsequently Henriette, a jealous and intriguing woman, was mixed up in plots to kill the king, and she had to be exiled from court after a silent reign which lasted ten years.

The marriage by proxy to Maria de Medici was fixed for 15 July 1600. A latent dispute with Savoy enabled the king to go south to meet his future wife. Before his departure Henriette d'Entragues gave birth to a son who lived for only a few hours. Considering himself freed from his promise of marriage to her, the king prepared to meet his new wife.

Maria de Medici landed at Marseilles on 3 November 1600. Henriette d'Entragues, who had followed the king, refused to leave him when the queen arrived at Lyons on 9 December. Using the excuse that he was already married to her by proxy, the king took the new queen to bed immediately, to Henriette's great rage. The marriage was celebrated at Saint-Jean de Lyon on 17 December 1600. Though Maria de Medici, 'the fat banker', was no beauty, she had many

children by the king, and the dynastic problem was solved as soon as 1601 by the birth of a son, Louis, the future Louis XIII.

During their stay in Lyons, Sully had solved the difficulties with Savoy. In return for the marquisate of Saluzzo, the duke of Savoy conceded Dombes, Bugey and Valromey to France; the Rhône became the frontier for the area around Lyons as far as Geneva.

The ten last years of Henry IV's life, though full of scandalous sexual adventures, were beneficial to the nation and to the state. The monarchy received the institutions which it kept until the Revolution, government took on a more absolute tone, reference to the Estates-General was not deemed compulsory, and the king more readily called simple assemblies of notables, which were much easier to manipulate.

On the whole Henry IV was hostile to municipal administrations, because he felt they represented a danger to the state. He therefore tended to centralize authority more and more. At a high level, problems were put to the Conseil des Affaires, which was under the Conseil d'Etat, which was set going by the Conseil des Finances. Ministers became the virtual heads of royal administration, and since there were only four of them, it was easy for the king to keep an eye on their activities.

Governors were named to represent royal authority in the provinces, and they were assisted by the Corps des Intendants, which had been temporary, but now became permanent. Henceforth the crown had a way of controlling and surveying local privileges, which in theory made it possible to neutralize revolts at an earlier stage.

Henry IV's financial policy, which was destined to revive a country ruined by civil wars, remains one of the most interesting aspects of his reign. To raise funds, the king put offices on sale, and revoked the former right to bequeath an official post to a chosen successor, making it subject to the payment of a yearly tax called the 'paulette', evaluated at one sixtieth of the purchase price of the office. This move, which made the magistrature into an independent caste, was to have heavy consequences in the eighteenth century, and the state was to perish because of it.

Though well versed in governmental matters and having a natural instinct for authority,

Henry iv was totally ignorant when it came to financial administration, and he had a tendency to approve of any measure which permitted him to satisfy his own expensive whims.

In financial matters he relied entirely upon his faithful minister Sully. Sully had found the treasury milked dry by the civil wars, and, worse still, had discovered that the revenue from the royal domain was heavily committed in advance. The fact was that returns amounted to 25 millions per year, and liabilities to 340 millions. Sully set about righting this disastrous situation. He had no hesitation in paying off the public debt by falsely devaluing the currency, causing it to lose a third of its value, increasing indirect taxation, and taxing the clergy.

These joint measures bore fruit: the State's resources grew from 25 to 34 millions of livres and the debt was reduced by thirty per cent between 1600 and 1610.

However, Sully's claim to fame was not this, but his idea of promoting agriculture. His was the famous statement: 'Farming and raising livestock are the two breasts from which France feeds, and her true Peruvian mines and treasures.' ('Labourage et pastourage sont les deux mamelles dont la France est alimentée et ses vrais mines et trésors du Pérou.') If one adds to this Henry iv's apocryphal comment about having 'a chicken in the pot every Sunday' ('la poule au pot tous les dimanches'), it is easy to understand how this economically difficult period, during which ruined France was rebuilt, has been remembered as a time of ease and happiness: the newly-won peace seemed to be the greatest bonus.

Sully, advised by Laffemas, promoted not only agriculture but also the manufacture of mirrors, glass and carpets. The famous factory of La Savonnerie owes its existence to him.

Though he was responsible for the building of the Place des Vosges in Paris, the Pont-Neuf and the Palais du Luxembourg, Henry iv was not a great builder. But he was an experienced colonialist, and his sending of Samuel Champlain to Canada was followed by the founding of Quebec. Such a tremendous achievement should have won him respect and put a stop to the intrigues and plots. But this was not the case, and the climate remained stormy. A dozen attempts were made on Henry iv's life, of which the last was fatal, and there were many conspiracies.

The most famous of these was undoubtedly led by his friend the duke of Biron, who, as governor of Burgundy, allied himself to Henriette d'Entragues to negotiate with the duke of Savoy, who was then on bad terms with France. Henry iv was prepared to pardon his old friend, but Sully demanded his head. Biron was tried by the Parlement and condemned to death; he refused to ask for mercy and Henry iv let him be beheaded.

Henry iv led such a dissolute private life while on the throne that his popularity with the masses often waned. His end was precipitated by a final sexual whim. During a presentation at court, he had fallen madly in love with one of the queen's maids of honour, the young Charlotte of Montmorency, who was just fifteen. The king was more than fifty-five, but he behaved like a young lover of twenty. He had the idea of marrying Charlotte to the prince of Condé, who had a reputation for lax morals, intending to take advantage of this situation to make Charlotte his mistress. But he was disappointed in this, as the prince of Condé, revealing himself to be jealous despite his habits, snatched his young bride from under the king's nose and took her to Belgium.

Public opinion insinuated, with only a modicum of truth, that Henry was prepared to go to war to get Charlotte back. The truth was more complicated, and has to do with the general background of foreign policy. While conciliating Spain, Henry iv was worried about Austria, whom he saw as a future enemy in war. According to Sully's memoirs, the king was working on a project called 'the Grand Design', which aimed to form a sort of League of Nations to conciliate when there was a danger of war, and to see to it that the imperial crown should not be the sole prerogative of one house. The entire project may have been an invention, but the fear of Austria was real, and the king was determined to limit any imperial encroachments.

An event of this nature took place at the beginning of 1610. At the death of the sovereign of Cleves and Jülich, who was heirless, Emperor Rudolf ii appropriated his properties near the eastern French marches. Without hesitation, Henry iv undertook a military expedition to reconquer the two duchies. He equipped three armies, and gave one to Marshal Lesdiguières to fight in Italy and the second to La Force to invade

The assassination of Henry IV by Ravaillac, 1610.

Spain. The king himself commanded the third, which headed for the Netherlands. This gave rise to rumours that he was waging war to recover Charlotte of Montmorency. Expecting to be away for a long time, the king decided to make Maria de Medici regent; the consecration of the queen was fixed for 13 May 1610.

Chronicles and testimonials of the time reveal that Europe was severely disturbed by the news of the impending war. Some preachers attacked Henry IV in strong terms, accusing him of stirring up trouble and protecting the countries upholding the Reformation. These diatribes strongly influenced certain fanatical spirits.

The day after the queen's coronation at Saint-Denis, the king went to visit Sully, who was ill at his quarters in the Arsenal. The royal carriage was open, and it is said that the king got into it apprehensively, surrounded by La Force, Montbazon and Epernon. A jam, possibly contrived, brought the coach to a halt in the narrow rue de la Ferronnerie, and a man who had been following the carriage for some time leapt onto it and stabbed the king twice with a dagger. Henry IV bled to death almost immediately

(14 May 1610).

The murderer's name was François Ravaillac. He was a teacher from near Angoulême whose head had been turned by the sermons of fanatical preachers, and who hoped, by murdering the king, to prevent the war and defend the Catholic faith. He died that month, quartered, after a speedy trial which came nowhere near uncovering the truth. It has since been thought that the king may have been the victim of a plot fomented by members of the League.

The sovereign's body was returned to the Louvre.

'The king is dead,' said Maria de Medici to Chancellor Sillery.

'Madam, in France kings do not die,' he answered sharply, pointing to the dauphin.

Though often criticized during his lifetime, Henry IV was universally mourned at his death. Shortly before being assassinated he had said: 'They will see what I was worth when I am gone.' His prophecy came true, and his reign of reconstruction and able administration was followed by an incredible period of disorder, under the regency of Maria de Medici.

✄ LOUIS XIII ✄
(1610–1643)
AND ANNE OF AUSTRIA

KING LOUIS XIII WAS A STRANGE FIGURE. As a child he had been sulky, morose, secretive and shy. But he was like a smouldering fire, and at the age of sixteen he revealed himself to have a very violent personality, which made of him an absolute monarch. His character is well summed up by one of his pronouncements: when he was asked to pardon Montmorency, he replied: 'A king should not have the same feelings as a private man.'

The strangest aspect of Louis XIII was his love life. Some historians have claimed that he was a homosexual. It seems more likely that he was simply not a very physical person; his only favourites were platonic ones. His marriage to Anne of Austria remained unconsummated for four years, and they only had children after being married for twenty years. This strange person would have left little mark on history had he not been served for about twenty years by one of the greatest politicians in world history, Cardinal Richelieu.

Louis XIII's youth, during the regency of his mother, Maria de Medici, was a particularly sad one; the young king was virtually abandoned. His mother handed over power entirely to the husband of her foster-sister, Leonora Galigaï; he was an Italian adventurer, a handsome man, able and cunning, called Concini. The queen's favour made him Marshal d'Ancre, even though he had never borne arms.

The political situation became very difficult after Henry IV's death. Deciding not to abandon the expected war completely, the queen and Concini swiftly had Juliers occupied, and the town was handed over to the German princes, to the annoyance of Emperor Rudolf. To conciliate Spain, they negotiated the marriage of the Infanta Anne of Austria to the young king Louis XIII.

Anne of Austria was one of France's most interesting queens: virtually ignored by her husband, she adopted a reserved and dignified bearing; it is sometimes claimed that the duke of

Buckingham was in love with her, but their relationship, if there was one, was platonic. By chance, one stormy night in 1637, Anne of Austria was visited by her husband in bed. The result was the birth, in 1638, of the future Louis XIV, to be followed two years later by the birth of the duke of Orléans. There were some strange rumours about these births. Widowed at the age of forty, Anne of Austria was an able regent, with the help of Cardinal Mazarin. There were even unproven rumours that they were secretly married. Hers was, evidently, a far from ordinary life.

But the queen played no role in Louis XIII's minority, nor did the king. Sully, who had argued against the marriage plans for the king, was not listened to, and resigned at the beginning of 1611. Henceforth Concini was master of French politics.

The situation was a difficult one, since the Protestant faction, which had a hundred strongholds in France, had an army more powerful than the royal army. Another danger presented itself in the form of the princes and grandees, who formed a league led by Mayenne and Vendôme, ready to wage war against the crown. The sly Concini negotiated with them, and the princes were granted pensions, which put the treasury in difficulties.

To raise money and strengthen their own position the princes demanded a meeting of the Estates-General. The queen and Concini were obliged to agree. This meeting of the Estates, in 1614, was the last before that of 1789. They revealed the conflict between the three orders, and the privileged classes were offended by the egalitarian pretensions of the Third Estate. However, the principle of monarchy was not questioned, and since the deputies had no reforms to propose, the crown triumphed.

The most striking feature of this meeting was the appearance of a vitally important ecclesiastical figure, Armand du Plessis de Richelieu, the future cardinal. The queen introduced him into

the Council of State, and he and Concini dismissed Henry IV's old ministers, had Condé imprisoned, and pacified the Protestants.

Louis XIII was watching all this from the shadows and, probably encouraged by his grand falconer, Charles d'Albert de Luynes, he ordered the captain of the Guard, Vitry, to arrest Concini. When Concini resisted, he was killed (24 April 1617). His wife was condemned to death as a witch, and the regent was removed from power.

'Now I am king,' said Louis XIII. He dismissed Richelieu, recalled his father's ministers, and handed over real power to Luynes, whom he made a duke and high constable. Luynes, a poor politician, got on the wrong side of Richelieu and Maria de Medici. The result was that mother and son took up arms against each other, and Richelieu saved the situation by the treaty of Ponts-de-Cé (August 1620).

Difficulties arose abroad: Ferdinand of Styria, elected emperor, announced that he could not renounce the throne of Bohemia, and called on Catholic France for solidarity (1619). This was quite a problem for Louis XIII, since France had to choose between helping Austria, and a Protestant victory in Germany. Luynes advised mediation. The emperor defeated his enemies at the battle of the White Mountain (8 November 1620) and the house of Austria became a grave danger.

Louis XIII therefore became the defender of the Catholic cause, and proceeded to attack the Protestant faction at home. This caused a new war of religion which, badly led by Luynes, resulted in a defeat at Montauban. The Protestants, under the leadership of the duc de Rohan, a relative of Sully, ravaged Languedoc, and the king was forced to lay siege to Montpellier. Luynes died of scarlet fever, and the king signed the treaty of Montpellier (18 October 1622), by which Protestants were forbidden to hold political assemblies.

But this did not solve France's foreign problems, since the emperor, to be sure of having links with his possessions in Italy, occupied the Valtellina, a deep valley of the Adda, which was a dependancy of the Swiss canton of Grisons, a Protestant fief. This caused a highly complex conflict. Without Luynes' help, and faced with an internal situation as difficult as that abroad,

Louis XIII was reduced to calling to the ministry his mother's favourite Richelieu, whom she had just had appointed cardinal through her Italian connections.

Richelieu's entry into the ministry on 29 April 1624 was one of the crucial events in the history of France, and it turned Louis XIII's reign into a truly great one politically. The situation was virtually unique in the history of France: his was a dictatorship exercised by a first minister with the enforced agreement of the king, who stood back and accepted the design and wishes of his minister whenever he thought the nation's interests demanded it.

Born in 1585 to a noble family of Poitou, Richelieu was obliged by his family to enter Holy Orders. In 1606, at the age of twenty-one, he was made bishop of Luçon by Henry IV but, convinced that a great destiny lay ahead of him, he made every effort possible to leave this miserable bishopric. At the Estates-General of 1614 he revealed his true personality, which was henceforth to grow and grow.

A convinced Christian and a strict priest, Richelieu had greatly impressed the Sorbonne by his theological theses, and was now to astound France with his political expertise. Though he used every means possible, even the most dubious, to attain power, he exercised it with an extraordinary feeling for affairs of state.

His programme is well known, though it was in fact only his political testament. It consisted of three points; to ruin the Huguenot party, to bring down the pretensions of the great nobles, and to humble the house of Austria. This programme was carried out point by point.

Priority was given to putting the great nobles in their place, as this facilitated government action. Richelieu began by ousting from the Council all the ministers who stood in his way; he had the superintendent of finances, La Vieuville, arrested, accusing him of embezzlement, and dismissed Sillery, which won him permanent hatred.

Louis XIII's second-rate and jealous younger brother, Gaston of Orléans, immediately rose up against Richelieu, and was the spirit behind the conspiracies aiming to discredit the cardinal. In 1626, urged on by César de Vendôme, who wanted to make Brittany an independent fief once again, he fomented a conspiracy in which

Anne of Austria, wife of Louis XIII, by Rubens.

Anne of Austria was possibly involved. The conspiracy was brought to light, and Richelieu proved merciless: Marshal d'Ornano was imprisoned in the Bastille; the comte de Chalais, one of the Talleyrand family, who was deeply implicated in the affair, was tortured and confessed. He was condemned to death and executed in a particularly atrocious way.

Another execution caused even more of a stir, that of the count of Montmorency-Bouteville, who was beheaded on 22 June 1627 for having infringed the edict forbidding duels. Louis XIII refused him a pardon, ostensibly opting to respect the law.

Great men began to tremble: to keep them in check, Richelieu ordered the dismantling of all private fortresses suspected of harbouring pockets of resistance. This decision, though governmentally a wise one, was a bad one environmentally, since it deprived France of some admirable buildings.

Having put the yoke upon the great nobles and checked them for the moment, Richelieu came to the second point of his programme, which was to reduce the power of the Protestants; his idea was to leave them freedom of worship, but to deprive them of military power. This was a far-reaching plan which was not judged fairly by the majority of the French people: the Counter Reformation was in full swing, and public opinion attached more importance to fighting the schism than to neutralizing one faction within the state. Events in the future, however, were to prove that Richelieu had read the situation aright, and that his policy was a wise one.

The Protestants were still receiving help from England, even though Charles I had married Louis XIII's sister, Henrietta Maria. The duke of Buckingham landed English forces on the Ile de Ré in 1627, and organized a link with the Protestant stronghold of La Rochelle, whose authorities without doubt were planning to establish a Protestant republic in the old English territories. This republic, consisting at least of Aunis and Saintonge, was to be put in the care of the duc de Rohan.

The danger seemed so great that Richelieu decided on civil war. From October 1627 to October 1628 there took place the famous siege of La Rochelle. After capturing the town and

dismantling its fortifications, Richelieu attacked a Protestant bastion in the Cévennes.

A truce, not a peace treaty, was signed at Alais on 28 June 1629. It re-established the Edict of Nantes as regarded freedom of worship, but abolished the strongholds, which put an end to the internal political power of the followers of the Reformation.

On returning from this expedition, Richelieu personally took Montauban, the last Protestant citadel (20 August 1629).

As he promised the king, Richelieu had managed to 'remove the faction from the midst of his subjects; the rest was a task which would have to come from Heaven, and no violence should be used other than leading a good life and setting a good example'.

The most remarkable aspect of Louis XIII's and Richelieu's policies seems to have been the judicious way in which the struggle against Austria was conducted. The Thirty Years' War was raging in Europe, but Richelieu wisely kept out of it, refraining from intervening until the opportune moment when the exhaustion of the combatants would give him the advantage.

It was necessary, however, to have certain guarantees before entering the fray. One of these was the expedition against Piedmont: it ended with the occupation of Pinerolo and Saluzzo, which fell easily after Montmorency's victory at Veillan (10 July 1630). Casale was then besieged: at this point an Italian horseman rushed out between the lines and demanded that hostilities cease, as a peace had just been signed at Regensburg; he was none other than Jules Mazarin, the future first minister.

Louis XIII's health had been badly affected by the rigours of the campaign. On his return he had to take to his bed at Lyons, and it seemed he was dying. Maria de Medici and Anne of Austria came to him, complained about Richelieu's excessive power, demanded that he be dismissed. The cardinal was informed of this and discovered, to his dismay, that if the king died he would be imprisoned by Maria de Medici. His character was such that he put a good face on it, but his standing was seriously undermined, and the great nobles, led by Gaston of Orléans, joined together against him.

Maria de Medici judged that the moment had come for her triumph. On 10 November 1630

Portrait of Richelieu by Philippe de Champaigne.

The siege of La Rochelle (1627–8).

she invited her son to come and see her, and demanded that the cardinal be dismissed. Richelieu, informed of this by his *éminence grise*, the famous Father Joseph, came to the Petit-Luxembourg, the queen mother's residence, and dared to enter the room in which he was being attacked. When Maria de Medici saw him, she hurled insults at him and thought she had won the day.

Richelieu did not give up. He came back to see the king, and spoke to him so cleverly that he won back all his confidence, and regained all his former authority. This was the famous Day of the Dupes, which resulted in the queen mother being exiled and severe measures being taken against the grandees: Gaston of Orléans was accused of *lèse-majesté* and had to take refuge at Blois, the duke of Guise was sent into exile, and Marshal Bassompierre was imprisoned together with Marshal de Marillac, who was later beheaded.

The cardinal thought that these measures would settle the great nobles for good, but he was wrong. Gaston of Orléans, furious, called on Henry de Montmorency to avenge the offence that had been done to him. Montmorency, the governor of Languedoc, who for financial reasons was in open conflict with Richelieu, rallied some of the southern nobility and occupied the territory from the Rhône to the Garonne. He had overestimated his own forces: they were defeated by royalist forces at Castelnaudary (1 September 1632).

Montmorency was taken prisoner, condemned to death, and executed in the courtyard of the Capitol at Toulouse. Louis XIII refused to grant him pardon, saying severely: 'One should not pity a man who is about to suffer his punishment, one should only pity him for having deserved it.'

His was not the last attempt by the great nobles, who were only finally defeated during the revolt of the count of Soissons. He won a military battle at La Marfée in 1636, but was killed in the battle, which put an end to these problems.

It is fair to wonder, in the face of all these revolts on the part of the nobility, whether wrong was really all on one side, and whether Richelieu may not have been too harsh in putting down a class which represented the backbone of the nation. Some historians claim that Richelieu's fight against the high nobility was one of the distant causes of the Revolution. But it could be answered that threats from abroad called for absolute unity at home.

Richelieu did not merely observe the course of the Thirty Years War: once he had regained his authority in 1630, he took part in it on a diplomatic level.

The emperor had put his operations in the charge of a famous *condottiere*, Wallenstein, and his military talents almost brought about German unity at the expense of the Habsburgs. The emperor felt strong enough to demand, at the treaty of Regensburg, that his son should be named king of the Romans (1630).

Richelieu sent Father Joseph on a mission: he demanded that Wallenstein be dismissed, and that the nomination of the king of the Romans should be overruled. Moreover, Richelieu went as far as to sign an alliance with the champion of the Protestant cause, Gustavus Adolphus, king of Sweden. He entered the war, but was killed at the victory of Lützen (16 November 1632). The Swedes were defeated at Nördlingen (1634), and the German princes resigned themselves to peace.

If it was signed, France would be in the greatest danger from Austria. To avoid this, Richelieu had Louis XIII declare war on the king of Spain, who supported the Empire. French Catholics found themselves obliged to fight for the victory of the Protestant princes.

This bold policy was not a success to begin with. In 1636 the Spanish crossed their northern frontier, seized the citadel of Corbie, and sent scouts towards Paris. Public opinion turned against the cardinal, who once again faced it. He gathered together a powerful army, and put it under Marshal de la Force, who, accompanied by the king, managed to recapture Corbie. But this success did not put an end to hostilities, which were to continue for more than ten years. The siege of Arras (June–August 1640) and the taking of Breisach allowed the French to maintain their forces along the Rhine. There was also a campaign in Piedmont.

But the most important act of the end of Louis XIII's reign was a diplomatic one. France, ally of the Braganzas, helped them by secret manoeuvres to regain the throne of Portugal.

Rifletteran al mondo i lumi tui

Segnan con l'ombra tua i Fatti tui

P. Jevin Fecit

This coincided with the fall of the Spanish chief minister, the all-powerful Olivares.

Having accepted the title of count of Barcelona, Louis XIII was obliged to intervene militarily in the Roussillon sector. Before he set out, a *lit de justice* removed the right of remonstrances from the Parlement, a step which favoured absolutism. The journey to Roussillon was marked by a serious conspiracy, once again the secret work of Gaston of Orléans. Using one of Louis XIII's favourites, d'Effiat, marquis de Cinq Mars, Gaston had approached Olivares to overthrow the cardinal with the help of Spain, to whom territories were promised.

Louis XIII and Richelieu arrived at Narbonne, with the intention of besieging Perpignan. When they discovered the plot, Cinq Mars was arrested, confessed, and went as far as to compromise his intimate friend, François de Thou, who had not taken part in the plot but had not denounced him.

Richelieu was ill, and wanted to return to Paris: he took with him the two prisoners, in chains. Condemned to death at Lyon, Cinq Mars and de Thou were beheaded there on 12 September 1642. Then, borne on a huge litter, Richelieu returned to the Palais du Cardinal, where he died two months later. His last words have passed into legend: to the priest who was confessing him and asked if he forgave his enemies, he replied proudly: 'I have none but the enemies of the state.'

This grandiose statement ended one of the most important careers in history. Unfortunately nothing remains of Richelieu's political achievements, the consequences of which would probably have surprised him. On the other hand we owe him one of France's oldest intellectual institutions, the Académie Française, which he founded in 1635, and which received letters patent from King Louis XIII. This company has kept all the splendour which it owes to its famous founder.

After Richelieu's death, public opinion expected great changes. The cardinal's enemies breathed again, and Cardinal de Retz even said that Louis XIII seemed happy, as if he had been set free. But in fact, apart from the release of some prisoners of state, nothing changed, and the ministers remained.

The king was as ill as the cardinal: he was thinking about the succession, and about his son's minority. By the declaration of 20 April 1643, he restricted Anne of Austria's powers as regent as much as possible, and then he died piously on 14 May 1643. Five days after his death, on 19 May, the duc d'Enghien, the future 'Great Condé', won a resounding victory against the Spanish at Rocroi, which augured well for the end of hostilities.

It is difficult to judge Louis XIII's personal actions, eclipsed as he was by Richelieu's personality, but it is fair to say that he always supported his minister, and took decisions with him.

Having examined the king's domestic and foreign politics, it is worth talking about his colonial achievements. These were many, and, thanks to a resurgence of the navy, distant conquests were discreetly made.

Champlain had consolidated Canada, to which many French people emigrated. France gained a foothold in Senegal, established a base in Madagascar, Fort Dauphin, and conquered several islands in the Caribbean, including Saint Lucia and Saint Christopher. Commercial links were established with the new colonies, and the creation of the *grandes compagnies* was undertaken. The pious Louis XIII completed his colonial policy by the development of missions, mainly in Canada.

In France religious foundations increased in number: Saint Francis of Sales founded the order of the Visitation with Saint Jane of Chantal, M. Olier founded the seminary of Saint Sulpice, and Monsieur Vincent, chaplain of the galley slaves, was canonized as Saint Vincent de Paul. He was the foremost spiritual figure of the time.

An important part was also played by another movement, also spiritual in essence: this was the abbey of Port-Royal, where an elite of thinkers and writers gathered. They were out of favour with the authorities, as they were accused of favouring Jansenism, a kind of schism, non-hostile to Catholicism, which was named after the bishop of Ypres, Jansenius. His doctrines on grace were propagated in France by Duvergier de Hauranne, abbot of Saint-Cyran, whom Louis XIII had imprisoned.

To complete the picture of the king, we must note that he not only favoured the Académie Française but was very interested in literature

OPPOSITE ABOVE The refectory of the abbey of Port-Royal des Champs, which was reformed under Louis XIII. OPPOSITE BELOW A meeting of the Académie Française, founded in 1635 by Richelieu with letters patent of Louis XIII.

and writers. The very different masterpieces of Corneille's *Le Cid* (1636) and of Descartes' *Discours de la Méthode* (1637) date from his reign.

Louis XIII can therefore fairly be considered as a very great king, to whom history has not done justice. With the help of his minister he paved the way for a hegemony which was to place France at the head of Europe for over a century.

ᘓ LOUIS XIV ᘓ
(1643–1715)
AND MARIA THERESA

THE REIGN OF LOUIS XIV, the longest in the history of France (it lasted for seventy-two years) falls easily into three parts; the first consists of his youth, up to his marriage, the second corresponds with the life of Queen Maria Theresa, and the third with that of Madame de Maintenon.

Youth (1643–1661)

When Louis XIII died, Louis XIV was only ten. On 18 May 1643, Anne of Austria went to the Palais de Justice with her son and had conferred upon her 'the free, absolute and complete administration of the kingdom's affairs during the minority'; but Gaston of Orléans had to be named lieutenant-general of the kingdom.

Power was in fact exercised by Cardinal Mazarin, Richelieu's assistant, who had been papal nuncio in France. Mazarin, who was to be first minister for about twenty years, was a shrewd politician and a cunning man who worked very successfully for the greatness of France. Since he was not a priest, it is not impossible that he contracted a morganatic marriage with Anne of Austria, who was very attached to him and placed her complete trust in him.

The victory at Rocroi had given rise to peace negotiations at Münster and at Osnabrück. These went on for four years and resulted in a triumph for France. The treaties of Westphalia, which fragmented Germany, assured the French hegemony in Europe. But in domestic politics this was a time of great difficulties, which were to end in civil war, the Fronde.

Because taxation had had to be increased, the Parlement made trouble again, with the support of the great nobles. Mazarin put a stop to this by imprisoning the duke of Beaufort at Vincennes. The Parlement refused to give in, and for three years things got worse. However the situation abroad had become excellent, since the victory of Lens (August 1648) won by Condé resulted in the signing of the peace (October 1648).

The immense diplomatic success of the peace of Westphalia, the greatest in French history, should have brought about internal peace. Paradoxically, it marked the beginning 'of the Fronde. As a result of the edict of 13 May 1648, which re-established the tax called the Paulette, the Parlement rose against Mazarin; Mazarin, feeling more powerful after the announcement of the victory of Lens, had one of the leaders of the Parlement, the councillor Pierre Broussel, arrested.

This strong measure provoked the revolt of Paris, and barricades went up everywhere (August 1648). Mazarin arranged for the secret escape of Anne of Austria and Louis XIV from Paris and installed them at Rueil under Condé's protection, and then on 7 January 1649 the queen and her sons were taken to the château of Saint-Germain-en-Laye.

The queen and Mazarin promulgated an ordinance exiling the main figures of state to the provinces. They retaliated by declaring Mazarin a public enemy. Civil war broke out. Parlement formed an army, commanded by the prince of Conti. In the queen's name, Condé besieged Paris. The rebels entered into negotiations with Spain. Parlement, not wanting to collude with a foreign country, submitted, even though the Parisians had tried to bribe Marshal Turenne to persuade him to turn the army against the king.

Cardinal Mazarin, first minister to Louis XIV for nearly twenty years.

This revolt, which failed, is known as the Fronde Parlementaire.

The king returned to Paris on 18 August 1649, but the troubles were far from over. The princes of the blood revolted and demanded the arrest of Mazarin. During the night of 9–10 February, Gaston of Orléans attacked the Palais Royal under the pretext that the king had been kidnapped. Anne of Austria confronted him and showed the assailants her sleeping son. The young king was woken up, and was permanently marked by this scene. It inspired in him a hatred of Paris and a horror of disorder, and explains both the strong measures he took and his desire to move the capital from Paris to Versailles.

Mazarin had to leave the country; disorder broke out. The queen had Louis XIV crowned and gave the Seals to Mathieu Molé, president of the Parlement. A meeting of the Estates-General was wisely cancelled. At that point Condé changed sides, and, going over to the Spanish, roused Bordeaux to revolt.

To put an end to the disorder, Mazarin returned to France at the head of an army. Condé allied himself to Gaston of Orléans, and Turenne, who had returned to the service of the crown, tried to recapture Paris, but was kept back at the Porte Saint-Antoine by Gaston of Orléans' daughter, the Grande Demoiselle, who had cannons fired at the royal troops from the towers of the Bastille.

On 4 July 1652, the Parlement was besieged by the troops of the Fronde, the Hôtel de Ville was set alight and Broussel was named provost. Condé thought he had won, and Mazarin had to leave again. Louis XIV saved the day by promising a general amnesty, and then by addressing a delegation from the town of Paris in strong terms, reminding them that all authority lay with the king alone.

Paris had virtually been recaptured, but the civil war continued in the form of the siege of Bordeaux in 1653. Condé went over to the Spaniards, Cardinal de Retz, who had supported the rebels, was removed from the archbishopric of Paris, and the Fronde could be considered as finished.

Mazarin had triumphed, and the king became master of his kingdom, but only after five years

of bloody struggle which had harmed the country more than a foreign war or a revolution. Nevertheless royal authority came out of it consolidated, and from 1653 to 1661, Louis XIV, confirming Mazarin's authority, allowed him to become a virtual dictator, in much the same style as Richelieu.

With the war with Spain dragging on, Mazarin took the bold step of allying himself to the English under Cromwell, even though he was a Protestant and had been responsible for beheading Charles I, Louis XIII's brother-in-law. The Protector put his navy at France's disposal and France thus acquired naval superiority. The war was ended near Dunkirk by the battle of the Dunes in 1658. Condé, at the head of the Spanish forces, was beaten there by Turenne, head of the French armed forces.

The conflict was ended in the following year by the peace of the Pyrenees. Cromwell had been promised Dunkirk, but since he died at an opportune moment the promise was not kept, and Louis XIV supported General Monk in his struggle to re-establish the Stuarts. By the treaty of the Pyrenees, France received Roussillon, Artois and isolated strongholds along the northern border.

The main clause of the treaty was a matrimonial one: the signing of the peace was conditional upon Louis XIV's marrying Philip IV's daughter, the Infanta Maria-Theresa. This clause deeply upset Louis XIV, who was passionately in love with Marie Mancini, Mazarin's niece. This drama, which inspired Racine's *Bérénice*, broke the king's heart but, aware of his duties, he bowed to reasons of state. Louis XIV's wedding was celebrated at Saint-Jean-de-Luz after the signing of the peace treaty on the Ile des Faisans, on the Bidassoa.

While Mazarin lived, the king handed over the reins of office to him. But in 1661 the cardinal fell ill and died. On 10 March 1661 Louis XIV called together his council and announced that he intended to reign himself, without a first minister, and that he would deal with all affairs in person, down to the simple granting of passports. And so began his personal reign, which was to dazzle the world for fifty-four years, and which would bring France to the peak of its power.

IO SOCIOS, QVI FORTIBVS ARMIS
T LÆSAQVE IVRA DEI

Louis XIII receives Glory's crown, by Philippe de Champaigne.

Louis XIV with the Grand Dauphin, the duke of Burgundy and (it is assumed)
his second son, and the Duchess de Ventadour, by Nicolas de Largillière.

Louis XIV and Maria Theresa (1661–1683)

Queen Maria Theresa was not an attractive woman; she was small, swarthy, and lacking in personality. She gave the king several children who died in infancy and one mediocre son, known as the Grand Dauphin. But apart from these births, she did not play an important part in the king's life. (Hence his famous remark at her death: 'It is the first grief she has ever caused me.')

Louis XIV's dissolute life caused the queen a great deal of suffering, but she put up with his infidelities with great dignity. Since these affairs were notorious and played a great part in history, it is impossible to ignore them. Louis XIV has been described as a seducer, probably because he was an all-powerful king. The truth was that he was physically plain: slightly below medium height, he wore high heels and huge wigs to make himself look taller. Since he is thus accoutred in all his portraits, it is hard to know what he really looked like. But even in official portraits one can see his harsh gaze, hooked nose and receding chin, a type which has since been called 'Bourbon'.

It would appear that Louis was of average intelligence, had common sense, great harshness of heart, and was an indomitable egoist. To counteract these mediocre qualities, he had a profound feeling for his royal duties (he professed that the job of king was delightful), and such a strong feeling for the state that he has had attributed to him the famous statement 'L'Etat c'est moi'. He has been remembered as the Sun King, even though the second half of his reign was by no means as brilliant as the first.

The first was dominated by his private life, which was strewn with amorous adventures. Shortly after his marriage, the king had fallen in love with one of the queen's ladies in waiting, Louise de la Baume-Leblanc, whom he made duchess de La Vallière. They had children together, and she loved him sincerely. When he abandoned her, she retired to a nunnery. She had been rapidly ousted by an intriguer, the beautiful Athénais de Rochechouart-Mortemart, marquise de Montespan, who ruled the king's affections from 1667 to 1679 and gave him many children, among them a daughter, Mlle de Blois, whom Louis XIV married to his nephew the duke of Orléans, the future regent.

Madame de Montespan was in turn ousted by Angélique de Scoraille, duchess of Fontanges, who soon died, possibly poisoned. For a scandalous affair, called Affair of the Poisons, troubled the reign, and the importance of such people as Madame de Montespan herself and of the poet Racine was compromised. Apart from these three great favourites there were many other fleeting romances.

The king's scandalous private life shocked the clergy but was accepted by his contemporaries: they hardly ever dared to contradict the king, who allowed no comment, however well founded.

The beginning of Louis XIV's personal reign was marked by two acts of very violent authoritarianism.

First of all he wanted to hold sway over his ministers, remarkable men who numbered among them Colbert and Louvois. But the most powerful of them initially was the superintendent of Finances, Fouquet, an impudent man who had acquired an immense fortune, partly at the state's expense. Having made the mistake of throwing a sumptuous party for the king in his château of Vaux-le-Vicomte, he was accused of extortion, arrested and given a rough trial. It was conducted in iniquitous circumstances, and Fouquet's head was only saved thanks to the courage of Councilor d'Ormesson. Condemned only to banishment, Fouquet's sentence was made more severe by Louis XIV, who imprisoned him at Pinerolo, where he died after more than fifteen years of harsh captivity.

It must be admitted that the harshness of Fouquet's treatment secured internal order for more than half a century. Along with Fouquet, certain financiers were obliged to pay up, which slightly appeased the penury in the treasury.

As well as the financial powers, Louis XIV also attacked the spiritual powers; he had Port-Royal condemned, with the support of the pope, to punish the nuns for their independence of spirit.

Louis XIV unnecessarily provoked the European states in the hope of holding sway over them. For trivial questions of precedence he acquired in less than four years the enmity of Turkey, England, the Empire and the Papacy. With such a haughty and intransigent master, the nobility had to bow down very low. Some of them, who wished to maintain their positions, remained at court in servile fashion. The

Madame de Montespan and her children.
(French school, sixteenth century)

independent spirits cut themselves off in their properties, where they were deliberately forgotten.

These difficulties were compensated for by the way in which the king carried out his duties of state. He tried to restore the finances and let Colbert handle the public debt by repudiating or cancelling bonds, which ruined the bondholders, but restored for a while the balance of the budget, which was definitively broken from 1672 onwards by military expenditure. Louis XIV was, in effect, a warrior king, paying his armies personally and following an inflexible policy.

The first pretext for war was the king's marriage itself. Philip IV of Spain had died, leaving his crown to a degenerate, Charles II. He had excluded Maria Theresa from the Spanish throne in his will and had reserved its ultimate assumption for his other daughter, the wife of Emperor Leopold.

Maria Theresa's dowry of 500,000 golden écus had not been paid, and Louis xiv used this excuse to demand payment in territories; he demanded from Emperor Leopold that the Netherlands should immediately be handed over to Maria Theresa, without prejudicing the handing over of Spanish territories at the death of Charles ii, which seemed imminent, though in fact he was to live for another thirty years.

Thinking that the Netherlands would not be handed over to him without a show of force, Louis xiv, at the head of an army of 73,000 men, undertook a campaign of sieges which resulted in his winning of Flanders.

It seemed that this war, called the War of Devolution, had been won easily. But this was to underestimate the appetites of sovereigns. The Protestant nations of Sweden, Holland and even England joined together against Catholic France, even though Louis xiv had helped with the restoration of the Stuarts. A treaty was signed by the three powers at the Hague at the beginning of 1668, and war resumed in another Spanish bastion which Louis xiv was planning to attack, Franche-Comté. It was conquered in two weeks by Condé, which gave the king a second bargaining point in case Spain refused to sign a treaty.

He gave them the choice between Flanders and Franche-Comté. Spain preferred to give up Flanders and at the treaty of Aix-la-Chapelle France received Lille, Douai, Furnes and Armentières (2 May 1669). Moreover, the queen's rights to the Spanish succession were recognized; this was to have heavy consequences in the future.

Louis xiv, very vindictive by nature, resented Holland having taken sides against him, and made lengthy preparations for an expedition to take his revenge. While the troops were being armed for the expedition, a grand diplomatic offensive managed by the minister of foreign affairs, Hugues de Lionne, neutralized first England (the treaty of Dover, 1670) and then Sweden. Secret negotiations with some of the German princes gained for France bases on the Rhine.

At the head of a considerable army, numbering nearly 120,000 men, the king began a lightning war. By forced marches he reached the ford of Tolhuis across the Rhine, at the very gateway to Holland. The crossing of the Rhine has been immortalized by painters and poets.

It seemed that Holland was going to drop like a ripe fruit. But alas, Louis xiv engaged in lengthy siege warfare and, convinced that he was the stronger, refused the offers of peace which were made to him. At this point Holland rallied: its interests were put in the hands of William of Orange and the dykes which kept out the sea were opened, flooding the country.

In the face of this heroic resistance, Europe, sensing that things were going badly for France, united itself against her. The Empire, with the exception of Hanover and Bavaria, joined with Holland, and Charles ii, breaking the clauses of the treaty of Dover, rejoined the coalition, as he dreaded seeing the French establish themselves in Antwerp.

The French army was so powerful that it managed to resist: Condé defeated the prince of Orange at Seneffe in 1674, and Duquesne victoriously held off Admiral de Ruyter at sea.

The Imperial forces had invaded Alsace as far as the Vosges: they were driven out by Turenne, who defeated them at Turckheim (January 1675), then rebuffed them on the right bank of the Rhine, where he was unfortunately killed by a bullet at Salzbach (July 1675).

Since Holland had not been invaded, it retained the advantage, but the treaty which put an end to this war, signed at Nijmegen in 1678, brought enormous gains to France, at the expense of Spain. Louis xiv kept Franche-Comté, Valenciennes, Maubeuge and Cambrai. Holland gained certain concessions, not the least of which was the creation of the 'Barrier', its right to hold garrisons in a certain number of towns in the Spanish Netherlands. This defensive glacis was to cause France complications in later wars.

The peace of Nijmegen is generally considered as the high point of the reign, but it could equally well be thought to have been in 1681, when Louis xiv annexed the free town of Strasbourg, or in 1682, when he moved into the partly finished Palace of Versailles; or even in 1684, the date of the truce of Ratisbon, which guaranteed the treaties of Westphalia.

Louis XIV on horseback, probably painted in 1668, the year of his triumphant entry into Douai during the French invasion of the Netherlands. (Studio of Lebrun)

In the midst of these glorious days one tragedy occurred, the death of Queen Maria Theresa in 1683. Her role was not an important one, but it seems that she brought the king luck, since after her death difficulties and misfortunes were to build up during the last thirty years of the reign.

The beginnings, as we have seen, were brilliant; they consolidated the position of France, which became by far the foremost state in Europe. But it is important to point out that this greatness was not only the product of force and good administration; if France shone with unparalleled brilliance during this period, it owed it mainly to its intellectual and artistic primacy. In no other period of its history had France known such an abundance of talented men: one need only mention Corneille, Descartes, Pascal, Racine, Molière, La Rochefoucauld, Cardinal de Retz, La Bruyère, La Fontaine, Bossuet, Boileau and Fénelon to prove it.

Artistic primacy was equalled by intellectual primacy, and for the first time France outshone Italy, which since the Renaissance had been considered the mother of all the arts. This was such an established truth that the king first called on Bernini to complete the Louvre and begin work on Versailles, then realized that he could find quite as good in France, and recruited the prodigious team which had built and decorated Vaux-le-Vicomte.

At the head of these artists was the landscape gardener Le Nôtre, father of the French garden. Around him were gathered a galaxy of architects whose buildings put France ahead of the world in this field: it is enough to name Mansart, Le Vau, Libéral Bruant, d'Orbay, Hardouin Mansart and Claude Perrault, and to mention such remarkable creations as the Place Vendôme, the Château de Maisons, the colonnade of the Louvre, the Collège des Quatre Nations (the seat of the Institute of France), the Invalides, the terrasse of Saint-Germain, and hundreds of châteaux which contributed to making France a true museum of architecture.

At the head of all this was the most astonishing architectural achievement in the world, the Château de Versailles, and its park, which was copied with varying degrees of success by all the princes and kings of Europe. It took 30,000 workers forty years to build Versailles. The park was the most sublime manifestation of Le Nôtre's genius. The paintings were executed by le Brun, Mignard and Van der Meulen, and the sculptures by Girardon, Tuby, Coysevox. Lully was in charge of the music.

Versailles was to set the tone for Europe for more than a century, and the crown made it an instrument of domination over the servile nobility, failing to realize in time that the world's most beautiful palace was one day to be the tomb of the monarchy.

Louis xiv and Madame de Maintenon (1683–1715)

Louis xiv's last thirty years were dominated by the influence of a woman whom he married morganatically and who, unlike Queen Maria Theresa, played an important political role. Françoise d'Aubigné, granddaughter of the poet Agrippa d'Aubigné, was born in prison, where her parents were put for religious reasons. Very beautiful, but without any fortune, she had resigned herself to marrying the poet Scarron, an invalid, with whom she held a successful literary salon.

When she became a widow, Louis xiv asked her to bring up his children by Madame de Montespan. It is surprising that such a religious woman should have accepted this equivocal task. She carried it out to such perfection that, after the bastards were legitimized, the widow Scarron was admitted to court and given an endowment with which she bought the Château de Maintenon.

After the disgrace of Mme de Montespan and the death of the duchess of Fontanges, Louis xiv, who held Madame de Maintenon in great esteem, became physically interested in her, though she was well over forty. She probably became his mistress and he married her after the queen's death, at an uncertain date which is situated by historians at between 1685 and 1693.

When Madame de Maintenon entered the king's life the external political situation was a very interesting one: France's traditional ally, Turkey, had besieged Vienna, and the blockade had been raised by John Sobieski. The Turks had to withdraw, and their authority had waned. Momentarily deprived of its political counterweight in the East, France was open to threat from Austria. Louis xiv countered this by signing the Truce of Ratisbon in 1684, which guaranteed peace with Austria.

The only difficulties externally were now with the Papacy, which did not represent a military threat, but the possibility of a schism. The fight with the Papacy had begun with the condemnation of the Jansenists, which gave rise to resistance from the episcopacy.

The conflict became more acute during the affair known as of the *Régale*. It was the right of the crown to use the revenues of a bishop's see in the space between the incumbent's death and the consecration of his successor, and to make nominations for benefices, according to the Concordat of 1516. Two Jansenist bishops, to retaliate for the harsh treatment they suffered, called on Rome to intervene. Pope Innocent XI wanted to solve single-handed a difference which the king regarded as his province. At a general assembly of the clergy the declaration of 1682 was formulated by Bossuet, affirming that the Papacy did not have the right to intervene in the *temporel*. The pope pronounced this declaration to be void, excommunicated Louis XIV *in petto*, and left the bishoprics vacant.

This conflict lasted for about ten years, and was only settled after the pope's death. His successor, Innocent XII, accepted an arrangement which made it necessary to annul the declaration of 1682. This was a humiliation for the crown and the king did his best to cover it up.

He felt that right from the start of the quarrel he had made a generous move in favour of Catholicism, since, under the influence of Madame de Maintenon, he had decided to have all followers of the Reformation expelled from the kingdom.

From the beginning of his reign the king had restricted the liberties which had been granted to the Protestants by the Edict of Nantes, and this was even more unfair since the Protestants, deprived of their political muscle by Richelieu, no longer presented any danger to unity. They were in fact not numerous (less than six per cent of the population), and lived under the code of peaceful coexistence with the Catholics, even in regions where Protestantism predominated: Poitou, Saintonge and the Cévennes.

However, some Catholics still considered the Edict to have been a temporary expedient, and, seeing the king as the religious head of the country, considered the Protestants to constitute a political faction which was hostile to power.

Louis XIV, rather removed from these things, began by not considering the Catholics' wishes. It was only after the peace of Nijmegen that he waged an undeclared war on the Protestants, though without weighing up the deplorable consequences: forced conversions, often bought, *dragonnades*, financial persecution, and the closure of religious schools.

The ministers, to conceal the fact of these persecutions, ended up by persuading the king that the Protestants were being converted en masse, and that consequently the Edict of Nantes had lost its reason for existing. The king was only too ready to be convinced, and, without giving the matter sufficient thought, signed the edict of revocation at Fontainebleau on 18 October 1685; the text had been prepared by Chancellor le Tellier, father of the minister Louvois.

This act of intolerance, an iniquitous denial of Henry IV's promise, provoked a mass exodus, in difficult circumstances. It is estimated that more than half a million Protestants left the country, depriving France of part of its élite. Since not all Protestants were able to emigrate, even though the sovereigns of the countries of the Reformation opened their doors wide to them, an internal resistance grew up. Protestants worshipped in secret in remote places, but their deprivation of civil rights led to aberrations in the case of marriage or succession.

The attitude of the authorities was generally fairly merciless, and it provoked bloody revolts, of which the most famous was the war of the Camisards, which flared up in Languedoc at the beginning of the eighteenth century, and caused serious difficulties to France, which was engaged in the War of the Spanish Succession. Clandestine Protestantism became a political faction.

The immediate consequence of the revocation of the Edict of Nantes was to provoke the indignation of the German Protestant princes, who united in 1686 in the famous League of Augsburg, which brought together the elector of Brandenburg, the emperor, Venice, Russia, Poland, Spain, Sweden, Bavaria and Holland. Through his unwise religious policy, Louis XIV now found himself in danger of being surrounded.

Madame de Maintenon and her niece, by F. Elle.

He tried to negotiate, since the League's pretext was to contest the rights of the duchess of Orléans, the king's sister-in-law, over the heritage of her father, the Elector Palatine. Arbitration was referred to the pope in case the Germans failed. Watching the talks dragging on between the emperor and Philip von Neuburg, the heir to the Palatinate, Louvois advised Louis XIV to intervene.

The king offered withdrawal of the duchess of Orléans' claims against the renewal of the truce of Ratisbon, and made this ultimatum valid for three months. He took his precautions: to make the pope and the German mediators capitulate, he occupied Comtat-Venaissin, as well as the electorate of Cologne, Liége, Spires and Kaiserslautern, and the dauphin besieged Philippsburg and established bridgeheads at Mannheim and Heidelberg.

These preventive operations seemed to have placed France in a good position for negotiating, but the situation was about to be suddenly reversed. A revolution broke out in England, and the Stuart King James II was ousted and replaced by his son-in-law William of Orange; since he was a member of the League of Augsburg, England joined the League, which placed France in an extremely difficult situation.

Faced with the danger of war, Louvois ordered a devastation which was one of the most scandalous in history. The ravaging of the Palatinate, which reduced a whole territory to fire and blood, was to weigh heavily on the memories of Louis XIV and his minister, and gave rise to a long-lasting resentment.

Hostilities were to break out on numerous fronts: in Piedmont, Ireland, the Netherlands, Württemberg, Belgium and Provence, and they were to last for ten years, seriously weakening French finances.

The war of the League of Augsburg revealed some great military leaders: Catinat, the victor of Marsaglia (4 October 1693), and particularly Marshal Luxembourg, son of Montmorency-Bouteville, who had been beheaded by Richelieu. Thanks to his victories, particularly that of Neerwinden (29 July 1693), he earned the nickname of the *tapissier de Notre Dame* (the carpeter of Notre Dame: all the captured enemy standards were used to decorate the nave there).

The war was waged on sea far more than on land, and Colbert's navy was partly wiped out. The great man in this field was Admiral de Tourville, the victor of Beachy Head (29 June 1690). But he was also the victim of the disaster at La Hougue (29 May 1693).

Contrary to expectations, the war was not a disaster for France: though Louis XIV, at the treaty of Ryswick (1697), had to recognize William of Orange and abandon the Stuarts, he kept Strasbourg. At about the same time the Empire made a treaty with the Turks at Carlowitz (1699), and this increased the threat from Austria.

A new bone of contention was soon to arise in the shape of the Spanish succession; it was a cause in which Louis XIV had taken an interest ever since the war of Devolution. After many hesitations, the Spanish King Charles II made a will leaving all his crowns to one of Louis XIV's grandsons, the duke of Anjou, because it seemed to him that France was the only nation powerful enough to maintain unity. If France refused this heritage, he would turn to the Habsburgs, and they would be back to the state of affairs of Charles V's time.

Charles II died on 1 November 1700. Louis XIV, informed of the contents of the will, accepted the heritage. It was necessary to make some concessions to get the consent of the European states: the emperor, implacable, declared war immediately, but England and Holland recognized the duke of Anjou, who became Philip V. Strengthened by this relative success, Louis XIV had the Barrier strongholds along the frontier with the Spanish Netherlands occupied, and supported the rights of his grandson to the throne of France, against his own commitments.

Louis XIV now wanted his grandson to rule over all the Spanish possessions and remain heir to the throne of France – though he had previously promised that not all this power would be in the hands of the French king. This claim made Europe rise up in arms against the Sun King, who was reduced to only a few allies: Bavaria, the duke of Mantua, the duke of Savoy and Portugal. These allies were soon to prove inconstant.

The war dragged on for twelve years, and succeeded in ruining the country's finances, which were now in a catastrophic state. Louis XIV was reduced to having his silverware melted down, and to instituting new taxes of which one, the *capitation*, was aimed at the nobility also. In addition to this, more new official posts were instituted, but unfortunately even this did not help in any way to redress the financial situation.

The first three years of the war of the Spanish Succession saw French victories thanks to marshals Berwick and Villars; but they had much to contend with, as the coalition forces were led by the greatest military leader of the time, the Frenchman, Prince Eugene, son of the count of Soissons and of one of Mazarin's nieces.

Prince Eugene stopped the offensive in Piedmont, which was led by Catinat. In retaliation, Villars led an offensive as far as Ulm in 1702 and in the following year he had a resounding success at Wachstadt (alias Blenheim, September 1703). Eleven months later, on the same spot, on 13 August 1704, Prince Eugene and the English General Marlborough destroyed the French army, removing all possibility of an offensive on Vienna and turning the course of the war.

A naval front had opened in Spain; after defeating the count of Toulouse at Velez-Malaga, the English occupied the Rock of Gibraltar. After this they blockaded what was left of the French navy in the port of Toulon, and it was forced to scuttle some of its own ships to defend itself.

From 1706 onwards, the war became a purely defensive one. Villeroy was crushed at Ramillies by Marlborough (23 May 1706), a defeat which entailed the loss of the Netherlands, a threat to Provence, and the taking of Lille by Prince Eugene.

At Malplaquet (11 September 1709), Villars just managed in an indecisive and bloody battle to preserve the northern frontier, where over the next three years the situation got worse and worse; Prince Eugene, master of the Barrier, laid siege to Landrecies, the last fortress which guarded the road to Paris.

Louis XIV ordered Villars to attempt to free Landrecies, announcing that if they were checked he would forget his age and 'would place himself at the head of his troops to perish together or save the state'. Galvanized by the king's heroic stance, Villars' troops pierced through the Imperial front at Denain (18 July 1712). Prince Eugene retreated, and in the

following years Villars occupied the Palatinate and part of the country of Baden.

These last advantages made it possible to conclude a treaty at Utrecht and at Rastadt (1713–14). But though Spain was conserved for Philip V, which had been the main objective of the war, heavy concessions had to be made in other sectors. In particular, Louis had to recognize the perpetual separation of the two crowns of France and Spain, to admit the presence of an English commissary in Dunkirk, and to give back Pinerolo, which was compensated for by the return of Barcelonette. The English were the winners of the day, acquiring bases in the Mediterranean, Gibraltar and Minorca, as well as territories in Canada. Belgium was taken away from Spain and given to Austria. The settlement of 1713 was the only one of the reign to bring no advantages.

It is a fact that the end of the reign was a miserable one. The winter of 1709, one of the coldest in history, had frozen the wheat, olive trees and vines. Temperatures of $-30°$ were recorded in the Paris area, and people dropped like flies. This misery coincided with grave financial difficulties, which forced the king to have the last of his silver melted down.

In the midst of the death threat which hovered over the state, the royal family was struck by bereavement. On 14 April 1711, the Grand Dauphin died of smallpox. He was a mediocre prince who, since he had become a widower, had been living as man and wife with a lady in waiting, Mademoiselle la Choin, a kind of replica of Madame de Maintenon.

Since the dauphin had several sons, the damage did not seem irreparable. The duke of Burgundy, husband of Adelaide of Savoy, became dauphin in his turn. He was an excellent prince, perhaps unwisely schooled by Fénelon. But there was no opportunity to discover his merits: smallpox struck once again. The duchess of Burgundy died on 12 February 1712, followed by her husband on 18 February and by their eldest son, the duke of Brittany, on 8 March.

The heirs to the throne were a two-year-old child, the future Louis XV, and the last brother of the duke of Burgundy and of Philip V, the duke of Berry, who was of the dynasty. He too died, in 1714, and Louis XIV, overcome by dynastic despair, took the unheard-of step of declaring

Louis XIV presents the Blue Ribbon to the young duke of Burgundy,
who was to become the father of Louis XV.

that his bastards could succeed to the throne.

Obsessed by the risks he saw following upon
his death, Louis XIV made his will, then fell ill
and, tortured by gangrene, died piously on 1
September 1715.

Of the interminable reign of this king, so great
despite his faults, we can say, like Voltaire, that

'his name cannot be uttered without respect, and
without linking it to an eternally memorable
century'. He had indeed made France great and
powerful, and by its prestige, its art and its culture, it had become the first nation in the world:
but the edifice was a fragile one and the
eighteenth century was to see it crumble.

❦ LOUIS XV ❦
(1715–1774)
AND MARIA LECZINSKA

The Regency (1715–1723)

WHEN LOUIS XIV DIED the young Louis XV, his great-grandson, was only five; a few hours before his death, Louis XIV had asked for the child to be brought to him and had given him some words of advice. But because of the new king's youth a regency was indispensable until his legal majority, which would not come about until 1723.

The regency was taken over by the duke of Orléans, Louis XIV's nephew and also his son-in-law by his marriage to one of Mme de Montespan's daughters. The regent was one of the most astonishing figures in the history of France. He was a highly intelligent, undeniably charming, and very subtle man. But these assets were diminished in public eyes by his well-deserved reputation for debauchery, and also by the idea, probably unjustified, that he had had a hand in the numerous deaths which had afflicted the court, and which now made him, for the time being, master of the kingdom.

Louis XIV thought so little of his son-in-law that in his will he had laid down a restriction of his powers, to the benefit of his own bastards. Philip of Orléans very cleverly showed that Louis XIV's will contradicted the fundamental laws of the kingdom: he obtained its annulment by the Parlement, in return for recognizing the Parlement's right of remonstrance, a dangerous act which during the course of the century was to entail power conflicts, and can be numbered among the causes of the Revolution.

The regent dismissed Louis XIV's ministers and replaced them by small councils which allowed him to give a number of positions to his own friends. This system, called 'Polysynodie', did not work very well, but it kept the nobility happy, as it felt it was now playing the role of which Louis XIV had deprived it.

Very intelligently, the regent realized that this system was a deplorable one; he revised it in 1718 by naming actual ministers. However, the finan-cial situation had deteriorated to such an extent during the last three years that it now appeared insoluble. Certain measures advocated by the duc de Noailles, head of the financial council, helped to gain a few months, but after this they were once again faced with a yawning gulf.

The regent felt that he had the man available to solve the situation: he was a Scottish banker called John Law, an able financier, and a good man, but a gambler. He had fragmentary economic views which have wrongly been called a system. Law's chief idea was that there was a lack of currency to make the required payments, and that it was necessary, because of the shortage of specie, to create a fiduciary currency guaranteed and repayable in gold or silver, or for lack of these in government bonds. These arrangements, fairly orthodox on a financial level, were compromised in advance by the establishment of the forced rate of the bank-note.

To back his currency, Law set up companies to exploit the colonies: Senegal, the Antilles, Louisiana, Canada. Because of his success, he soon added to these a company for Africa and China. The regent, dazzled by these successes, made Law superintendent of finances on 5 January 1720.

But Law's actions ended in bankruptcy for the state. This may well have been a more honest state of affairs, but many people were ruined as a result, which did not increase the regent's popularity.

Philip of Orléans' foreign policy was just as strange as his financial methods. Wisely cautious of English power, which had manifested itself during the war of the Spanish Succession, he decided to reach an agreement with her. He took part in a quadruple alliance, with England, Holland and the Empire. This agreement was the work of the chief minister, Cardinal Dubois, the regent's old tutor, and one of the biggest scoundrels in history.

Relying on this agreement, it was decided to

But he was too intelligent not to realize the extent of his mistakes, and he must be credited with having tried to redress them during the last two years of his regency. The famous bankers, the brothers Pâris, were given the task of liquidating the after-effects of Law's system, and trying to reimburse at least the face value of his shares.

The regent's religious policy favoured the Jansenists, and he obtained from the pope a relaxation of the Bull *Unigenitus* which had condemned them anew from 1713.

In February 1723, Louis xv was declared of age, and crowned at Rheims Cathedral. The first minister Dubois was dead, and the young king virtually made Philip of Orléans first minister. But this system did not last long; the regent, exhausted by his debauchery, died of apoplexy at the home of his mistress the duchess of Falari on 2 December 1723. The duke of Bourbon, head of the Condé household, became a candidate for his ministry and obtained it without any difficulty.

Louis xv could not, in fact, govern alone, and for about twenty years he gave his ministers a free hand. Nevertheless things went better than during the regency, but its excesses had left their mark on the century and seriously weakened the monarchy.

Maria Leczinska (1723–1745)

The king was legally of age: he was so handsome that he won everyone's heart. By nature he was timid and violent. The duke of Bourbon judged rightly that he could not wait until his Spanish fiancée reached marriageable age. There was a dynastic problem to be faced, as well as that of the king's sexuality.

With the help of his mistress, Madame de Prie, Bourbon persuaded Louis xv to send his fiancée back to Philip v, an affront which could have caused a war with Spain, and to seek among the princesses of Europe the one who could most rapidly provide him with children. The Infanta was taken back to the Spanish border and a search was instituted for a possible bride. The choice was not an easy one, and they were reduced to accepting the daughter of the dethroned king of Poland, Stanislaus Leczinski, who lived in miserable exile at Wissenburg. The princess was already twenty-three, which was a

The coronation of Louis xv at Rheims in 1723.

declare war on Spain because of an alleged conspiracy fomented by the Spanish ambassador Cellamare. Spain was the only country whose navy could have helped France; ignoring this sensitive consideration, the regent sent Marshal Berwick to Spain, where his troops destroyed all the naval dockyards, while the English Admiral Byng dispersed the Spanish fleet in the Mediterranean.

In order to conciliate Spain, the regent decided that the Infanta, Philip v's only daughter, should marry the young king, and the little girl was brought to the French court. One searches in vain for Philip of Orléans' motives in this: it seems he had set himself the task of destroying Louis xiv's achievements.

Louis xv, by Maurice Quentin de la Tour.

considerable age difference for a young man of fifteen. Louis xv received his sexual initiation from Madame de Falari, and the marriage was celebrated on 4 September 1725.

Maria Leczinska, who was to give her husband ten children in ten years (eight girls and two boys, of whom only one survived, the dauphin, Louis xvi's father), was a very touching figure. She was good, sweet, moderately intelligent, and at first was an admirable wife. Louis xv, in the ardour of his youth, found her inimitable at first. Then, when she had lost her figure through childbearing, and for reasons of health she refused to fulfil her marital duties, she was deceived in the most blatant manner. We will return to the subject of Louis xv's mistresses later, since they influenced history.

The duke of Bourbon soon became very unpopular because he established a kind of income tax, though it was only of about two per cent. Moreover, the price of bread trebled because of the bad harvest of 1725, and reduced people to starvation. On the advice of his old tutor, Louis xv dismissed the duke and replaced him with Cardinal Fleury, who was to manage the government wisely until his death in 1743 at the age of ninety.

Fleury, the son of a tax collector, was born ambitious; nevertheless he had to content himself for a long time with the modest bishopric of Fréjus, where he felt he had been sent, as he said, 'by divine indignation'. His role as the young king's tutor was to decide the direction his career was to take, and the king, who trusted him implicitly, gave him a free hand.

Assisted by Maurepas in the navy, by Saint-Florentin in foreign affairs and by Le Blanc in matters of war, his achievement was a considerable one, and quite beneficial for France.

Very interested in religious matters, Fleury was an implacable enemy of Jansenism, and he undertook to put an end to it by the Council of Embrun (1729), which made a scapegoat of the pious bishop of Senez, Jean Soanen. He constituted *Unigenitus* a law of the kingdom, and the Parlement was freed of ecclesiastical clauses by a *lit de justice*.

Well versed in financial affairs, Fleury, advised by the Pâris brothers, fixed the price of the golden louis at 24 livres, and had the currency reminted. This operation, which seems a minor

one, was in fact very beneficial, and in contrast with Louis xiv's time, where the value of the louis changed about fifty times, the new value stood firm until the time of the *assignats*.

Then Fleury reconstituted the general system of tax farming by indexing the payment required from the Farmers General to the nation's productivity. This very new idea was a great success and there were no serious financial problems for the rest of the ministry. It is also important to note that on the advice of superintendent Orry, Fleury introduced a ten per cent tax on income to finance expenses of war. Moreover he founded the Corps of Bridges and Highways (*Ponts et Chaussées*), a service which made the major roads throughout the kingdom drivable.

Pursuing Law's ideas, he encouraged the big colonial companies, stressed the importance of Canada and Louisiana, and encouraged the plantations in the Caribbean. It can therefore be said that on the whole Fleury's policies would have been perfect if he had not – to his great regret, for he was a pacifist – had to wage wars which brought disadvantages as well as successes.

A *casus belli* presented itself in 1732; the queen's father, Stanislaus Leczinski, wanted to win back the crown of Poland, and he managed to get himself elected king by 60,000 votes, ousting the king of Saxony, Augustus iii, who only got 6000. But Augustus iii, who had the support of Russia, Austria and the Netherlands, was not prepared to give up. He had himself proclaimed king of Poland, and Stanislaus Leczinski had to take refuge in Danzig. Fleury sent a fleet and reinforcements to Danzig, but the operation failed and Leczinski had to flee.

To uphold the honour of the queen's father it was decided to attack Austria, since they could not attack Russia, and England's neutrality was bought. Berwick attacked in Germany, Villars in Italy, and both of them, after bringing home appreciable successes, died. French progress continued in the Trentino, in the direction of Vienna, and this made it possible to sign an armistice in 1735.

Peace negotiations, led by Chauvelin, went on for three years, and then a treaty was signed at Vienna (1738). This treaty was a success for Fleury; the duke of Lorraine, the emperor's son-in-law, gave up his duchy in return for Tuscany. Lorraine was given to Stanislaus Leczinski for

Maria Leczinska by Nattier.

life, but was to return to France at his death. This arrangement made it possible to settle the eastern frontier in a peaceful way.

But the war was not over, since Austria and Russia then attacked Turkey. Fleury helped France's traditional ally, and, at the peace of Belgrade in 1739, Turkey recovered part of the territories which she had lost to Prince Eugene. France was now strengthened by its advantages in the east, and it seemed that a new period of peace was about to begin. But this was not the case, and the year 1740 saw an upheaval in the whole of European politics. Frederick II the Great became king of Prussia, Elizabeth, daughter of Peter the Great, became Tsarina, and Maria Theresa, the emperor's daughter, ascended the throne of Austria.

The emperor had assured his daughter's accession by a solemn act making Europe adhere to the Pragmatic Sanction of 1713. As payment for

The Galerie des Glaces at Versailles during the celebrations for the wedding of the Dauphin Louis (Louis XV's son) in 1745.

his consent, Frederick II suddenly occupied Silesia.

An anti-Austrian party was agitating in France, led by Fouquet's grandson Marshal Belle-Isle, in support of Frederick II. Despite themselves, Louis XV and Fleury were obliged to go to war. An attack was made in the direction of Vienna, and a success was won in the capture of Prague (1741).

With this success behind them, the French imposed the election as emperor of the elector of Bavaria, Charles Albert, whose dynastic rights in the male line had precedence over those of Maria Theresa. But this election did not have the hoped-for result. Maria Theresa, supported by the Hungarians, invaded Bavaria and concluded a separate peace with Frederick II, giving him Silesia. Under attack from the Hungarians, the French had to evacuate Prague in the middle of winter, and the retreat was terrible.

Seeing that France was in an impasse, Fleury wrote secretly to Maria Theresa to try to reach an agreement. The letter was discovered. Fleury lost face and disavowed the letter but, overcome by his misfortune, died shortly afterwards (29 January 1743).

The war continued for another three years, but before describing all its convolutions it is important to mention Louis XV's private life during this period.

Since the queen had closed her bedroom door to him, Louis XV, who was only thirty, went to seek consolation elsewhere. He had famous affairs with the four de Nesle sisters, of whom the most remarkable, the duchess of Châteauroux, thought, at Fleury's death, that the king should rule alone and cover himself with glory by military exploits.

After the evacuation of Prague it was decided to give up trying to occupy Austria. An army was left in Germany, but in 1743 the coalition, in which England had now joined, attacked the French army successfully at Dettingen. The French army had to cross the Rhine, and Alsace was defended by Maurice de Saxe, a bastard son of Augustus, the Polish king, and of Countess Aurora von Königsmark.

The defence of Alsace was so effective that by the treaty of Frankfurt (22 May 1744) Frederick II offered an alliance to France and to Bavaria. Thus fortified, Louis XV took charge of hostilities in person. He attacked the Netherlands and took Menin, Ypres and Furnes.

Austria retaliated with an offensive in Alsace and Louis moved his headquarters to Metz. There he fell seriously ill, and his life was in danger. On the advice of his confessor he made honourable public amends, sent away the duchess of Châteauroux, and was reconciled with the queen.

But he recovered and resumed the campaign; he lifted the blockade on Alsace and took Freiburg im Breisgau on 6 November 1744.

On 20 January the Bavarian emperor died in Munich, and this might have made possible a compromise treaty, had Frederick II not resumed hostilities. Maria Theresa's husband, Francis of Lorraine, easily took over the imperial crown.

After his success in Alsace, Louis XV had returned to Paris, and despite his promise had renewed his relationship with the duchess of Châteauroux, to great public indignation. A few days later she died, possibly poisoned.

Unable to stand his solitude the king began a relationship with a bourgeoise, Jeanne Poisson, wife of Le Normant d'Etioles; he was to make her marquise de Pompadour. She was a very attractive girl, clever and ambitious, who made all sorts of sacrifices to maintain her position until her death in 1764. This liaison with a girl of humble extraction scandalized the nobility, and Madame de Pompadour was in an even more difficult situation since, being frigid, she could only keep her place by procuring for the king numerous mistresses.

Her 'reign' was to last for nineteen years, and she would play an important role in the whole of French politics.

Madame de Pompadour (1745–1764)

Madame de Pompadour had no part to play, however, in the last years of the war of the Austrian Succession.

With Alsace freed from danger, the theatre of war reverted to the Netherlands. Louis XV took part personally in a large number of the operations, which were conducted with great talent by Marshal Maurice de Saxe, who on 11 May 1745 crushed Cumberland's army at Fontenoy. This, the finest battle of the eighteenth century, was marked by the famous exchange: 'French gentlemen, fire first.' 'English gentlemen, we never fire first. You fire.' And Louis XV made the very human reflection to his son on visiting the battlefield: 'Look at the cost of this triumph: our enemies' blood is still men's blood, true glory is to spare it.'

As a result of Fontenoy, part of Belgium fell into French hands. A peace could have been signed, but Frederick II signed a separate one with Austria at Dresden, which guaranteed him the possession of Silesia.

The war with England and Austria continued. On 20 February 1746, Maurice de Saxe seized Brussels. This success was neutralized by a reversal which took place in England, where the Stuart pretender supported by France was crushed by Cumberland at Culloden (16 April 1746). This English victory renewed a struggle which did not confine itself to Belgium, as fighting also went on in the colonies, in Canada and in India, where Dupleix and La Bourdonnais fought magnificently.

Belle-Isle tried to recapture Piedmont but he was defeated in the Alps, at the Col de l'Assietta. But Maurice de Saxe was piling success upon success. He won victories at Raucoux in 1746 and Laufeldt in 1747, while Lowendal, in Holland, took the impregnable citadel of Berg-op-Zoom.

The taking of Maastricht by Maurice de Saxe in the spring of 1748 was the pretext for a peace conference which was held at Aix-la-Chapelle. There was no obvious winner, and reciprocal concessions were made. Madras was exchanged for Louisbourg, and Francis of Lorraine was recognized as emperor. Maurice de Saxe demanded the enormous reward of Belgium as a personal proconsulate. Louis XV, who was determined to 'make peace like a king, not a shopkeeper', gave it back to Austria, which gave rise to the proverbial sayings 'as stupid as the peace' or 'to work for the king of Prussia'. Indeed, as possessor of Silesia, Frederick II was the sole beneficiary of the peace.

All in all, since the national territory had been saved from invasion, the prosperity of France was not affected by the war. A dynamic minister, the superintendent of finances, Machault d'Arnouville, wanted to institute a permanent income tax of five per cent and also to

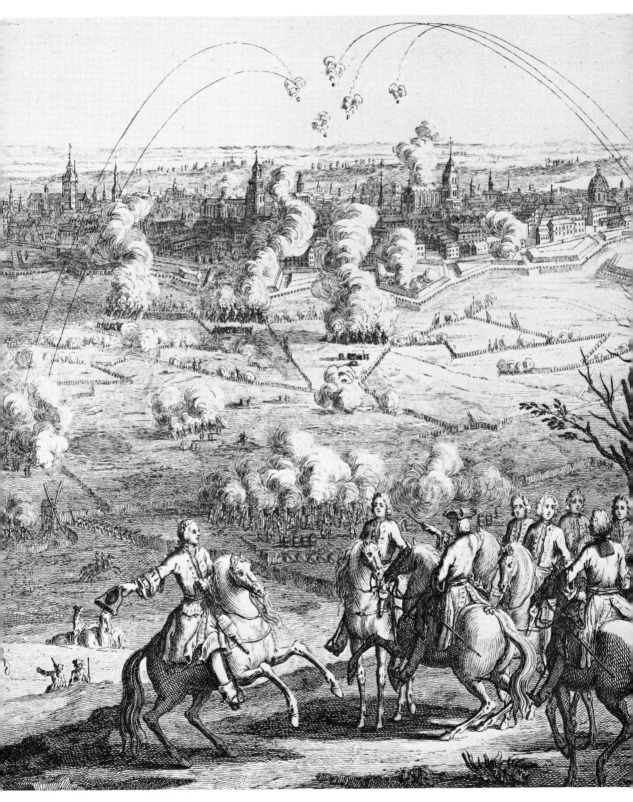

The siege of Brussels, February 1746.

Madame de Pompadour, by François Boucher.

tax the clergy, who were virtually immune from taxation. Since Louis XV's private life made it impossible for him to alienate the clergy, these fiscal reforms were not instituted, and Machault had to resign. This was a very important event, and one of the causes of the Revolution.

Abroad, the situation was getting worse because England, with a strong navy, persevered in her intention of seizing the French colonies to preserve her own hegemony. Louis XV, aware of the danger, sought an alliance with Spain (1754).

Then, in 1755, Maria Theresa used Mme de Pompadour's political influence: she had her spy out the possibilities of an alliance. Cardinal de Bernis, minister of foreign affairs, thought it wise to study the possibilities of this project. The empress proposed to place Louis XV's son-in-law, Philip of Parma, on the throne of the Austrian Netherlands in the hope that they might revert to France, as Lorraine had done.

These secret negotiations had a no less mysterious counterpart. Prussia, on learning that England had contracted a treaty for a defensive alliance with Russia, was wary of being encircled, and, without warning Louis XV, signed the treaty of Westminster (16 January 1756).

Since this defection left France isolated, it became possible to follow up Maria Theresa's proposal, which up to that point had seemed contrary to the honour of France. And so an alliance with Austria was signed on 1 May 1756. It has been called the Reversal of Alliances, and had serious political consequences. As soon as England found out about the treaty, she declared war (8 May 1756), and Frederick II entered the campaign without a declaration and occupied Saxony. At that point Russia took sides with France.

The war began successfully: in 1756 Richelieu and La Galissonnière took Minorca, then Richelieu forced Cumberland to capitulate at Closter-seven, and Frederick II was defeated by the Austrian Marshal Daun at Kolin (June 1757).

The year 1757, which had begun so well, was marked by an assassination attempt on Louis XV perpetrated by a half-mad man called Damiens. This revealed that the king's popularity was waning, and indeed it was badly affected by the reversal of fortunes which was about to take place.

In one month, Frederick II inflicted two bloody defeats on the French at Rossbach (5 November 1757) and on the Russians at Leuthen (5 December 1757).

France in turn won a few local successes in the Hesse-Westphalia sector thanks to Marshal de Broglie at Hastenbeck and Bergen, and to Marshal de Castries at Clostercamp (16 October 1760). But disaster followed upon disaster in the colonies: Montcalm, charged with the defence of Canada, was defeated at Quebec and died there on 3 September 1759. Levis, his second-in-command, was unable to prevent the fall of Montreal in 1760. In India, Lally-Tollendal succeeded in ruining Dupleix's achievements, a mistake for which he was to pay with his head.

On the advice of Mme de Pompadour, Louis XV had made the duke of Choiseul, the ambassador to Vienna who had negotiated the Reversal of Alliances, his first minister. He carried out this task with great energy for about twelve years.

Since France had lost what was left of her navy at the battles of Lagos (1759) and des Cardinaux (1759), Choiseul had the idea of giving France the benefit of the Spanish navy by negotiating an alliance with all the European Bourbons, the Family Pact (1761). This act of diplomacy was neutralized by the defection of Russia, whose new Tsar, Peter III, signed a separate peace with Frederick II. France was obliged to submit to peace under deplorable conditions.

The treaties of Paris and of Hubertusburg (1763) put an end to hostilities. Maria Theresa finally gave up Silesia. The conditions for France were exceptionally severe, though her territory remained intact.

The real disaster, which at the time was not fully appreciated, took place in the colonies. Nothing was left of Canada, which went to England in its entirety, and France's only bases left in this sector were the small islands of Saint-Pierre and Miquelon; in India, apart from five trading stations – Pondicherry, Chandernagor, Yanam, Mahé and Karika – most of the territory was incorporated into the British empire. Louisiana went to Spain to compensate for the loss of Florida, which went to England. The colonial achievement of two centuries had been wiped out, apart from the possession of a few islands in the Caribbean, Martinique, Saint Lucia, Guadeloupe and, in Senegal, the small island of Gorea.

It would be wrong to think that Louis XV was not fully aware of these disasters. As soon as the treaty of Paris was signed he began to study the possibilities for revenge, sent secret missions to America, and began to rebuild the fleet.

But these praiseworthy activities were overshadowed by a private life which was deemed scandalous even by the liberal eighteenth century. From 1750 onwards Mme de Pompadour was just a good friend. To maintain her position she had to resign herself to providing her royal lover with mistresses. There was a famous house in Versailles, near the deer park, where the king went every night to meet beautiful girls. Some of them did not even realize that they were meeting the king. Others lasted, including the famous Morphise, who gave the king one of the few bastards in whom he took an interest. Much has been said about these adventures, which were probably no more scandalous than those of Henry IV and Louis XIV.

There is no doubt that Mme de Pompadour's influence, even though the reversal of alliances did not have the hoped-for success, was beneficial on the whole. She encouraged painters, sculptors and architects, and France's heritage owes a lot to her: one need only name in this context the Place de la Concorde, the Ecole Militaire, and the Petit Trianon.

Mme de Pompadour died, probably of a chest infection, in 1764. After her death the king con-

Madame du Barry by Madame Vigée-Lebrun.

tinued his debaucheries and, at the death of the queen, in 1768, took an official new favourite who scandalized Europe, the Comtesse du Barry.

The Reform of the Parlements (1764–1774)

The last years of Louis xv's reign partly made up for the mistakes which marked the early ones in the eyes of public opinion. This opinion was sometimes unjust, as Louis xv was the most conscientious of sovereigns and had a hand in all the affairs of state, but he was often hampered by running into very delicate international situations.

To restore France to its former position, Choiseul made elaborate plans: to obtain the necessary credit it was important to conciliate the Parlement, which had become more and more powerful. The concession had to be made to them of sacrificing the order of the Jesuits when Father La Valette went bankrupt in 1764.

This painful concession did not make the Parlements any more sympathetic, and little by little they reached an attitude of permanent revolt, of which the most striking example was the famous Aiguillon-La Chalotais affair in Brittany.

Despite this resistance, Choiseul gradually reconstituted the navy and the army, seconded by Guibert, Castries and Gribeauval. They bought Corsica from the Genoese, and the subjection of the island was undertaken by Marshal de Vaux (1768), giving France a solid naval base in the Mediterranean.

In 1768, Louis xv named Maupeou, president of the Paris Parlement, chancellor. He was a sombre man, sly, and devoted to duty. His ideas were the opposite of Choiseul's. He thought that the Parlements should be forced to obey, while Choiseul was for increasing their power, so as to win the absolute monarchy into a constitutional monarchy.

This conflict of influences was to dominate the years 1768–77. Choiseul had the upper hand at first, by negotiating the marriage of the dauphin, the future Louis xvi, to the Archduchess Marie-Antoinette, Maria Theresa's daughter, which consolidated the alliance with Austria. Choiseul, who had been the creature of Mme de Pompadour, was on the best of terms with the new dauphine, but could not bear the Comtesse du Barry, and his relations with her became strained to the point of irritating the king. Louis xv would not have dismissed his first minister for a court intrigue, but he used the excuse of an act of disobedience by Choiseul, who armed an expeditionary force to the Falkland Islands without telling the king, to disgrace him suddenly on 24 December 1770.

The crisis of the Parlement took on a serious tone. The king had to hold several *lits de justice*, and on 3 December 1770 he published an edict affirming the royal prerogative: 'We hold our crown from God alone. The right to make laws by which our subjects can be led and governed belongs to us alone, without dependence or sharing.' This was adopting Maupeou's position against that of Choiseul, which also explains the fall from favour of a chief minister who had become so powerful that he had been nicknamed 'the coachman of Europe'.

The magistrates of the Parlement, jealous of

their independence, refused to register the edict of 2 December. In Choiseul they had lost their last champion, and the king solved the problem by a coup d'état. During the night of 19–20 January 1771, the members of the Paris Parlement were asked in person to answer yes or no to whether they wanted to resume their work, and to put it in writing. Since the majority replied in the negative, the king broke up the Parlement by an order of the Grand Council and exiled its members. This manifestation of absolutism came too late, for it was not in the spirit of the century. Choiseul probably had the right ideas, and if Louis xv had established a constitutional monarchy himself the Revolution would probably have been avoided.

Since the king was only sixty when he carried out his coup d'état, he had a right to hope that he still had time to see the consequences of his reform. He constituted a new Parlement whose functions were reduced to judicature, and he ordered that offices were no longer to be venal; the members of the new Parlement would be named by the king and appointed, thus ending the sale of official posts which had succeeded in restricting royal power.

The majority of the privileged classes proved hostile to the reform. A war of *libelles* broke out and the king confined the new system to the Paris Parlement, leaving the old habits to linger in the provinces.

The ministry which served the king during the last years of his reign was called the Triumvirate, since it consisted of Maupeou, Terray and the duke of Aiguillon. Aiguillon, like Maupeou, was a born enemy of Parlement. Terray, an abbot, was superintendent of finance, and he tried to reduce the abuses in that field. He lowered the more flagrant taxes, organized an equitable way of collecting the *vingtième* and came up with the idea of the *contribution mobilière* (tax on personal property), an equitable system of taxation.

Aiguillon failed in foreign policy and lost his authority at the time of the first partition of Poland between Prussia, Russia and Austria (1772). This partition marked the failure of a mysterious policy called the King's Secret, conducted by Louis xv unknown to his ministers with the intention of placing on the throne of Poland a Frenchman, the prince of Conti.

Increasingly concerned by the internal reform, Maupeou probably was aware of its futility, because of the king's age. It would have taken fifty years of stability to have the new institutions accepted, and he was wondering whether the new dauphin, a heavy, slow boy, would have the strength for it.

The dauphine, despite the repeated comments of her mother, Maria Theresa, was in a state of permanent conflict with Mme du Barry, and from this resulted scenes which affected the relations between Louis xv and his grandson and heir, for the king's son and daughter-in-law had both died within a short space of time of each other, at the same time as Queen Maria Leczinska.

Mme du Barry certainly was all-powerful over Louis xv, but only in the field of the senses; she was an experienced and beautiful young girl who had given back the illusion of youth to a mature man, exhausted by his physical excesses. It seems fair to say that she was not an evil woman; she was charitable and generous, and, apart from her differences with Choiseul, she did not interfere with politics.

Possibly exhausted by his excesses and by the cares of government, Louis xv showed signs of a decline. Occasionally he talked apprehensively about the frightening account he would have to make to God. But, with his mind still set on amorous adventures, he decided to go and spend a week alone with Mme du Barry at the Grand Trianon. As soon as he got there he developed a high fever, and his doctor had him hastily brought back to Versailles.

After a few days it became clear that the king had smallpox, a disease which would not spare a man of his age, in the state of medicine at that time. When told of the seriousness of his condition, Louis xv sent Mme du Barry away, called the court chaplain Abbot Maudoux, to whom he made his confession, and made public and honourable amends for the disorders of his private life.

He died on 10 May 1774, leaving the throne to his twenty-year-old grandson, King Louis xvi.

Before moving on to him it is worth making a general judgement on Louis xv's reign. Despite the colonial losses, which were made a big issue, Louis xv's reign can be considered a great one. During this period, France set the tone for

Europe, and continued to dazzle the world, even when her chances of hegemony had more or less disappeared. The national territory had been increased by the acquisition of Corsica and Lorraine, which were considerable and strategically important gains.

It could not be said that France was displeased with its government: the unpopularity which surrounded Louis xv in the last years of his reign was directed against him personally. In his youth he had been adored, and when he fell ill at Metz he had received the nickname 'well-beloved'. It was his private life which made him unpopular towards the end of his reign, and his almost clandestine burial gave rise to scandalous demonstrations.

In contrast, his successor was at first to enjoy such fabulous popularity that one is still amazed that in less than twenty years his reign ended up with the destruction of royalty.

❦ LOUIS XVI ❦
(1774–1793)
AND MARIE-ANTOINETTE

Louis xvi before the Revolution (1774–1789)

KING LOUIS XVI has become a particularly moving figure in history because of his martyrdom. Physically, he was a thick-set man, with a puffy face and prominent eyes, and short-sighted. He loved hunting and manual work, particularly lock-smithing, but he was also highly educated, particularly in geography. Full of good intentions, but incapable of carrying them out, he was, after a brilliant beginning to his reign, to see the state crumble in his hands and the resulting downfall of the monarchy.

Because he had a slight genital malformation, he did not consummate his marriage for seven years, which deeply hurt the pride of his wife Marie-Antoinette. She was more majestic than truly beautiful, had an inimitable bearing, a certain stiffness of manner, a great deal of arrogance, and occasionally a wounding sense of irony. Isolated as a wife, she tried to make a private life for herself and often went to balls without her husband. These imprudences caused her to be vituperated as much as Louis xv's mistresses had been but her adventures, apart from the attachment of Count Fersen, were probably imaginary. The unfortunate thing was that the nation believed all the criticism against her, and she lived in a climate of unpopularity which in part accounts for her misfortunes.

Who could have foreseen the sombre future at the death of Louis xv, when the new king was greeted with a fervour that had not been seen since Henry iv's time? Nevertheless the young couple, in their twenties, seemed to guess the future straight away, and they immediately said: 'God watch over us, protect us: we are too young to reign.'

Louis xvi had a moral testament from his father which advised him on the choice of a first minister. He hesitated between Machault d'Arnouville, whom he rejected as being hostile to the clergy, and the comte de Maurepas, whom he chose. Maurepas was one of Louis xv's old ministers, who had fallen from favour because he had failed to show due respect to Mme de Pompadour, and this weighed heavily in the choice. Maurepas, who had only been consulted, took over the duties of first minister with rigour; in less than three months, Louis xv's ministers fell from favour, and were replaced by new men who were not without their merits, principally Vergennes in foreign affairs and Turgot in finance.

Maurepas' first action was to advise Louis xvi to go back on the reform of 1771, and to re-establish the Parlement; it was a mistake to disavow Louis xv, unless the intention had been to establish a constitutional monarchy, which was far from being the case. It is worth quoting Maurepas' profound and prophetic words, when

OPPOSITE Louis xvi by Duplessis.

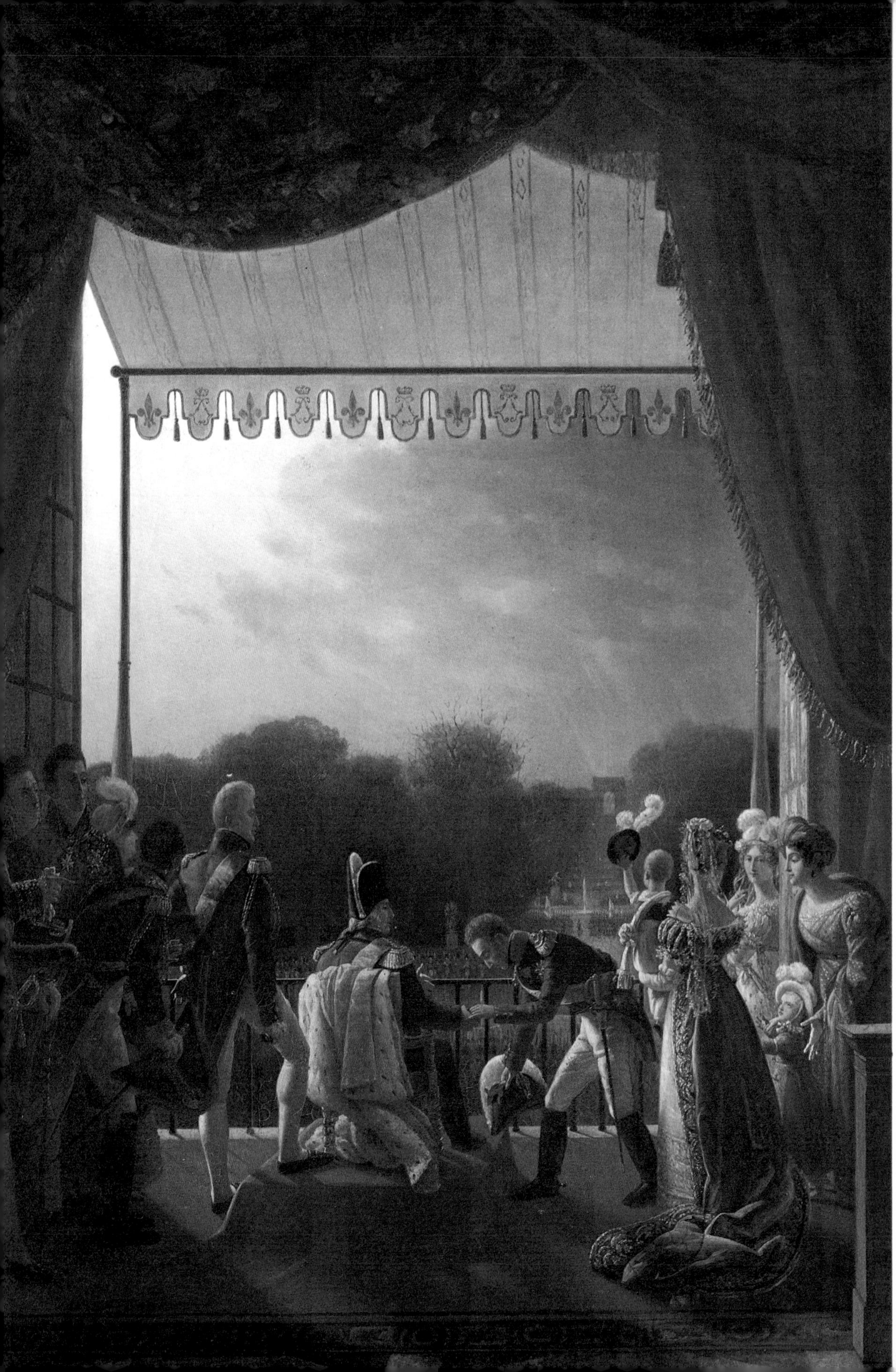

he was disgraced: 'I had made the king win a case which had been going on for three centuries: if he wants to lose it again, he is the master.'

The two ministers who were to direct policies in turn were Turgot and Vergennes, but Maurepas played the important role of adviser throughout, and Louis XVI, who valued him highly, dubbed him his mentor.

Turgot's method was expressed in this simple formula: 'No bankruptcy, no increases in taxation, no borrowing,' which of course was fanciful. But as a pupil of the Physiocrats, Turgot believed that material difficulties stemmed from the constraints imposed by commerce. In 1774 he therefore decided on free circulation for grain. The harvest had been a poor one, the price of bread rose in unfavourable social conditions, and the reform provoked the trouble known as the 'Flour war'.

This setback did not discourage Turgot who, going back on his programme, wanted to establish a new tax, the land subsidy, for which the quota was to be established by assemblies of landowners. This idea seriously offended Louis XVI and was one of the reasons for Turgot's disgrace.

Without realizing how unpopular he was, in 1776 Turgot pursued his reform by suppressing the *corvée* and replacing it with a land tax, abolishing guilds, and giving liberty to industry and commerce.

The Parlement rebelled against all this; the king had edicts registered, then went back on them. This hesitant policy boded ill, and was to bring about his downfall. Turgot was disgraced, and before leaving he said to the king: 'Remember, sire, that it was weakness which put Charles I's head on the block.'

Marie-Antoinette had applied heavy pressure on the king to dismiss Turgot; but the same went for Vergennes, who was hostile to Turgot because he had assured him that the state of the country's finances made any war out of the question, while Vergennes, who was keeping a close watch on the revolt of the English colonies in America, saw therein the battlefield on which to avenge the disgrace of the treaty of 1763.

Vergennes was right. Since 1773 a conflict over the excise on tea had split England and her colonies, and they sent an emissary to Versailles, Silas Deane, to ask for French support. On 4 July 1776 the English colonies proclaimed their independence, which made it possible, with good will, to recognize them as a sovereign state.' In the spring of 1777 a young aristocrat, the marquis de La Fayette, went to join up in the American army, and was given a command there, which was a very significant move for the future.

To enter into the war represented a great financial risk, but the new controller-general, the Genevan banker Necker, judged that it was possible to take it. His attitude encouraged French participation in the war in America. On 6 February 1778 a treaty was signed in Paris between the American representative Benjamin Franklin and Louis XVI. This friendly treaty was in fact a defensive alliance.

When England found out about the treaty she declared war, and it was engaged in the Channel by the incident of la Belle-Poule and the battle of Ushant. Simultaneously, Louis XVI sent a fleet to help the Americans, under Admiral D'Estaing. This fleet, which bore the first French ambassador to the United States, Conrad-Alexandre Gerard, reached the American coast in July 1778, but it failed at New York and at Newport, which meant that the war was going to be a long one.

Indeed, it took more than three years to end English resistance in America. In 1780, an expeditionary force under Rochambeau was sent to the United States, but it was unable to operate effectively because of a lack of manpower. It was only in 1781 that a new minister for the navy, Marshal de Castries, solved the problem by sending reinforcements and by appointing Admiral de Grasse to head the intervening naval force, and Suffren to head the campaign in India.

The combined forces of Washington's army, Rochambeau's expeditionary force and Admiral de Grasse's navy succeeded in 1781, and the fall of Yorktown on 19 October 1781 marked the success of American independence. However, the treaty which ended the war was not signed at Versailles until 3 September 1783. It represented a huge moral success for France, but she had not won any important material advantages, and her finances were in ruins.

The financial crisis caused by the expenses of war had broken out in 1781, and Necker had thought it wise to publish his *compte rendu*, the account of the financial situation, which brought about his disgrace.

OPPOSITE From a balcony in the Tuileries, Louis XVIII, together with Monsieur and the duke of Angoulême, watches the army's triumphant return from Spain, on 2 December 1823. (*Painting by Louis Dubois*)

ABOVE Rochambeau and Washington at Yorktown, 1781.

His successors, Joly de Fleury, then d'Ormesson, could do no better than he, and in 1783, Louis XVI thought he had found an adequate superintendent in Count de Calonne. Calonne was a good financier, but he was also a courtier, and for three years he offered favours at court to get the programme of reforms which he presented to Louis XVI in August 1786 accepted.

This plan, rather judiciously, incorporated a programme of loans and of new taxation; since Calonne feared resistance from the parlements, he advised Louis XVI to call an assembly of notables and to impose his wishes on them.

The notables gathered in February 1787, the day after the death of Vergennes. Calonne put forward his projects, which included a stamp tax and a land tax which would have made it possible in time to restore the state's finances. But, tricked by the notables, Calonne was forced to

resign and the king replaced him by an impudent prelate, Cardinal Loménie de Brienne, archbishop of Toulouse, and then of Sens.

Since the treaty of Versailles France had been shaken by an internal crisis which revealed that authority was beginning not to be observed. A very unfortunate affair, the affair of the Necklace, unfairly compromised the queen and discredited the royal family. A clumsy foreign policy, in which France refused to support her Dutch allies, also contributed to the weakening of the government, to an extent which Lómenie de Brienne was incapable of controlling.

Brienne began by applying the programme which the notables had voted for: he made the Parlement accept the principle of provincial assemblies, but they clashed when he asked them to register the stamp tax and the land subsidy.

Louis XVI finally decided to take a firm hand:

OPPOSITE The young Marie-Antoinette.

227

on 14 August 1787 the members of the Parlement were exiled to Troyes. Loménie de Brienne was made first minister, with discretionary powers, which provoked the departure from the ministry of the Marshals de Castries and de Ségur, accompanied by the superintendent Laurent de Villedeuil.

Loménie was to govern alone for a year, but he negotiated secretly with the Parlement, even though it demanded a meeting of the Estates-General. When the Parlement agreed to authorize a loan of 485 millions, which was indispensable to overcome the financial deficit for the next five years, he promised them a convocation of the Estates, to take place in 1792. When Louis XVI expressed his reservations about this, Brienne explained to him that this was only an empty promise, which would not be carried out.

A tortuous policy was beginning. In order to win the Parlement's agreement to the loan, the new keeper of the seals, Lamoignon, tried to buy the most influential parliamentarians. At this point the two first Estates grouped themselves around the duke of Orléans, in whom they saw a possible alternative king. The sitting to register the loan took place on 19 November 1787. A procedural error was made, and the duke of Orléans, who had stood up to demand that legal procedures be adhered to, received from Louis XVI the reply: 'It is legal because it is what I want.'

The Parlement had to submit, but as soon as the king had left, the parliamentarians refused to transcribe the texts. At this point the king jibbed and tried to lead a revolution in favour of the crown. He signed two *lettres de cachet* against the most virulent parliamentarians, and exiled the duke of Orléans.

Since this act of authority failed to compel the parliamentarians to respect their duties, Louis XVI carried out a coup de force reminiscent of that of Louis XV in 1771. He made preparations to dissolve Parlement, but before the decree had been published the parliamentarians assembled and took an oath to maintain the status quo. On 5 May 1788, the king had the instigators of this, d'Eprémesnil and Freteau de Saint-Just, arrested, then he called a *lit de justice* and instituted a plenary court which was to replace the Parlement.

It is likely that, had these measures been applied, the crown might have won the day. But Louis XVI had already exhausted all his energies. The plenary court was not constituted, and a tragic situation developed, as the provincial parlements rose up in turn. An assembly of the provincial Estates at Vizille demanded fiscal equality, and a meeting of the Estates-General.

This troubled atmosphere added to the difficulties of the public finances: Loménie de Brienne asked the clergy for help, but in vain, and on their refusal he took out an order on 8 August 1788 calling a meeting of the Estates-General for 1789. This admission of weakness, which marked the failure of the attempt at a royal revolution, provoked such a crisis in the treasury that Brienne, realizing that he was incapable of paying the dues for the end of August, had to resign (24 August 1788).

So Louis XVI, who believed he was falling in with the nation's wishes, resigned himself to calling on Necker and making him chief minister. The Genevan's credit was such that public funds increased once again, and a massive subscription for the treasury was obtained. But though Necker's presence had re-established confidence, the new first minister could envisage no programme of reforms other than the establishment of a constitutional monarchy, which was a total contradiction of Louis XVI's views.

Louis XVI *and the Revolution (1789–1793)*

The formal session of the Estates-General opened on 5 May 1789. The opening speeches, made by Louis XVI and by Necker, kept to general topics, and they avoided the question of whether the vote would be taken by head or by order.

The nobility, which was experienced in these matters, rushed to establish its power so as to be able to take measures which would become law; the clergy, torn between trying to maintain its privileges and its sympathy for the third estate, hoped for a compromise; the third estate, realizing that nothing could be decided without it, remained cleverly inert and waited.

After a month the king ordered conferences of conciliation between the three orders. The third estate, thinking that this was a bluff, sent its doyen, the astronomer Bailly, to ask for an explanation, but the king, worried about the health of the dauphin, who was dying, refused to grant him an audience.

At this point the third estate, exasperated, decided to operate the verification of their mandates in common, and when the privileged classes failed to answer their call they constituted themselves alone and called themselves the National Assembly.

Louis XVI, outraged at this behaviour, had the conference hall closed; the deputies of the third estate, gathered together in the room of the Jeu de Paume at Versailles, swore an oath to give the country a constitution (20 June 1789).

On 23 June a royal session, presided over by the king, annulled the decision which had been taken by the third estate and ordered it to retire to deliberate separately. Resistance was organized straight away, and the marquis of Mirabeau replied to Dreux-Brezé, who warned the third estate to evacuate the room: 'Go and tell those who sent you that we are here by the will of the people, and that we will only leave at the point of the bayonet.' Then a vote was taken in favour of legal immunity for deputies.

Not only did Louis XVI not take any steps against them but he changed his mind yet again and ordered the three estates to assemble again, on 27 June 1789, to deliberate together, a gesture which established de facto constitutional monarchy.

Louis XVI's retreat had alarmed the court. Then the king changed his mind again. He called his troops, dismissed Necker on 11 July and called on Breteuil to constitute a ministry of war, prepared to face bankruptcy if the Assembly did not vote him the necessary credit to re-establish his finances.

Hearing of this, Paris rose against him and bands of rioters seized the Bastille and killed its governor, Launay, as well as the provost of merchants, Flesselles (14 July 1789).

In a new about-turn, Louis XVI recalled Necker and on 17 July he came to Paris, where he was received by the new mayor, Bailly, and by the commander of the National Guard, La Fayette, who decorated the king with the tricolour cockader, combining the white of the royal flag with the colours of the town of Paris.

The Assembly continued to sit, and took measures the most important of which came during the night of 4 August 1789, when the vicomte de Noailles had a vote passed abolishing privileges and feudal rights, a generous decision

which was to give rise to many complications. Then, while the Assembly was working at formulating a constitution, Louis XVI gathered his troops at Versailles, probably with the intention of staging a coup.

But the rioters outmanoeuvred him. On 5 October 1789 a troop of women, swelled by men in disguise, marched on Versailles despite La Fayette's attempts to dissuade them. They invaded the Assembly room and sent a delegation to the château. Louis XVI received the delegation amicably, thinking that this would be the end of it. But this was only an illusion. During the morning of 6 October, the rioters invaded the château and Marie-Antoinette was nearly killed. She owed her life to the presence of mind of La Fayette who, by kissing the queen's hand on the central balcony of the château, disconcerted the crowd. But the mob demanded that the king come to Paris; the journey was made in horrible conditions, and the royal family found itself virtually prisoners in the Tuileries. This captivity was to last for nearly three years.

In this difficult situation the king looked for support; he found it in La Fayette, and also in Mirabeau, who became his secret adviser and thought that one possible solution was the king's flight into the countryside where, with the help of the army, he could try to dissolve the Assembly and resume the reins of power.

Necker, who had become first minister again, tried, together with the Assembly, to restore the financial situation, which was becoming increasingly precarious. He tried to borrow, without success, and ended up by agreeing to the principle of a solution proposed by the bishop of Autun, Monseigneur de Talleyrand.

It consisted of confiscating the clergy's immense fortune and giving them in return bills called *assignats*. On 2 November 1789 the Assemblée Nationale, which now sat at the *Manège* in Paris, voted a sanction for this principle, and several hundred millions of bills were put into circulation, which helped the treasury but were consumed in six months. This made a new issue necessary, followed by several others, which brought about the collapse of the exchange rate of the *assignat*.

Had they kept to these purely financial measures it is likely that they would have had no further difficulties with the clergy. But the

The Oath in the Tennis
Courts, 20 June 1789,
after David.

The Storming of the Bastille, 14 July 1789. (A contemporary engraving)

Assembly, which had dubbed itself 'Constituent', was about to go much further. It worked for the establishment of a civil constitution for the clergy, which anticipated the appointment of curates and of bishops by election. Since the papal territory of Comtat-Venaissin had been annexed, Pope Pius VI was disinclined to accept reforms which made him run the risk of losing his authority over the French clergy.

1790 saw a period of relative calm: on 14 July, a festival of the Federation took place on the Champs de Mars; the king, surrounded by a huge mass of people, swore an oath to the constitution, and many people thought that the revolution was over. But this was not the case, and a few days later the king signed, not without reservations, the law giving a Civil Constitution to the clergy.

Papal reaction was severe, and by the Bull *Quod aliquantum* (10 March 1791) Pope Pius VI condemned all the intended reforms. But it was already too late. From November 1790 the Constituent Assembly demanded that the priests and bishops should take an oath of loyalty to the constitution. The oath affected more than half of the clergy, and a large number of monks and nuns returned to the laity.

The bishops showed more restraint, and only four of them, plus three coadjutors, agreed to swear. Talleyrand agreed to inaugurate new bishops, and in April 1791 all the bishoprics in France found themselves run by dignitaries who were forbidden by papal condemnation to carry out their functions.

Europe began to be worried about these disorders, and to palliate them Louis XVI formulated a secret policy: he charged the baron de Breteuil with conducting a system of secret diplomacy with the sovereigns of Europe, and with the numerous nobles and priests who had emigrated and had their seat at Koblenz, under the authority of the count of Artois, Louis XVI's second brother, and the future Charles X.

It goes without saying that this double-dealing was fraught with the gravest dangers. Mirabeau, who approved of it, died suddenly, on 2 April 1791, leaving Louis XVI without an adviser.

At Easter 1791, Louis XVI wanted to go to St-Cloud to take communion from the hands of a non-oath-swearing priest. The mob refused to let him leave the Tuileries, and he then had the idea of putting into operation the plan for his flight thought out by Mirabeau.

The flight was organized by Count Fersen. During the night of 20–21 June 1791, Louis XVI, disguised as a lackey, Marie-Antoinette, provided with a Danish passport, the dauphin, dressed as a girl, Madame Elizabeth, the king's sister, and Madame Royale, managed to leave the Tuileries in secret. A rather too ostentatious coach took them in the direction of Montmédy. At the same time, the count of Provence had taken the road to Brussels and reached there without any impediment.

On the morning of 21 June, Paris was astounded to hear the news of the king's flight. La Fayette, to avoid the worrying possible consequences of it, announced that the king had been kidnapped and sent his messengers after him with a warrant for his arrest.

Because of unwise moves, the king had been recognized on the road. A postmaster called Drouet caught up with him and made the coach stop at Varennes-en-Argonne, where La Fayette's emissary, Romeuf, arrived just in time to make the arrest. The royal family had to return to Paris in a difficult three-day journey.

The Assembly suspended all the king's powers and locked him up in the Tuileries. There was tremendous mass unrest, and on 17 July La Fayette and Bailly were forced to open fire on the demonstrators, killing about fifty of them.

This act of authority restored calm for a while, and the Assembly, fearing for its own survival, thought it wise to make the king the guarantor of any reforms; it amended the constitution favourably for the monarchy. Louis XVI, with his authority re-established, agreed to swear an oath to the new constitution (14 September 1791). Shortly afterwards the Constituent Assembly was dissolved, leaving way for the assembly which the constitution had established and which was called the Legislative Assembly. This consisted of young, absolutely new men (since the deputies at the Constituent Assembly had decided to make themselves ineligible for re-election), but also of men with a great deal of political experience.

The Legislative Assembly began its work on 1 October 1791. It was faced with a difficult situation because of the religious crisis, and the problems in the treasury.

It split into factions: the constitutional monarchists, called *Feuillants*, on the right; and on the left two groups, the Girondins, led by Vergniaud and Brissot, and the Jacobins, with Carnot and Gambon, who were quite simply republicans. The mainstream group of undecided people, representing a third of the deputies, was called the Marais.

Since deputies could not be ministers, Louis XVI instituted a 'Feuillant' ministry, under the count of Narbonne, who favoured a war which would distract attention from the internal crisis. By a curious paradox, the Jacobins were in agreement with this, but they hoped that the upheaval of a war would clear the way for a republic. These various military intentions suited those who had emigrated, gathered at Koblenz under the comte de Provence; they wished for a war so that they could bring foreign support to bear to re-establish an absolute monarchy. The war finally resulted from this immoral mixture of extremes.

A reason for conflict soon arose with the question of the *princes possessionés*. They were minor German sovereigns whose territories were situated in Alsace, and whose inhabitants were demanding the benefits of the revolutionary reforms.

Louis XVI, feeling that war was imminent, because the ultimatum offered to the *possessionés* had resulted in an Austro-Prussian alliance, was forced to order all those who had emigrated to return to France under pain of confiscation of their goods, and he was weak enough to send the minister of foreign affairs, Valdec de Lessart, who was in favour of peace at all costs, to the high court.

The Feuillant ministry disintegrated after the dismissal of Narbonne, and Louis XVI was obliged to constitute a Girondin ministry, in which Roland de la Platière became minister of the interior, and in which the war was put in the care of a royalist soldier, General Dumouriez. He decided to save the monarchy by any means possible, but ran up against hostility from Marie-Antoinette.

Gustavus III, king of Sweden, who supported the émigrés, was assassinated in March 1792, and at the same time Emperor Leopold, the queen's brother, died. The ultimatum which had been sent to him was renewed for his son, Francis II.

Without waiting for Austria's reply, Louis XVI, who saw in war his last hope of salvation, proposed to the Assembly that it be declared (20 April 1792). After long deliberations the Assembly approved the declaration of war, making it clear that France was not after conquests, but only wanted to put a stop to the injustice of a king. From this decision resulted the twenty-three-year conflict which was to end only on the battlefield of Waterloo.

The war began with a series of setbacks; Rochambeau's armies scattered and the Imperial forces took the northern frontiers. Moreover, the coalition forces were preparing to form a powerful invading army, under the command of the duke of Brunswick, who was considered to be the leading general of the period.

While foreign policy seemed to dominate the situation, the Legislative Assembly worked on domestic policies; it made the sanctions against those who had emigrated more severe, and demanded measures of constraint and exile against priests who did not agree to the civil constitution of the clergy. Louis XVI vetoed these coercive measures. The Assembly retaliated by disbanding the king's personal guard, and by calling in from the provinces 20,000 federal troops to take over Paris. It would seem that Louis XVI did not grasp the danger presented by these decisions.

On 13 June 1792, the Girondin ministers handed in their resignation to protest against the maintaining of the veto. Chief minister Dumouriez, unable to save the king, also resigned, and the king constituted a Feuillant ministry, which was going against public opinion; a riot broke out on 20 June. The Tuileries were invaded, and Louis XVI had a red bonnet placed on his head and was forced to drink with the rioters. But he did not give in to violence and maintained his veto.

The king's determination seemed to restore the situation for a few days. La Fayette came to offer him his services and was clumsily rebuffed by Marie-Antoinette.

The foreign threat was becoming clearer. Francis II was crowned emperor at Frankfurt on 20 July, and Brunswick's army gathered near Mainz, at the same time as the federal troops

The execution of Louis XVI, 21 January 1792.

from Marseilles were making their entry into Paris.

Before taking the offensive, the duke of Brunswick issued a very clumsy manifesto threatening Paris with destruction if any attempt was made on the royal family. When this manifesto became known, at the beginning of August, it inflamed public opinion and a day of riots was organized for 10 August 1792.

This was the day on which the monarchy was to succumb. Since the Tuileries was virtually surrounded by rioters, Louis XVI and his people thought it wise to go to the Assembly and ask for asylum. The rioters, who had killed the head of the royal guard, Mandat, achieved their ends all the more easily because Louis XVI ordered his Swiss Guards to cease fire in order to avoid a massacre.

While the Tuileries were pillaged, the Paris Commune put pressure on the Legislative Assembly and made it order the imprisonment of the king and his family in the Tour du Temple. A provisional executive committee presided over by Danton replaced royal power, and at the beginning of September ordered horrible massacres of priests and aristocrats.

Then the Legislative Assembly disbanded, to be replaced by a national Convention whose first act, on 20 September 1792, was to abolish the monarchy.

On the same day, at the mill at Valmy, Dumouriez and Kellerman repulsed the duke of Brunswick. He decided to retreat, and this gave all power to the government of the Convention.

The Convention, not content with having abolished royalty, deemed it necessary to suppress its head, and the trial of Louis XVI was initiated by Robespierre and Saint-Just.

The discovery of papers in an iron chest in the Tuileries, establishing the collusion between Louis XVI and the émigrés, provided the prosecutors with the chance to try him for high treason. The outcome of the trial was obvious from the start, since it was far less a question of judging the king than of assassinating him legally.

The trial of Louis XVI lasted from 26 December 1792 to mid-January 1793.

The king displayed admirable dignity and composure. Despite the devotion of his defenders, Malesherbes, Trouhet and de Sèze, the king was condemned to death by three successive ballots; in one of them the vote was only 361 against 360, which weighed heavily on the memory of the duke of Orléans who voted for death, out of cowardice, it seems.

On 21 January 1793, Louis XVI was led to the scaffold in the Place de la Concorde. He died with great dignity, shouting to the crowd before he died: 'Frenchmen, I die innocent, and I pray to God that my blood will not fall upon my people.'

Queen Marie-Antoinette was to suffer the same fate as her husband, and, after an abject trial, she was guillotined on 16 October 1793.

However the monarchy was not dead: the dauphin Louis XVII became king as a result of his father's death. Imprisoned in the Temple, and put in the charge of the cobbler Simon, it appears that he died there on 8 June 1795. This death has taken on a legendary aspect, since after this there appeared many false dauphins, impostors who gave rise to much discussion until the middle of the nineteenth century.

And the dauphin's death did not in any case mark the end of the monarchy, since in exile the count of Provence declared himself king under the title of Louis XVIII.

THE PROCLAIMING OF THE REPUBLIC and the execution of the king interrupted the continuity of the monarchy. The dauphin, who became Louis XVII, resigned only nominally. At his death in 1795 his uncle, the comte de Provence, declared himself king and his theoretical reign lasted until 1814 when he came to the throne with the Restoration.

The twenty-two years separating the proclaiming of the Republic, on 20 September 1792, and the Restoration of April 1814 saw the following régimes: the Convention Nationale (1792–1795), and the Directoire (1795–1799). On 18 Brumaire the Directoire was overthrown by a coup d'état led by General Bonaparte; he instituted the Consulate which, in May 1804, was replaced by the Empire. Since Napoleon was an emperor and not a king he does not feature in the list of the kings of France.

Part Six

THE RESTORATION OF THE BOURBONS

1814~1830

The false spring

The arrival of Louis XVIII
at Calais, 24 April 1814.

⚬❀❀ LOUIS XVIII ❀❀⚬
(1814–1824)

LOUIS-STANISLAS-XAVIER DE BOURBON was the third son of Louis XV's dauphin and of his second wife, Marie-Josèphe de Saxe. He was born in 1755, one year later than Louis XVI. Since the eldest of the sons died prematurely, Louis XVI became dauphin and his brother took the title of Monsieur, count of Provence.

He was a studious child, fond of literature and poetry, which made him very popular with his grandfather Louis XV. When Louis XVI ascended the throne, Monsieur was heir presumptive, and he remained so until the birth of the dauphin in 1781. Feeling, with reason, that he was more intelligent than Louis XVI, he was jealous of his older brother and some historians say that he even tried to get rid of him. The future Louis XVIII was married to a princess of Savoy, very ugly, and who was destined to have a miserable life. Monsieur had a physical deformity, and it is probable that the marriage was never consummated. The prince consoled himself with numerous platonic relationships, with both men and women.

A man with a sense of self-importance and an active life, the count of Provence began to have a political role in the Assembly of Notables, where he preached double representation for the third estate.

Worried by the king's concessions at the beginning of the Revolution, he encouraged him to resist. He also organized a conspiracy with the help of the marquis de Favras to intern the king, and for him to become lieutenant-general of the kingdom. The affair was discovered, and the count of Provence abandoned Favras, who was hanged (1790).

On the day when Louis XVI began his flight, which ended at Varennes, the count of Provence reached Brussels without difficulty and then installed himself in Koblenz with the count of Artois, and placed himself at the head of the émigré movement with such virulence that his actions put the royal family in peril; but this seemed not to worry him overmuch.

He took part in the Brunswick campaign and, after the retreat, took refuge at Hamm, in Westphalia, where he organized the semblance of a government. At the death of Louis XVI, he proclaimed himself regent, and tried to join up with the English at Toulon. Napoleon Bonaparte's successes made him change his plans. He established himself at Verona, and, when he heard of the death of the dauphin, who had become King Louis XVII, he proclaimed himself king in turn and always dated his reign from June 1795.

This fictitious reign was an interesting one, full of adventures, manifestos and plots. Louis XVIII's errant life in exile took him from Verona to Blankenburg (1796), and from there to Mitau in the Latrian duchy of Courland (1798), from which Tsar Paul I expelled him. He installed himself in Warsaw in 1801, then came back to Mitau in 1805 to settle definitively in England from 1808 onwards. He led the life of a recluse at Hartwell Castle, where his wife died in 1810.

It was at Hartwell that, at the beginning of April 1814, he heard that he was king of France. He replied majestically: 'Have I not always been?'

On 24 April 1814 he landed on French soil, then took up residence in the château of Saint-Ouen, where he received a delegation from the Senate. He reached a compromise with them: he was returning by divine right, but he consented to grant his subjects a Charter establishing a constitutional monarchy on the model of England. The king alone held executive power; legislative power was shared between him and the two chambers, one elected by restricted suffrage, and the other nominated by him, the Chamber of Peers.

The first problem to be resolved was to clear national territory of the Allied forces. A peace treaty was discussed, and the king obtained very advantageous conditions: France returned to its 1792 frontiers, plus Savoy and Venaissin. There was to be no occupation, and no war indemnity.

The treaty was signed at Paris on 30 May 1814. A few days later, the Chamber of Peers met and the Charter was promulgated. The National Assembly, which had been elected at the end of the Empire, was preserved.

Louis XVIII by Paulin Guérin, 1820.

Major allied figures at
the treaty of Paris,
1814: Metternich,
Hardenberg and
Castlereagh.

The territorial problems in Europe were handed over to an international congress which took place in Vienna and where Talleyrand brilliantly represented French interests. The first success was won as soon as January 1815, when an agreement was signed with England. Further progress was in view when the news exploded like a thunder clap that Napoleon had left Elba, had landed at the Golfe Juan, and was marching on Paris.

The Restoration government had not pleased everyone: some supporters of the Empire lost their jobs, which were given to émigrés, or to faithful royalist subjects. Since part of the army had been disbanded, the officers were placed on half-pay. Bonapartist plots broke out occasionally. This critical atmosphere facilitated the operation which the emperor was attempting.

Louis XVIII concentrated his troops at Lyons under the direction of his brother, Monsieur, the count of Artois. Since resistance proved impossible, the troops went over to Napoleon's side as he advanced. The defection of Ney at Auxerre opened the road to Paris.

Louis XVIII left Paris during the night of 19–20 March 1815 and took refuge in Ghent. Less than twenty hours after his departure, Napoleon made his entry into the Tuileries and resumed the government of France.

An attempted military resistance by the duke of Angoulême, son of the count of Artois, failed in the southern provinces, and Napoleon was momentarily master of the country. But risings were breaking out in the west.

At Ghent, Louis XVIII formed a provisional government and waited to see what would happen. The sound of cannon brought him the news of the battle of Waterloo.

Since it had not been anticipated in the final act of the Congress of Vienna (9 June 1815) that the king of France would recover his throne, Louis XVIII decided to do so himself. He left Ghent and returned to Paris, exactly one hundred days after leaving it. Napoleon had abdicated and was heading for the Atlantic coast.

Even though he had made unfortunate proclamations threatening exemplary punishment to those who had betrayed him for Napoleon, Louis XVIII was able to take France in hand without too many domestic problems. The real problems stemmed principally from the new invasion, and the very harsh conditions which the Allies intended to impose on France, because of its new defeat.

All these problems were resolved in the first years of the reign. To make sure of internal peace, and to put an end to the troubles called the White Terror, troops had to be used. Exceptional tribunals, the *cours prévotales,* were set up, which condemned more than nine thousand people. The most famous of the victims were Colonel de la Bédoyère and Marshal Ney, who were court-martialled.

A severe purge replaced nearly a quarter of the civil servants, and seventy prefects were suspended. The Chamber of Peers was completed and the peerage became hereditary.

An electoral law was promulgated by edicts: it established electoral colleges based on a property-owning qualification. Following on this very restricted system of suffrage, an assembly was elected in August 1815; it numbered such an overwhelming majority of royalists that Louis XVIII dubbed it the 'unfindable chamber' (*chambre introuvable*), meaning that it was beyond his wildest dreams.

Using the pretext of difficulties with the Allies, Talleyrand provoked a ministerial crisis. Louis XVIII opposed him with composure: he got rid of Talleyrand and Fouché and gave the job of first minister to a great seigneur and former émigré, the duc de Richelieu.

Richelieu, a friend of Tsar Alexander I, made it a point of honour to negotiate a peace treaty, which was signed at Paris on 20 November 1815. This treaty was much harsher than the previous one: France lost Savoy and its strongholds in the north and east. More serious than this was that it allowed for the occupation of the country until heavy war indemnities had been paid. France had to pay 700 millions in gold, 130 millions a year as occupation costs. Long discussions were needed to bring the cost of war damages down to 265 millions. This represented a total charge amounting to more than a whole annual budget.

Since the *chambre introuvable* proved very stubborn in the presence of these financial difficulties, the Allies became alarmed and, giving in to pressure from them, Louis XVIII dissolved the chamber, even though it had not voted the ministry out. It seems that this act of authority, though not illicit, was to compromise the system of parliamentary government. Only one person protested, and that was Chateaubriand, who in his pamphlet 'Monarchy according to the Charter' criticized the measure and was immediately disgraced.

A new and much more reasonable chamber was elected, and Richelieu attacked the problems which had been posed by the war indemnity with the help of the minister of finance, Corvetto. By wise measures they managed to stabilize the currency, to speed up the payment of indemnities, and to free the country of occupying troops sooner than had been expected.

Richelieu, who had brought about admirable results, was rewarded with royal ingratitude, and he resigned. He was replaced by General Dessoles as titular first minister, but the government was exercised by Louis XVIII's favourite, Decazes, the ex-prefect of police, and an able politician.

Richelieu's administrative achievement was an important one: an electoral law allowing for the renewal of the chamber by fifths had been passed in 1816. The second basic law was military in nature: conceived by Marshal Gouvion-Saint-Cyr, it established a sort of conscription by lot, but in particular it removed the granting of promotion from the nobility's hands, thus destroying the only privilege which had survived the night of 4 August 1789. They also tried to abrogate Bonaparte's Concordat, but the project failed in its broad outline, and all that is left of it is the distribution of bishoprics.

The elections of 1819 revealed the discontent of the nobility, which often voted with the left, so creating a strong opposition faction in the Assembly. This opposition brought about a governmental crisis from which Decaze emerged victorious. He was not president of the council for long.

On 13 February 1820, the duke of Berry, second son of the count of Artois, and third in line of the heirs presumptive, was assassinated coming out of the Opera by a fanatic called Louvel. The Ultras, led by Chateaubriand, tried to accuse Decazes of having instigated this crime. Under the pressure of opinion, Louis XVIII had to dismiss his favourite: he made him a duke, and ambassador to London, then he recalled Richelieu.

To maintain their power, the royalists restricted the freedom of the press and instituted the law of the double vote, which favoured the better-off. The law was adopted through the intervention of a deputy from Toulouse, the Count Villèle, who was soon to have a very important role to play.

On 28 September 1820, the duchess of Berry gave birth to a child, Henri-Dieudonné, who received the title of count of Bordeaux. Since the succession was hereby assured, the monarchy felt stronger. However, internal ferment showed that the opposition was making progress. A liberal movement, secretly stirred up by La Fayette and La Charbonnerie, was working for the establishment of a republic.

These agitations proved useful for Louis XVIII. He used them to implement a right-wing policy and to take measures of a clerical nature which placed secondary education under the control of the Church.

Difficulties in internal policies led Richelieu reluctantly to abandon his foreign policy. Though France was present at the Congress of Aix-la-Chapelle in 1818, she was absent from the Holy Alliance's conferences at Troppau (1820) and Laibach (1821), during which the Allies extended their power in Europe.

Richelieu was being secretly opposed by the count of Artois, though he had promised his support after the assassination of the duke of Berry. He was obliged to resign again, and the king's brother replaced him by Villèle.

Villèle, who was to be president of the council for more than six years, was a good minister, and most of all an excellent administrator; but he was a narrow, blinkered royalist, and did not have an expansive enough foreign policy, which earned him a great deal of opposition. He was soon to find himself in a situation contrary to his principles, and would be obliged to compromise them to keep his position.

On 9 March 1821, the king of Spain, Ferdinand VII, had been forced by an insurrection to swear to introduce a constitution. He attempted a coup which resulted in power going to the extreme left. The king became a prisoner, as Louis XVI had been in the Tuileries. The royalist northern provinces instituted a regency and the resistance government established itself at Seo de Urgel. This sparked off a civil war for the liberation of Spain.

Europe was divided. The Tsar and Metternich were for intervening to stop revolutions. England remained aloof and opposed French intervention in Spain. Louis XVIII was all the more embarrassed because the decision was in danger of falling to him in the end.

A congress of the Holy Alliance was to be held at Verona at the end of 1822 to deal with the question. While the minister for foreign affairs, Mathieu de Montmorency, took it upon himself to send arms secretly to royalist Spain, the king and the count of Artois sided with Villèle's neutral policies. Montmorency represented France at Verona, but Louis XVIII sent Chateaubriand with him, having forbidden

The entry of the French, under the
duke of Angoulême, into Madrid, 24 May 1823.

Montmorency to bring the Spanish question
before the congress. Montmorency disobeyed,
and the king did not disavow him, to Villèle's
great fury. Chateaubriand had gone the same
way as Montmorency, and had had a word with
Tsar Alexander.

On Christmas Day 1822, Louis XVIII supported Villèle's position before the council of
ministers. Montmorency, feeling that he had
been disavowed, resigned. To calm public
opinion, which favoured an intervention in
Spain, Louis XVIII was forced to make
Chateaubriand minister for foreign affairs. He
opted for war, and Villèle, against his wishes,

had to make the necessary finance available (10
February 1823).

This Spanish war, which Villèle considered a
dangerous adventure, was instead a tremendous
success. On 7 April 1823, the duke of
Angoulême crossed the Bidassoa with ninety-
five thousand men. It was a mere military stroll.
On 23 May the French army entered Madrid; on
31 August King Ferdinand, who was being held
prisoner at Cadiz by the Cortes, was freed, after
the decisive battle of the Fort Trocadero.

Angoulême tried to contain the excesses of the
Spanish royalists, and returned to Paris triumphant. There is no doubt that the Spanish war

245

brought Louis XVIII great prestige. To take advantage of this prestige, Villèle dissolved the chamber, where resistance often showed itself, and went on to hold a general election on 6 March 1824.

These elections were conducted with rare partiality, and the most dubious means were used to secure success. When it came, it surpassed expectations: the opposition collapsed, and La Fayette was defeated. The government won 411 seats out of 430. 'The chamber is found again', peacefully announced Louis XVIII. It was his last, famous, pronouncement.

To consolidate this success Villèle had a septennial law voted through, which was only to apply to the next election. But the crushing majority still did not produce the hoped for results, and Villèle only got a small majority when he tried to put forward a plan to convert the revenue, which was rejected by the Peers.

Needing a scapegoat, Louis XVIII held Chateaubriand responsible for this defeat and brutally disgraced him. This, the king's last act of authority, turned out to be a big mistake, for the furious Chateaubriand went over to the opposition, and his interventions in the press helped later to bring about the fall of the Restoration regime.

Louis XVIII's health was declining rapidly: at the end of August 1824 he was unable to leave his bed. His last days were tragic, as he suffered a living death from gangrene. He died on 16 September 1824, with few illusions about the outlook for his successor, the count of Artois, who became Charles X.

Louis XVIII was the last king to die while still on the throne, which merits him particular consideration. Nevertheless his contemporaries were not kind to his memory, and it is only with hindsight that we can do him justice.

Despite his faults, about which there is no doubt, he had a high ideal of the royal function, and of the duties implied by it. For nineteen years of exile in very difficult circumstances he had maintained the principle of royalty, and he had been rewarded for this by regaining his throne in 1814 with the minimum of concessions. Once he became truly king, he achieved a tremendous amount. He built a rich country out of ruined France, and gave back to this humiliated land its primacy in Europe.

But there are reservations to be added to the homage paid to this considerable achievement. The king was not expected to be good, nor even to be fair, but simply to be far-sighted. In creating the *cours prévotales,* in using exceptional tribunals without appeal, Louis XVIII showed that he was still a man of the *ancien régime.* His political liberalism had not killed his prejudices in juridical matters. This tendency manifested itself by a limiting of the franchise in the public domain of which the system of property qualification was a typical example.

The apparent emancipation of the state was paid for by a tighter hold at the departmental and communal levels. By continuing to nominate mayors and municipal councils, Louis XVIII managed to deprive himself of the liveliest forces in the nation. His heredity and education made it impossible for him to see that these reforms were necessary, and one should not reproach him for this too much, as he was a king of great quality, to whom history has not granted the admiration due to him.

❧ CHARLES X ❧
(1824–1830)

THE REIGN OF KING CHARLES X, which ended in revolution, marks the end of the monarchy by divine right. The prince's life surpassed in adventure and romance even that of his brother Louis XVIII.

Charles-Philippe de Bourbon, count of Artois, was born in 1757. He was a handsome man, but whimsical and obstinate. After his rather ordinary education he threw himself into a life of pleasure strewn with amorous adventures, particularly with actresses. He was married to a princess, Clotilde of Savoy, sister of

Louis xviii's wife, and she gave him two children, the duke of Angoulême, born in 1775, and the duke of Berry, born in 1778. After the death of Louis xviii they were heirs presumptive to the throne of France. The count of Artois' marriage was not a success; his wife was not attractive, and he was constantly unfaithful to her until her death in exile in 1805.

His liaison with Mme de Polastron, sister in law of the duchesse de Polignac, Marie-Antoinette's favourite, began in about 1784 and was to play a vitally important role in the future Charles x's behaviour. When Madame de Polastron died in London in 1805 she made her lover swear to give up his debaucheries, and to come closer to God. He swore to do so, and the rest of his life was edifying on both moral and religious levels. Henceforth pious to the point of bigotry, he let himself be confined by his mistress's confessor, Abbé Latil, whom he subsequently made a cardinal, and followed his advice blindly. This eventually led to his undoing.

In his youth he had been on the friendliest of terms with his sister-in-law Marie-Antoinette, and she took his advice willingly, and generally took notice of him, which was not a good thing. At the Assembly of Notables in 1787 and 1788 the count of Artois proved himself hostile to any reform and determined to defend the princes by divine right. His attitude became even clearer at the meeting of the Estates-General, and it was partly due to his influence that the royal session of 23 June 1789 was held, which was so unfortunate for the monarchy. He encouraged Louis xvi to take forceful measures against the Constituent Assembly, which led directly to the reaction of 14 July and the storming of the Bastille.

Louis xvi felt that his brother had compromised himself to such an extent that he made him leave France on 17 July 1789. The count of Artois established himself with his father-in-law at Turin and there organized, with Calonne, the first gatherings of the émigrés. He continued his policies at Koblenz with his brother, the count of Provence, and took part with him in the Valmy campaign.

In exile at Hamm in Westphalia, he did not follow his brother to Verona, but, after many difficulties, established himself in London. After the disaster at Quiberon he led an expedition in the Vendée, but contented himself with landing on the island of Yeu, from whence, having achieved nothing, he headed back to London. There he lived until 1814. In March of that year he went to Vesoul in France; he was joined there by an able man, the baron de Vitrolle. Together they negotiated with the allies and in April 1814 the count of Artois made his entry into Paris as lieutenant-general of the kingdom. He was to administer France, without the least skill, until the return of Louis xviii.

During his brother's reign, he completely disapproved of the concessions which had been necessary to recover the throne, and he was at the head of a faction, called the *pavillon de Marsan*, which constantly complicated Louis xviii's policies. He had a hand in the fall of Decazes, and in Richelieu's resignation, and he had complete confidence in Villèle, whom he was to keep as his first minister when he came to the throne on 16 September 1824.

With these political views in mind, it seemed that the reign of Charles x was to prove a stormy one. Nevertheless he began very successfully, and for a few months, thanks to his fine presence and to certain liberal measures, including the abolition of censorship, he was truly popular. But the euphoria was short-lived. A few months after his accession, Charles x alienated the army by forcing some of the Empire's generals into retirement, and instituted a law against sacrilege reminiscent of the Inquisition.

To make it quite clear that he intended to affirm the continuity of divine right, he had himself crowned at Rheims. This coronation ceremony, the last in the history of France, was conducted with extraordinary pomp, but its symbolism became the laughing-stock of the pamphleters and of the chansonniers.

Charles x's policies were to be made clear by the institution of two laws which created a great stir, and were not fully appreciated. The first, which was called *Milliard des émigrés*, pertained to the granting of indemnities to those émigrés who had been deprived of their goods by confiscation in 1792. In the minds of Villèle and Charles x, this was a question not only of repairing an iniquity, but of definitively guaranteeing their national rights. This quite reasonable law, which only compensated people in small part, was the object of lively criticism, and was only adopted by a tiny majority.

The second law, of primogeniture, was rejected by the Peers, who would have been the first to benefit from it, because it aimed at strengthening the sharing out of goods resulting from the Code Napoleon, and to favour the elder sons.

A wave of anticlericalism denounced the abuses of the 'priest' party, and of the Congregation, a religious association which combined politics and religion a little too closely. Charles x answered the attacks on his policy by restricting the freedom of the press. This weakened Villèle's authority.

Villèle, a good administrator, was more interested in the state of the budget and of the treasury than in a policy of foreign expansion. In particular he refused to intervene against the Turks after the drama of the massacres at Chios, then he was forced to do so by public opinion, and even though the French fleet won a resounding victory at Navarino (20 October 1827), he never regained his popularity.

A demonstration by the National Guard during one of its reviews scandalized Charles x and resulted in its being dissolved. This measure made the ministry very unpopular. To regain his majority, Villèle had Charles x appoint a batch of new peers, then, on 24 October 1827, he took the unwise step of dismissing the *Chambre Retrouvée,* hoping that he would do well in the elections. Even though pressure was brought to bear, the 1827 elections placed Villèle in a minority, and he resigned, because the king would give no firm undertaking to support him.

The king was no longer in agreement with the Chamber of Deputies and it in turn was no longer loyal to the monarchy. A new first minister, the comte de Martignac, a subtle politician, failed to disarm the opposition even though he made large concessions to them, particularly in the clerical field, where he made the king sign the ordinances which forbade Jesuits to teach.

An attempt at electoral reform brought about such an uproar that Martignac had to retire. Charles x felt the moment had come to show that the constitutional system would lead to an impasse and, instead of handing over power to the opposition, which would have been logical, he made one of his dearest friends, Prince Jules de

Polignac, president of the council. Polignac was devoted to divine right, and faithful to the king until death. His ministry, which contained Bourmont, the traitor of 1815, and La Bourdonnaye, who had been in charge of the purge, was very badly received by public opinion.

The truth was that Polignac had no policy to follow other than carrying out the king's wishes, and these aimed at a return to absolutism. The speech from the throne of 1830 was extraordinarily unfortunate and Charles x said, among other things: 'If guilty manoeuvres should place obstacles in the path of my government which I do not wish to foresee, I would find the strength to overcome them in my determination to maintain public peace, in my just faith in the French people and in the love which they have always shown for their king.'

This was taken by the deputies as a declaration of war, and the Address to the king was full of implicit threat.

> The Charter lays down as a right the country's intervention in the deliberation of the public interests. It maintains that a permanent concurrence of the political views of your government and of the views of your people should be the indispensable condition for the running of public affairs. Sire, our loyalty forces us to say that this concurrence does not exist at present.

This famous text has been called the Address of the 221, representing the number of deputies who voted for, against the 181 who voted against. Royer-Collard, president of the Chamber, brought the Address to the Tuileries. Charles x took it very badly: a few days later, he announced the dissolution of the Chamber, and decided to hold new elections. This measure seemed so inopportune that the wisest ministers resigned.

Polignac thought again: he was counting on foreign policy to help him out, because he was organizing a prestige expedition against the dey of Algiers who was guilty of having struck the French consul Deval with a fly-swatter. This worthwhile plan was to result in a resounding success, but it did not help to save the threatened throne of Charles x.

The elections disavowed his internal policy.

Charles x in coronation robes, by Gérard.

202 of the 221 were re-elected, and the opposition numbered 270 votes against the crown's 150. The indications were clear: the ministry must be given to the opposition, in accordance with the terms of the Charter.

But the interpretation of Polignac and Charles x was to lead to the opposite concept: basing themselves on article 14 of the Charter, which, they claimed, granted them full power where the safety of the state made it necessary, they decided to resolve the situation by the Ordinances which were signed at Saint-Cloud on 25 July 1830.

These ordinances, which so vitally affected the course of history, were four in number: the first suppressed the freedom of the press, the second illegally dissolved the Chamber, which had not yet met, the third restricted the franchise, and the fourth fixed new elections for the 6 and 13 of September 1830. The programme was completed by an important measure of changes in the civil service.

Charles x and Polignac were so sure of their authority that they did not take the necessary measures to keep order in Paris, in case the Ordinances gave rise to trouble. This lack of forethought brought about a revolution. It was to last for three days, and to mark the end of monarchy by divine right.

On 27 July the deputies of the opposition met in consultation. On the 28th the revolt broke out and Marshal Marmont was put in charge of keeping order in Paris. The capital was covered in barricades; bells were rung and the armed populace took to the streets. Marmont divided his troops into four columns; firing began, but his troops fraternized with the rebels. The deputies of the majority sided with the people, feeling that the monarchy had betrayed them.

It seemed that they were heading for the proclamation of a republic on the American model, under the probable presidency of La Fayette, who had just been given command of the National Guard by the commune of Paris. But things were to turn out differently, with the birth of a new monarchy, rather as had happened in England in 1688.

A young journalist, Adolphe Thiers, whose daily newspaper the *Constitutionnel* accurately reflected public opinion, felt that it would be more in France's interests to have a liberal monarchy under the duke of Orléans, Philippe-Égalité's son. He was named lieutenant-general both by Charles x and by the Paris commune. On 29 July the rebels were masters of Paris and Charles x, who had finally realized his mistake, accepted Polignac's resignation and gave the duc de Mortemart the task of forming a new ministry, with the opposition's approval.

During the night of 29–30 July, Mortemart left Saint-Cloud to announce Polignac's resignation and the retraction of the Ordinances. When he managed to bring the acts to the Hôtel de Ville he was told he was too late; Thiers had already offered the crown to the duke of Orléans.

The duke, after many hesitations, decided to come to the Hôtel de Ville, where he was received by La Fayette, who took him out onto the balcony, draped him in the tricolour, and presented him to the people saying: 'This is the best of republics.'

The royalist forces retreated to Saint-Cloud. Charles and his people took refuge in the Château de Rambouillet. Troops were sent there to intimidate the king, and they succeeded. On 2 August Charles x resigned himself to abdicating in favour of his grandson, the duke of Bordeaux, and the duke of Angoulême also abdicated in favour of his nephew.

The situation now seemed perfectly clear. Charles x ordered the duke of Orléans, the lieutenant-general, to announce the accession of the duke of Bordeaux under the name of Henry v, and to assume the regency. The duke of Orléans contented himself with conveying the royal order to the archives of the Assembly, and letting the French people elect a king on 9 August 1830.

All that was left for Charles x to do was to take the road to exile. He did this with great dignity, and a long and majestic cortege led the fallen king to Cherbourg, where he set sail on 15 August 1830.

He survived for six years after his fall. He was received at first by an English lord, and was then offered the hospitality of the English crown at Holyrood in Edinburgh, where he spent two years. His daughter-in-law, the duchess of Berry, tried in a ridiculous adventure to win back the crown for her son. She failed, and was imprisoned in the citadel of Blaye, where it was

The meeting of the deputies to protest against
Charles X's ordonnances, 26 July 1830.

realized that she was pregnant. This brought her
into disrepute.

Charles X broke off relations with her. He left
Edinburgh and established himself in Prague, in
the Hradcany Palace, where he was to spend four
years, supervising the education of his grandson.
In 1836, so as not to be an embarrassment to the
Austrian sovereign, who was going to be
crowned king of Bohemia in Prague, Charles X
and his people headed for Görz (now Gorizia),
which had a reputation for its healthy climate.

He caught cholera as soon as he arrived there,
and died in November 1836, having ruined his
destiny by his stubbornness and narrowness of
spirit but, also, one must say, by his loyalty to
the tradition of divine right.

'Liberty regained.'
The revolt breaks out
in Paris, 28 July 1830.
(From a popular engraving)

Part Seven

THE ORLÉANS

1830~1848

King of the French

A medallion with a portrait of Louis-Philippe.

✤ LOUIS-PHILIPPE I ✤
(1830–1848)
AND MARIE-AMÉLIE

Louis-Philippe before his reign (1773–1830)

THE FIRST FIFTY-SEVEN YEARS of the life of King Louis-Philippe are important, since they throw a good deal of light on his character and his behaviour.

The son of the duke of Orléans and of Princess Louise Adélaïde de Penthièvre, a Bourbon, though not of the direct line, Louis-Philippe, duke of Chartres, was born at the Palais Royal in 1773. His father entrusted his education to an intelligent intriguer, his mistress Félicité de Genlis. This education gave the pupil a remarkable training; he learned several languages, was well informed, and became very adaptable.

Surrounded by the opposition who gravitated around his father, the duke of Chartres naturally adopted the new ideas. He became a member of the Jacobin Club, and was making a career for himself in the army, in the Vendôme garrison. After 10 August, Danton advised him to continue in this, giving him to understand that his time might come.

Under the orders of Dumouriez, the duke of Chartres played a valiant part in the victories of Valmy and Jemappes, which he always liked to recall. After the defeat at Neerwinden, Dumouriez, threatened with arrest, went over to the Austrians with the duke of Chartres.

Not wanting to serve under a foreign flag, Chartres went to Switzerland. He lived for a while at Bremgarten, then in order to earn a living was obliged to take a job as a schoolteacher in Reichenau, in the Rhine Valley. His virtual desertion brought about the arrest and sentencing to death of Philippe-Égalité, whose two other sons, the duke of Montpensier and the count of Beaujolais, underwent a severe captivity in Marseilles.

From Switzerland the duke of Chartres, who by his father's death had become duke of Orléans, established himself in Hamburg. He made a trip to Lapland, then headed for America,

where his two brothers joined him after being freed. Then in 1800 the three brothers settled in London; a reconciliation with the Bourbons took place at the home of the count of Artois.

The duke of Orléans lost both his brothers in turn; their health had been ruined by their captivity. The count of Beaujolais died in Malta, and from there the duke of Orléans went to Sicily, whose king, after some hesitation, gave him the hand of his daughter, Princess Marie-Amélie, in marriage. She was a very virtuous and highly dignified person. They had a very successful marriage and had ten children, of whom five sons and two daughters survived.

After taking part in operations in Spain, the duke returned to Paris in 1814, but in 1815 Louis XVIII, who had feared at the time of Waterloo that he might steal the crown from him, sent him into exile in London for two years. When he returned to Paris in 1817, the duke, who had recovered some of his possessions, gladly took charge of his affairs with the help of the lawyer Dupin, and built up a considerable fortune. But he was constantly kept at arm's length by Louis XVIII, who distrusted him and caused him a great deal of trouble.

Things changed when Charles X came to the throne. He was kind to his cousin, gave him back the title of royal highness and maintained good relations with him.

Charles X's political mistakes inclined public opinion in favour of the duke. Articles and literary works sang the praises of the English 'Glorious Revolution' of 1688, which had saved the principle of monarchy by substituting a younger liberal branch for an old reactionary one.

Thiers, who was one of the propagators of this idea, therefore logically called on the duke in July 1830, but he protested his loyalty to Charles X, and this attitude has puzzled historians. Invested with the title of lieutenant-general of the kingdom both by the commune and by the king, it seems that he attached more importance to his first commission than to his second.

Louis-Philippe (on the sofa) and his family, by E. Lanu.

Given the mission by Charles x of proclaiming the duke of Bordeaux king, he merely took the royal order to the archives of the Assembly, which was one way of declaring it void.

Chateaubriand, summoned by the duke of Orléans, read in his eyes the desire to be king. It seems that the duke only wanted to avoid another exile, and the loss of his goods, and agreed to accept the crown which La Fayette had practically forced on him.

On 7 August the Chamber voted the devolution of the crown to the duke of Orléans by 219 votes out of a total of 428 deputies. The peers agreed, despite Chateaubriand, and on 9 August 1830 the duke was crowned as Louis-Philippe, King of the French.

Reign and Second Exile (1830–1850)

The monarchy, which had been hereditary, became elective, and it began with a small majority. The royalist party split into two factions, 'Carlist' and 'Orleanist', which did not make the new king's job any easier.

In these difficult circumstances, the beginning of the reign was remarkable. The job of deciding the fate of Charles x's old ministers fell to the minister Laffitte. A famous banker, he was the instigator of a progressive political movement called simply 'the Movement'. Conservative by nature, Louis-Philippe sided with the rival party, that of the 'Resistance'. The trial of the ministers ended with a sentence of life imprisonment. Since public opinion felt that they deserved death, Laffitte's popularity waned, and the king thanked him, getting rid of the party of the Movement. He also got rid of La Fayette, taking away from him the general command of the National Guard.

He then handed over the government to the head of the Resistance, Casimir-Périer, a remarkable statesman whose early death made it impossible to assess his achievement.

The crisis of 1830 had had repercussions

throughout Europe. Belgium successfully revolted against the king of the Netherlands, and offered the crown to the duke of Nemours, Louis-Philippe's son. Wisely, to avoid incurring England's hostility, the king refused this proposal. Leopold of Saxe-Coburg, widower of the heiress to the throne of England, was elected king of the Belgians and married Louis-Philippe's daughter, Louise of Orléans. Talleyrand, ambassador to London, obtained a treaty guaranteeing the perpetual neutrality of the new kingdom of Belgium.

These successes in foreign policy were balanced out by the internal difficulties. Riots broke out in Paris: in February 1831 the Archbishop's palace was sacked, and at the end of that year a revolt broke out in Lyons and it was necessary to call out the troops. Casimir-Périer restored order in the country and led a successful foreign policy. He intervened militarily against a Dutch invasion of Belgium, where Marshal Gerard occupied Antwerp, and a punitive expedition was sent to Portugal. These successes, which strengthened the government, did not avert the necessity of making concessions to the Movement. The most notable of these was the abolishing of the heredity of peers in 1831.

Louis-Philippe, who had an almost unhealthy lust for power, did not miss a minister whom he felt to be too strong-willed, and he was happy to see a floating ministry. From 1832 to 1836 the president of the council changed many times, and there was a succession of first ministers, of whom the most important was the duc de Broglie.

The duchess of Berry's escapade ended in fiasco in 1833 and the instability of the government caused serious rioting in Paris. The king was the victim of several assassination attempts, of which that of Fieschi on 29 July 1835 killed about twenty people and seriously upset public opinion.

The instability of the ministry resulted in the fall of the duke of Broglie, on an insignificant point of procedure. In response to public opinion, Louis-Philippe thought it wise to hand over power to the Movement, and he made Thiers president of the council (22 February 1836).

Thiers, whose main policy was opposition, did not have a real programme to implement. He tried unsuccessfully to negotiate the marriage of the duke of Orléans with an Austrian princess, and, considering that France had been offended by the refusal, he decided to wage war to teach Metternich a lesson. Louis-Philippe disowned him; Thiers offered to hand back his portfolio and it was accepted without hesitation on 6 September 1836. Free of the Movement, Louis-Philippe nominated a first minister after his own heart, Count Molé.

The year 1836 was marked by two other events: the death of King Charles X, which dissolved the legitimist party, and the attempt by Louis Napoleon Bonaparte to seize power in Strasbourg, which did the Bonapartists no good. Prince Napoleon was sent to America without a trial.

The Molé ministry won a popular success by negotiating the marriage of the duke of Orléans to Princess Helen of Mecklenburg. Despite the new duchess's qualities, it was not a good match, but with the birth of a son, the count of Paris, in 1838, the succession was assured. This permitted Molé to stay in office, and for a while consolidated Louis-Philippe's position. But Molé was not popular: he was felt to be haughty and distant, and not to favour social progress. To maintain his majority he was reduced to nominating a handful of peers and dissolving the Chamber.

These political operations did not achieve all the hoped-for results, because Molé was strongly opposed. A parliamentary coalition led by Thiers, Guizot and Odilon Barrot was rising against him. To counter them, Molé dissolved the Chamber again in 1839, but as the elections did not favour him, he retired.

At that point occurred the most serious political crisis of the reign. For three months Louis-Philippe sought in vain to form a ministry. The forces of disorder felt that the time was ripe to intervene. A conspiracy called the conspiracy of the Seasons was formed by Barbès, Blanqui and Martin Bernard. The rebels managed to seize the Hôtel de Ville, and the troops were called in. Pressed by necessity, Louis-Philippe got Marshal Soult to form a ministry (12 May 1840), and the guilty men were imprisoned on the island of Mont-Saint-Michel.

Thiers, enraged, ostensibly retired from public life, but his retirement was to be a short

Marie-Amélie visits wounded soldiers in hospital.

one, for the Chamber refused to vote the endowment requested for the marriage of the duke of Nemours. Soult was forced to resign, and Louis-Philippe had to resign himself once again to handing over power to the Movement, in the person of Thiers.

Thiers, believing that he had triumphed, saw himself as first minister for life, but he was mistaken, as Louis-Philippe's fondest wish was to get rid of him. Thiers started again with a new idea which won him great popularity: he proposed to bring back Napoleon's ashes to France, and took advantage of the effect of this on public opinion to bury electoral reform and to refuse the National Guard the right to vote.

A crisis in Europe suddenly made everyone forget these miserable parliamentary considerations.

The Eastern Question, which was the name which Europe gave to her desire to control Turkey, entered a difficult phase. Mehemet Ali, pasha of Egypt, had declared war on Sultan

Mahmud and had crushed him at Nezib (24 June 1839). An international conference held in Vienna opposed the dismembering of the Ottoman Empire as demanded by Mehemet Ali as the fruit of his victory. And so Thiers, looking for an opportunity to make his presence felt, suggested that France support Mehemet Ali to the point of declaring war, to defend the position of this dangerous ally.

France did not have the material means to conduct this war, nor the possibility of declaring it without uniting the whole of Europe against her. And Louis-Philippe was determined to maintain peace at all costs, even at the price of the national honour, which had been heavily hit by the treaty of the Four Powers; this treaty had been signed in London without France's knowledge, and it had the effect of stirring up Paris opinion.

Louis-Philippe maintained his position and did well to do so, since at the very first battle Mehemet Ali was crushed. Thiers, full of warlike projects, nevertheless prepared a very aggressive speech from the throne. When Louis-Philippe refused to accept its terms, Thiers resigned, which freed the king once again from the Movement party.

At the peak of the ministerial crisis, the pretender Louis-Napoleon, hoping to take advantage of the publicity surrounding Bonapartism, because of the return of the ashes, attempted another expedition; he landed at Boulogne on 6 August 1840 and tried to stir up the garrison, but, clumsily, got himself arrested.

This time Louis-Philippe had had enough, and brought the pretender before the High Court. He was sentenced to life imprisonment in a fortress in the continental territory, and imprisoned in the fort of Ham. A few days after his incarceration Napoleon's funeral and burial in the Invalides were celebrated (15 December 1840).

From 1840 to the fall of Louis-Philippe, France was to live through a period of political stagnation, due mainly to the king's position. Isolated by power, Louis-Philippe, who had lived through the *ancien régime*, and had been an émigré, reverted to conceptions of absolutism and no longer took advice from anyone. He rid himself of all his troublesome adversaries by deception, but he did not realize that he had moved further and further away from public opinion in the country. In 1840 he supported the peace, while the young of the country, eager for glory, wished for war. During a period of social progress he remained shackled by narrow conservatism. An aristocrat at heart, and only a bourgeois for appearances' sake, he believed in the virtue of the owning classes and forgot that, under his régime, power no longer stemmed from divine right, but from the popular will. By refusing to fall in with the masses, he forgot the very principle of his salvation. The ruling class, self-centred to the end, demonstrated the faults of any oligarchy.

A dynastic phenomenon, the accidental death of the heir to the throne, the duke of Orléans, in 1842, underlined the contrast between the populace, and the old sovereign.

From 1840 to 1848, royal policy was supported by his henchman François Guizot, a strict Protestant, and an adherer to the principle that 'the throne is not an empty armchair'. He supported the king with admirable fidelity, but failed, like him, to discern the prejudice and obstinacy which would finally bring about the fall of a régime which could have been saved by a few concessions, because its principle was in fact quite close to the aspirations of the French people.

One must not think, however, that nothing at all happened during this period, which Lamartine summed up in the sentence: 'France is bored' (*La France s'ennuie.*). Though Louis-Philippe refused to risk a European war which might have broken the deadlock of the treaties of 1815, but which might also have placed France in danger of dismemberment, he did not balk at military operations when he felt they would be profitable and achievable.

It was thanks to Louis-Philippe, far more than to Charles X, that Algeria was conquered and pacified, and at the time this appeared to be an advantageous and virtally important operation. In the early years of the reign, the idea of outright war did not prevail, and the treaty of Tafna, signed by Bugeaud, was an attempt at finding areas of agreement with the emir Abd-el-Kader. Then, when the entente proved to be an illusion, military operations were resumed, of which the most famous was the taking of Constantine in 1837.

Louis-Philippe's sons took an interest in the

Algerian war: the prince de Joinville made a name for himself at Constantine, and later on in the war at sea, and the duke of Orléans forced the gorge of the Iron Gates in 1839. The duke of Aumale became famous through the capture of Abd-el-Kader's retinue in 1843.

From 1840 onwards, Louis-Philippe appointed Bugeaud governor-general in Algiers, and he undertook the methodical conquest of the territory. The conquest was not an easy one: it required a permanent staff of 100,000 men and an annual expenditure of 100 millions in gold. Gradually the occupation spread to the west, and England became alarmed as the French neared Morocco. But the struggle continued, as Abd-el-Kader put up a desperate resistance, only surrendering in 1847 to General de Lamoricière, when Louis-Philippe had just handed over government in Algeria to his son, the duke of Aumale.

In internal policy, Guizot dissolved the Chamber in 1842, which exacerbated extremist tendencies, but the new assembly left in abeyance the question of electoral reform, as demanded by a great number of citizens. The duke of Orléans, who supported the principle of reform, died in a driving accident at Neuilly on 13 July 1842, and the problem was raised of an eventual regency, which the king's age brought into question. Though most people were for the nomination of the duchess of Orléans, who shared her husband's liberal ideas, the regency fell to the duke of Nemours by a huge majority, which greatly irritated the supporters of social progress.

This argument over the regency brought about a new rising of the legitimist movement, and the count of Chambord seriously worried the Orleanists by organizing a demonstration of loyalism at Belgrave Square in London (1843). Queen Victoria disavowed his actions and established closer links with Louis-Philippe. The two sovereigns visited each other, and this strengthened Anglo-French friendships, which had been affected by various colonial incidents.

But the Anglo-French entente was short-lived, and a quarrel blew up over the affair of the Spanish marriages. King Louis-Philippe married his last son, the duke of Montpensier, to the sister of the queen of Spain, Isabella II, in 1846 – a marriage to which England was strongly opposed. Disappointed by the English attitude, Guizot turned to Austria in the hopes of renewing an old alliance, confronting Prussia, and also probably of regaining for himself the vital international role which had been played for nearly thirty years by Metternich.

This policy was unpopular with the nation, which since the time of Marie-Antoinette and Marie-Louise had remained deeply anti-Austrian, but this alone could not have brought about the fall of the throne, which was due more to a series of political scandals, such as the murder of the duchess of Choiseul-Praslin by her husband, and his subsequent suicide, and even more to the king's obstinate refusal to accept electoral reform.

France was prosperous; useful initiatives had helped her to improve her channels of communication. But there were poor harvests in 1846 and 1847, which made the price of bread rise, and provoked social upheavals. This atmosphere, with the help of the parliamentary opposition, created a very bad political climate. A 'Campaign of the Banquets', led by Lamartine and Ledru-Rollin, roused public opinion. Instead of taking note of these troubles, in December 1847 the king gave an authoritarian speech from the throne, which revealed his great distance from public opinion.

The parliamentary session which opened on 24 January 1848 was to be a stormy one, and Guizot's obstinacy provoked a dangerous reaction from the majority. Neither the king nor his first minister realized how much their position had been weakened. The Campaign of the Banquets was suspended for the duration of the session, but a great banquet was organized for its closure on 22 February 1848. Guizot decided to ban the popular demonstration which was planned for the end of the meal, and he placed troops in position in Paris.

The deputies of the opposition called off the banquet and the demonstration, but this proved a futile move, and on 22 February processions began to move through Paris. Under popular pressure, an anti-governmental motion was tabled in the Chamber, and the National Guard, as a form of protest against its inability to vote, announced that it was ready to lay down its arms and fraternize with the demonstrators.

The taking of the Tuileries during the revolution of 1848.

A change of ministry seemed essential. Guizot, who suddenly saw the light, resigned, and the king called on Molé. He went to discuss things with Thiers, one of the organizers of the campaign, who logically demanded power for himself. On 23 February Guizot's resignation became public, and this should have calmed people down, but the mob which had taken to the streets, who could see no difference between Guizot and Molé, marched on the ministry of foreign affairs. The soldiers opened fire on the demonstrators, killing sixteen of them and wounding fifty. This drama increased the tension, as the dead bodies were paraded through Paris.

Louis-Philippe, warned of the situation, took Molé's advice and appointed Thiers as president of the council. He demanded draconian measures, which lost him several hours. Nevertheless Louis-Philippe agreed to everything and accepted the required reforms, which should logically have saved him.

But the appointment of Thiers and the royal concessions became public too late. Bugeaud had been named commander-in-chief in charge of keeping order in Paris, but he was in a difficult position, as the demonstrators had not laid down their arms. Before taking the decision of defending the Tuileries by steel and by fire, Bugeaud consulted Louis-Philippe. The king, who had said he was determined to resist, expressed reservations when he found out that violent repression was called for.

Because of a mistake by General Bedeau, the defence of the Tuileries was unsupported. Lamoricière was given command of the National Guard, but was unable to make himself obeyed. Thiers pleaded with the king to leave Paris to avoid being taken prisoner, but in vain. Louis-Philippe decided instead to review the National Guard, which jeered him.

And so he signed an act of abdication and escaped with the queen, hoping that the Chamber would proceed to crown his grandson, the count of Paris.

The duchess of Orléans came to the Chamber with the duke of Nemours to have the regency recognized. The situation was a tragic one, as a provisional commission established in the Hôtel de Ville appeared to have assumed government already. Odilon Barrot, designated by Louis-

Philippe, defended the rights of the monarchy, and Lamartine, supported by the legitimists, called for a republic. During this debate the Chamber was invaded by the rioters. The deputies scattered, and Lamartine went to the Hôtel de Ville to proclaim the republic.

Louis-Philippe's elective monarchy ended in a disaster which was quite the equal of that which brought about the fall of Charles X.

In very distressing circumstances, Louis-Philippe and Marie-Amélie managed to reach Honfleur, where they went to ground until a ship agreed to take them to England. The king of the Belgians, Leopold I, put his house at Claremont at his father-in-law's disposal, and there Louis-Philippe lived out his last years in peaceful retirement.

He had failed, as Charles X had done, to understand the democratic aspirations of the new France; a prince of the ancien régime, he had shown himself constantly hostile to the extension of the suffrage, which would have consolidated his position.

With him ended the reign of the Bourbon dynasty.

Queen Marie-Amélie was as great in suffering as she had been on the throne. She was to survive her husband by about fifteen years, and lived in retirement and devoutness until her death, which occurred at Claremont on 24 March 1866. With her disappeared the last queen of France.

THE REVOLUTION OF 1848 brings to an end the list of the kings of France, of which Louis-Philippe was truly the last.

But he was not the last monarch, since the president of the Second Republic, which succeeded to the monarchy, was Louis Napoleon Bonaparte, nephew of Napoleon I, who, in 1852, re-established the Empire. He was overthrown by the Revolution of 4 September 1870 and since then France has had only Republican régimes.

❧ GLOSSARY ❧

appanage The provision of lands within the royal domain, or in some cases of pensions, to the children of the royal family so that they might live in a style corresponding to their position in society. Appanages were established to provide for the younger brothers and sisters of the king but were also given to an heir to the throne before his succession, at which time the land was reannexed to the crown.

Campaign of the Banquets In July 1847 the opposition party circumvented the law against public meetings by organizing political banquets at which speakers agitated for liberal and electoral reform.

corps des intendants The body of direct representatives of the king in the provinces, instituted by Richelieu. They controlled the judicial, fiscal, police and even military administration.

cour des aides A court of law, including two presidents and two benches, each of twenty-six judges, which tried suits arising out of the collection, farming etc. of the taxes. It also had executive functions in connection with public works, payment and rationing of troops etc.

cour des comptes An administrative court, comprising ten presidents and sixty-two *maîtres de comptes*, which revised the public accounts of the kingdom, exercising jurisdiction over the accountants and even some measure of control over the king himself.

dragonnade The practice of billeting dragoons or other soldiers on communities or individuals whom it was desired to punish.

Estates-General The assembly, summoned from time to time (by the king only and at his discretion) of representatives of the three estates of the realm, i.e. the clergy, the nobility and the third estate, in practice the burghers of the towns of France. They were instituted by Philip the Fair, without powers of initiative or free discussion, to give support or ratification to the king's proposals.

farmers-general Under the *ancien régime* the office of collecting certain indirect taxes, which implied also the right to exploit them, was farmed out or leased for fixed periods to private persons. These farmers-general paid highly in the first instance for the privilege, which was frequently auctioned to the highest bidder, but they made such a good rake-off that they were able to amass very large fortunes.

fief A vassal's source of income, held from his lord in exchange for services. It normally consisted of land to which a number of peasants were attached; the land was supposed to be sufficient to support the vassal and to secure his knight service for the lord.

Fronde (Taken from a boys' game where *frondes*, or slings, were used.) Name given to two revolts against the absolutism of the crown, caused by the unpopularity of Mazarin and the fiscal measures adopted to finance the German and Spanish wars.

lit de justice A ceremony in which decrees were made law by an expression of the king's will, thus bypassing the Parlement. Usually the king resorted to a *lit de justice* only after the Parlement had refused to register a particular edict. The ceremony was rigidly set: the king rested on a number of cushions (from which the name *lit*, or bed), surrounded in a prescribed order by the peers of France, royal officials, and the parliamentarians.

Parlement The supreme judicial assembly, next after the *conseil d'état* or king's council. By 1789 the number of parlements had risen to thirteen: Paris, Toulouse, Grenoble, Bordeaux, Dijon, Rouen, Aix, Rennes, Pau, Metz, Douai, Besançon and Nancy. The Parlement of Paris was the most ancient; its jurisdiction extended over half of France and it comprised two hundred magistrates. These sat in general assembly only to consider the gravest questions of state, such as the verification and registration of the king's edicts required to give them force of law. The parlements of the other cities comprised fewer magistrates but were organized on the same plan. The officials of the parlements were unremovable. Their offices were hereditary and might be purchased. When the Parlement is spoken of without further designation, the Parlement of Paris is meant.

third estate The Commons who, in contradistinction to the other two (the clergy and the nobility) had to sustain the main burden of taxation.

Ultras The ultra-royalist party after the Restoration of 1815. They were uncompromising believers in absolute monarchy and the supremacy of the Church.

⚭ ACKNOWLEDGMENTS ⚭

The pictures in this book are supplied or reproduced by kind permission of the following (numbers are page numbers, italics indicate colour pictures):

Archives Nationales 61
Archives Photographiques 76 right, 107, 172
Bibliothèque Municipale, Boulogne-sur-Mer 78
Bibliothèque Nationale, Paris 10, 18, 20, 21, 22, 24–5, 27, *29*, *30–1*, 34, 36, 40, 44, 46, 49, 52, 57, 72, 79, *81*, *82–3*, *84*, 89, 95, 96, 98, 102–3, 108, 110, 112, 116–17, *121*, 134, 138, 140, 144, 179, 183, 210, 214–15, 236, 245, 251, 262–3
Bulloz 131, 169, 185, 187, 188, 220
Caisse Nationale des Monuments Historiques 163, 180
Cooper-Bridgeman (Reunion des Musées Nationaux) *223*
Mary Evans Picture Library 114, 162
John Freeman 208
Giraudon 14, 15, 66–7, 126, 139, 202, 232–3
By gracious permission of Her Majesty the Queen 150–1
Kunstammlung, Basel 156
Lambeth Palace Library 105

Lauros-Giraudon 92
Mansell Collection 76 left, 145, 155, 167, 176–7
Monza Cathedral Treasury 50
Museo del Prado 146
National Gallery of Scotland 218
Princess Margaret of Hesse and Rhine 226
Radio Times 128, 212
Reformationsgeschichtliche Museum, Wittenberg 151
Roger-Viollet 62–3, 205, 211, 227
Snark International *32*, 122 (Louvre), 148 (Louvre), *197* (Louvre)
Stiftsbibliothek St Gall 41
Archives Tallandier, Paris 65, 90, 125, 137, *147 top* (Musée Condé, Chantilly), *147 bottom* (Musée Condé, Chantilly), 157, 160, 164–5, 170–1, 190, 192 top, 195, 200, 217, *224* (Musée de Versailles), 230–1, 238, 241, 242, 248, 252–3, 254, 257, 259
The Wallace Collection (photo John Freeman) *198*
Weidenfeld and Nicolson archives 59, 71

Calligraphic titles by Freda Harmer
Artwork for family trees by D P Press Ltd

INDEX OF PEOPLE,
⚭ COUNTRIES AND COUNTIES ⚭